Reliving the Civil War

Could Clarence show haversack? See p. 27-8
AF food (N/S diff)
Think thru all our gear — how to defarb sleeping
eating, etc.

Reliving the Civil War

A Reenactor's Handbook

R. Lee Hadden

STACKPOLE
BOOKS

Copyright © 1999, 1996 by Stackpole Books
Published by

STACKPOLE BOOKS

5067 Ritter Road
Mechanicsburg PA 17055
www.stackpolebooks.com

First edition previously published as *Civil War Reenactor's Handbook: A Guide to Historical Interpretation, Teaching History, and Living History* by the author and HadCo Associates, Greenville, North Carolina 27834. Original Library of Congress Catalog Number:
91-76325

Quoted material appearing on the following pages is reprinted with permission of the fol-
lowing organizations: Pages 8 and 23, University of Illinois Press; pages 21–22, Harmonie
Associates; pages 24–25, American Association for State and Local History; pages 130–132,
Camp Chase Gazette; pages 169–86, American Civil War Commemorative Committee.

Front cover photo courtesy of the author

Back cover photo courtesy of Ralph Hocken

All photographs from author unless otherwise specified

Printed in the United States of America

10 9 8 7 6 5 4 3 2 1

SECOND EDITION

Library of Congress Cataloging-in-Publication Data

Hadden, Robert Lee, 1951–
    Reliving the Civil War: a reenactor's handbook / R.Lee Hadden.—2nd ed.
        p. cm.
    Includes bibliographical references (p.).
    ISBN: 0-8117-2912-5
        1. United States—History—Civil War, 1861–1865. 2. Historical
reenactments—United States Handbooks, manuals, etc. I. Title.
E468.9.H33 1999
973.7—dc21
                                                                                    99-38768
                                                                                          CIP

Contents

Acknowledgments

I want to thank the following people who have helped me in my reenactment training and in the preparing of this work. They have helped with advice and encouragement, and their suggestions and criticism are gratefully accepted.

Ted Alexander, National Park Service (NPS); Jim Burgess, NPS; Steve Bockmiller, 4th North Carolina; Larry and Kate Bopp, 4th North Carolina; Jann Calhoun, North Carolina Department of Cultural Resources; Paul Chiles, NPS; Jo Christen, the Living History Society of Minnesota; "Hawk" Crummey, 1st/11th North Carolina; Glenna Karl Fleckenstein, 4th North Carolina; John M. Gibney, 24th Michigan; William "Bill" Gwaltney, NPS; Ina Hanel-Gerdenich, Kempf House Center for Local History, Ann Arbor, Michigan; Tom Holbrook, NPS; Bill Holschuh, *Camp Chase Gazette*; Mike Littlerest, NPS; Mike and Suzanne Ludwick, 19th Georgia; Greg Mast, 26th North Carolina; Mark "Nero" Pangburn, 24th Michigan; Bill Potts, 1st/11th North Carolina; David Pruitt, 1st/11th North Carolina; Jeff Stepp, 26th North Carolina; and the many other members of the 4th North Carolina, 24th Michigan, and 26th North Carolina reenactment groups. Literally hundreds of other men and women reenactors and historians gave me the benefit of their time, knowledge, patience, and advice over the years, and I wish I could thank them all.

I wish to acknowledge the help and assistance I have received from the staff of the Loudoun County Public Library. Their ability to get needed items through interlibrary loan was a godsend for this work. I especially want to thank the interlibrary loan section, and the library reference staff, for their help in finding obscure, incomplete, and sometimes tangled references. Their professionalism shows what even a small public library can do with coopera- tive agreements with other research libraries.

I also want to publicly thank Brian C. Pohanka, who reviewed my manu- script for Stackpole Books and offered many valuable and insightful criti- cisms and suggestions.

Thank you to the reenactors of the 2nd U.S. Infantry and the 4th U.S. Infantry, of Sykes' Regulars, who patiently went through the manual of arms for me to photograph them at Harpers Ferry, West Virginia.

A special commendation to my "home" unit, the 4th North Carolina, CSA, Inc., and our commander, Capt. Larry Bopp. The 4th North Carolina has recently celebrated its 30th year of quality living history, and I'm proud to be a member of such a fine group of reenactors.

Kevin and Mimi Rawlings have been very patient and generous with their time and expertise. Mimi Rawlings has courteously loaned me some period photographs from her collection for this book.

I also want to thank my wife, Eileen, who has put up with my hobby all these years and helped in correcting and finishing this manuscript.

Introduction

This book is written for newcomers to the hobby of living history and Civil War reenactment. Much of the information in this book will be helpful to anyone starting out in reenacting from any time period. In scope, the book is aimed at the portrayal of Civil War infantrymen and their civilian dependents. My experience of more than twenty years has been as an infantry private, so I have only peripheral information about Civil War-period navy, marines, cavalry, and artillery. I also have little advice to give to officers in the field of reenacting.

People interested in other areas of historical reenactment or living history are encouraged to look in the bibliography section of this work for other sources. Your public library will also help out.

There is disagreement over the use of the term "Civil War." There are many other names for the conflict preferred in different regions of the country, but the most popular alternative is the War Between the States. I have intermingled the use of these terms in this book and sometimes I have shortened the terms to CW and WBTS. My Virginian grandmother simply referred to it as "the Late Unpleasantness."

Welcome to reenacting. I hope you will enjoy the hobby as much as my wife and I have.

1

Reenactment, Living History, and Teaching History

HISTORY OF REENACTING

Reenacting is as old as human society, religion, and drama. Most plays are, in a sense, simply reenactments of past lives and events.

Many primitive people reenacted great events in their lives, such as hunting experiences, over and over again, both as a form of entertainment and as instruction to other members of the tribe. By showing and demonstrating a successful hunting trick, technical knowledge would be passed on to others in the tribe, to the benefit of everyone. Even today, many people learn things "manually," by seeing a physical demonstration, or "reenactment," of a special technique or skill.

Manual learning is often much more effective than book learning. I could read drill manuals all day and study the illustrations, and still not learn as much as a few minutes working with a good noncom on how to hold the rifle: "No, no, put the index finger *here* under the trigger guard, and the base of the thumb *here* on top of it," "Place the left thumb securely over the ramrod so that it doesn't fall out when you are marching," or my favorite, "If it feels comfortable, then you aren't doing it right!"

Aside from entertainment and instruction, reenactment is often used to commemorate religious events. Christians reenact the Last Supper during

Holy Communion; Jews reenact the Passover meal during the Seder; and Moslems reenact significant events of the life of Mohammed during Hadj, their pilgrimage to Mecca in Arabia. These are opportunities for common men to experience a sense of oneness with the divine. The spiritual connection between life in the present and life in the past is made through reenactment of historic events, and the importance of this connection is recognized and valued by the entire community.

Many reenactors started out as boys dressed in bathrobes and cotton-ball beards, portraying the journey of Joseph to Bethlehem in Christmas pageants. This was my own first taste of drama. I reveled in the approving smiles of the church ladies, the sympathetic grins of the church men, and the worried frowns of the much-aggrieved and put-upon Sunday-school teacher. I remember seeing "Mary" stick her tongue out at me when I flubbed my one and only line, while all the "angels" in white gauze and tinfoil halos, offstage left, giggled like mad demons.

Because of this connection to religion, many reenactors have a mystical bent toward the hobby. Ghost stories and supernatural events are discussed around the campfire. Many reenactors openly discuss visions or weird experiences on battlefields and historic sites. Unknown reenactors visit campfires, and then vanish with morning light. Extra soldiers are recorded on film marching in lines, who aren't recognized or remembered by the troops marching next to them. Living historians camping at historic sites mention hearing unexplained gunfire at night, smelling gunpowder fumes, and seeing apparitions.

Whatever the beliefs, reenactors cling to their units and uniforms in mystical ways. A surprising number have been buried in their uniforms, and even more have been married in uniform. Reenactors undoubtedly sense an attractive dramatic connection with the past.

Reenacting in America is an old tradition that predates the Civil War as a "sham fight" or "sham battle." Like today's reenactments, there is noise, confusion, heat, and lack of shade. Indeed, in a pamphlet printed by Henry Clark, "An Historical Address Delivered at Hubbardton, Vermont, on the Eighty-Second Anniversary of the Battle of Hubbardton, July 7, 1859," the author mentioned that roads for many miles around were choked by the traffic of incoming spectators. According to Clark, a speaker of the ceremony dedicating a new monument to the Revolutionary War battle was interrupted by a sham fight performed between members of a militia battalion, the Allen Greys of Brandon. Surprisingly, there was only one injury during the reenactment that had so many safety violations.

I was unable to hear as distinctly as I could have wished, owing to the noise and confusion occasioned by the "sham fight," which interrupted his speech, between Colonel Bush, with a small detachment of the "Greys," representing the British, and Captain Cook, with the rest of the "Greys" representing the Americans. This was one of the more interesting incidents of the day, although Mr. Walton's speech was interrupted for half an hour. The British were forced to retire until reinforced by a company of American Indians, commanded by the artist Hope [James Hope, the poet-painter], of Castleton, when they rallied and drove the Americans back as far as the speaker's stand. The smoke of the battle and rattle of musketry was really quite exciting, and involuntarily led one to inquire what the realities of grim war must be if mimicry is so stirring. It is understood that prodigies of honor were performed—although I have seen no official bulletin from Colonel Bush or Captain Cook. Major Hayward, of the staff, was the only one who was placed *hors de combat,* as far as I could learn, and his injuries were not severe, I believe. After the fight was over Mr. Walton concluded his speech amid great applause. . . . The day, as you well remember, was intensely hot, and there was not an approximation of shade within a stone's throw of the speaker's stand.

Harriet Beecher Stowe in *Poganuc People (1878),* in the section "Dolly's Fourth," also wrote some interesting observations on reenacting a sham fight, when men were still reenacting the Revolutionary War. Her account sounds surprisingly modern, including the famous question about using bullets in the muskets:

> "Hulloa boys, there's going to be a sham fight; Hiel told me so," said Bob Cushing. "Some are going to be British and some American, and the Americans are going to whip the British and make 'em run."
>
> "Tell ye what," said Jake Freeman, "there'll be banging' and poppin' won't there boys?"
>
> "Oh," said Dolly, who was irrepressibly following her brothers into the throng, "they won't really shoot anybody, will they?"
>
> "Oh, no, they'll only fire powder, of course," said Bill majestically, "don't you know that?"

The dramatization of past events is often used to define a common heritage and to give a sense of origin and community. During the past seventy-five years, the growth of outdoor theater dramas for local-history pageants has been phenomenal. Today there are almost fifty major outdoor pageants that demonstrate and reenact important, trivial, and infamous episodes of American history in thirty-three states.[1]

Civil War reenacting was done almost from the beginning of war, as soldiers demonstrated to family and friends their actions during the war, in camp, in drill, and in battle. Veterans organizations recreated camp life to show their children and others how they lived and to reproduce the camaraderie of shared experience with their fellow veterans.[2]

Large reenactments were done as military training exercises on the battlefield, such as the U.S. Army field maneuvers on the Manassas battlefield in September 1904. On the 72nd anniversary of Chancellorsville, in May 1935, cadets from the Virginia Military Institute, the U.S. Cavalry, and the U.S. Marines reenacted this battle.[3] Even today the Army War College takes officers over the Civil War battlegrounds so that the officers can appreciate the tactics and strategy of the past, which are still relevant.

During the Civil War Centennial in 1961, Manassas was again visited by the U.S. Army, which dressed up soldiers in blue and gray costumes and let them go at each other with Garand carbines and printed cardboard cartridge boxes.[4] Authenticity then was only a vague concept; mostly this was an attempt to entertain an audience of fifty thousand on temporary football bleachers. Interestingly, though, this reenactment of the battle was, militarily speaking, perhaps the most authentic reenactment of Manassas that has ever been carried out, although the soldiers were dressed in "costumes" and had the most inappropriate gear imaginable. The term "sham battle" was used at that time.

Without a doubt, Civil War reenactment got its boost during the centennial, which also saw the birth of the North-South Skirmish Association (NSSA). These individuals began competitive shooting with original and reproduction black-powder firearms (including cannons) and produced a lucrative market for equipment and uniforms that sparked the modern reenactment hobby.

There was a great deal of interest in the 1960s in sham battles. President John Kennedy enjoyed them a great deal. He was invited to attend the reenactment of the Gettysburg Address in November 1963, but he declined because he wanted to mend political fences in Texas. On the weekend planned for the centennial commemoration in Pennsylvania, President Kennedy went to Dallas instead, and met his fate at the hand of an assassin.

The sixties also saw the rise of the one-man impersonation show. Hal Holbrook began a full two-hour show impersonating Mark Twain. He did serious research on the writings and presentations of Mark Twain and gave an authentic re-creation of America's foremost humorist and wit. Since then there have been many of these shows, some successful, others failures.

By the end of the 1960s, the reenactment hobby split from the black-powder shooting community, and the two began to develop individually. Events were still small, and equipment either handmade or inappropriate. German leather cartridge cases from World War II were worn on Sears work-belts as cap boxes, Knights of Columbus swords were worn by officers, and many soldiers carried round Boy Scout canteens with painted covers. Work boots were common footwear. Few reenactors knew about army life in general, let alone their individual regiments or specific uniforms.

By far the biggest impact on reenacting was the Bicentennial in 1976. The increase in Revolutionary War reenactments, along with the quest for accuracy in uniforms and equipment, boosted the authenticity movement in Civil War reenactment tremendously. Research began on uniforms and equipment, and manufacturing of good reproductions was started. Reproduction weapons were made, although some were intended for wall hangings rather than shooting.

One problem for Civil War reenactment in the 1970s was the extensive reproduction of pistols, black-powder shotguns, and two-banded muskets. These short-barrelled weapons are dangerous in military formations and have caused many accidents. Nevertheless, they became ubiquitous in reenactments because they were so plentiful and cheap. Even through the 1980s and into the 1990s, these weapons were used by infantry reenactors.

During the late 1970s, some manufacturers began to make authentic reproductions. Antiques were still fairly cheap at this time, and this was an interesting but short-lived period during which reproductions were often more expensive than the original items. Good brogans from Lund's and Jarnigan's were becoming available, and the trend moved away from polyester blends in uniforms. Some 1870s military equipment was still around at the end of the 1970s and early 1980s, still very cheap, and passed off as original Civil War equipment by the unscrupulous. By 1979, many reproduction items were so good they needed identifying marks to prevent them from being resold as antique originals.

A split began during this period between the professional historians and the reenactors, which has continued to this day. Up until this time, reenactments had been small and did not attract more than local attention. As the reenactment movement started gathering steam, however, disagreements erupted between professional historians and reenactors.

The main argument between the two camps was the acceptance of amateur historians as authorities in history. Professional historians, trained to see the overall picture and the interrelation of events, rightly criticized reenactors for being too narrow in their focus and concentrating more on the actual events than the significance of those events.

Reenactors insisted that the historians did not have a monopoly on interpretation and, indeed, had lost some of their relevance with the public in promoting local and national history. Reenactments may not be the most accurate portrayal of history, but they certainly gave history life, taste, and smell, something significantly missing from dry academic tomes.

The main difference between reenactors and historians is the product of their research. Historians write down on paper their thoughts and interpretations of history, and their writings last for generations. Reenactors and living historians, on the other hand, put on a performance that is as ephemeral as the event they are portraying. Once done, it cannot be recaptured, unless it is captured on film. In this sense, reenactors are closer to professional actors than they are to historians. It is not surprising that there is such a difference in outlook and room for misinterpreting each other and each other's work.

Historical research is based on the study of grand events and trends in history. Reenactment and living history are interested in the human stories of individuals, and how to interpret the events of a particular time period to modern people through storytelling, living history, and historical presentations.

In 1986, the first of the 125th Anniversary battles was held near the original battlefield of Manassas. More than anything, this mega-event sparked an interest in the Civil War and reenacting. The massive gathering of reenactors from all over the world demonstrated the extent of the hobby and showed that decent profits can be made from historical reenactments. More than six thousand reenactors showed up in sweltering heat and camped out on an extensive ground with a three-sided reconstructed Henry house.

The Manassas event was a tremendous hit, and stock footage shot during the reenactment is still being used in movies and Civil War documentaries. *Time* magazine estimated that in 1986 there were more than fifty thousand reenactors of all sorts in America.[5] During this time, several miniseries on the

Civil War, including "The Blue and the Gray" and "North and South," were shot using reenactors as extras.

A popular series of documentaries by Classic Images used reenactors to stage battles and often had trailers showing life in camp as a reenactor. The trailers for the 125th Manassas and Gettysburg documentaries were both instructive and amusing.

By 1989 and 1990, some of the 125th Anniversary events began to lose their luster, as the twin demons of profit and liability began to predominate. An explosion at the Crater was so muted by the event coordinators, who were afraid of lawsuits, that many people did not recognize the explosion when it happened. At other events, local support organizations, such as volunteer rescue squads and fire departments, were stiffed. Profits were not as high as expected, and competing events divided the reenactors and the public. Both the reenactors' registration fees and the public fees were raised. Sutlers began to feel the pinch of higher fees at reenactments, as well as from competition with local, nonauthentic merchants. Straw, ice, parking, and sometimes powder, which before had been given away free by the organizers, now became income generators for an event.

Another change was in the movie industry. Several movies and miniseries had been made where reenactors had been extras or advisors. The film *Glory* saw much of the change in reenacting for movies, as for the first time a major motion picture was made using reenactors extensively.

Later productions were noted for the lack of pay for reenactors, and lack of benefits, such as park restoration. Some reenactors are willing to work for free for the opportunity to be in a movie, and to have bragging rights. Although this is a godsend to movie producers, since they are not paid or contracted, many of these reenactors are unreliable. Other, more reliable reenactors want pay or recompense for being in a movie. While many are willing to forgo the pay if the money is put in a trust for historical preservation, such as was done for *Gettysburg,* far too many reenactors put up real money and give up their vacations to be bought off with vague promises.

Also, some reenactors want some say in the production so that the movie does not become too one-sided or historically inaccurate. This leads to frequent clashes between the directors and cast. A recent trend has been for the producers to hire an experienced reenactor to "handle" the extras. This person acts as a go-between and lets the producers know what can and cannot be done and what is safe.

Many regiments refuse to participate in moviemaking because of the problems of safety and lack of authenticity. The producers often do not care about the quality of the reenactors as much as they do the quantity and will frequently take people off the streets and dress them in costumes. These movies have become "farb" playgrounds and are noted for incompetent drill, dangerous practices, and injuries.[6]

My advice is not to participate unless the extras are paid a fair wage. This is for the good of the hobby, since if it becomes known that reenactors will work for free, abuse of the hobby will result. Keep a good eye on who will be working with the reenactors. If there is someone who is not a reenactor in charge of the extras, then beware—the script or action could be dangerous. Hollywood moviemakers don't know how dangerous muskets can be, or how to mix up reenactors, stuntmen, off-the-street extras, and "farbs" in a charging melee without causing injuries.

One last warning: A large movie production could ruin a summer of reenacting for a number of events. *Gettysburg* was filmed over several months and drew numbers of reenactors away from other living-history demonstrations. If you plan to put on a reenactment, keep an ear out concerning movies.

INTERPRETATION

Interpretation is a means of conveying the essence of history. Far more than a recital of facts, it is a way of opening up to understanding a time period that is different from ours. Living history and historical reenactment are two methods of applying the art of interpretation. Both are role-playing exercises, and they incorporate life and feeling along with fact into the portrayal of history.

Living history and historical reenactment can be very effective in special circumstances, such as presenting local history in museums. Both methods require a knowledge of history and period culture, both allow participants and spectators to experience life in the past, when people did things differently, and both are fun for participants and spectators alike.

Compared with the classroom, books, films, or gallery exhibits, the living history setting provides more ways to reach the public and stimulate interest in history. Their real power is in their multisensory approach. As John Kouwenhoven has noted, there are limitations to language and all thoughts are not best transmitted through words. "Just as there are sight-thoughts, "Kouwenhoven reminds us, "there are also feel-thoughts, smell-thoughts, taste-thoughts, and sound-thoughts." Living history museums can present texture, color, odor and sound. By engaging visitors' senses, living history museums can then broaden the imagination. And although such museums require skilled interpreters if they are to discourage misinterpretation and to show visitors how to learn from the sensory impressions about them, interpreters have a real advantage over history teachers since they have such interesting and varied teaching aids and instructional materials.[7]

In a talk given at Antietam for interpreters, artillery reenactor and history professor Tom Clemens stated that there are three different levels of Civil War knowledge. The first and highest level is the best and includes documented, detailed knowledge about the persona, company, regiment, and details of dress and equipment. Almost any question asked about the uniform or unit can be answered by citing an authoritative source. This is a very sophisticated level of knowledge, but one attained by many veteran reenactors.

Clemens gave the example of the inexperienced 17th Michigan Infantry at its first battle during the Antietam Campaign. The men had only a limited knowledge of army life gleaned from novels and color engravings. When called to combat, they changed from their usual fatigue uniforms into their dress uniforms, thinking they should meet the enemy in their best clothes. The men then went into their first battle in full dress uniform, with Hardee hats, brass scales on their shoulders, and white gloves. Because the engravings never showed the men wearing packs in battle, they left them on the road. They never went back for their knapsacks, and during the rest of the campaign they went without food, blankets, or a change of clothes. During a reenactment of the Antietam Campaign, members of this unit can wear dress uniforms, which will be different from all other Yankee reenactors, in order to document this difference from the norm. It would be inappropriate, however, for other Union or even other Michigan troops to follow their lead.

Many units bring a "proof book" to reenactments. This is usually a looseleaf notebook filled with the regiment's history, copies of uniform and flag photos, and anything else needed to document their impression. Whenever they differ from the usual uniform, they can show historical evidence to validate that difference. If they can't document the difference, they should not try to be unique.

The second level of knowledge is that most widely attained by reenactors. This is a general knowledge of WBTS-period dress and society. When you do not know the specifics of your regiment's uniform, you are safe in wearing the customary dress of the general soldier. For example, little is known about the uniform specifics of the Southern troops during the

Antietam Campaign, so general trends used by the Army of Northern Virginia are followed. As a result, there can be few exceptions from the normal uniform, because they can't be documented. There are many examples of both early- and late-war uniforms in photographs, but the middle-war period is not as well documented.

The third level is a general knowledge of the Civil War period. Many new reenactors fall into this category, with an interest in the WBTS and a great deal of miscellaneous knowledge. If you are at this level, you need to do some research, study photographs, and acquire a feel for the life of the common soldier in your unit. Someone once commented that this is the only hobby around where action on the field leads to reading in the library. Every unit should have a list of books, articles, and other materials that can be used by regimental members to increase their knowledge. Ask other unit members about any primary documents, such as written recollections by veterans and regimental histories. You also can talk with members of other units that historically brigaded with yours, or with enemy units that opposed your regiment in battle. You can learn a lot from the expertise of others, but the main key is to read, and then read some more. Then, when anyone passes your camp and asks questions about your uniform, you will be able to answer them and tell them where they can go to find out more information about your regiment and the Civil War.

Within these three levels of knowledge, there are three areas of sophistication needed for interpretation. The first is knowledge of the uniform and equipment. Just by being seen, you are giving out information, and ethically the reenactor must not give out wrong information. You must strive to wear the correct uniform and to wear it correctly. Learn how to use equipment properly, how to clean it, and when and where you would have received it.

The second area is an understanding of the nineteenth-century persona, attitudes, and lifestyle. Before becoming a soldier, everyone was a civilian. You need to understand where the soldier came from and what his life was like. People did things differently in the 1860s, and it is fun to explore these differences. What were people's beliefs and attitudes? What was home life like? Were you a farmer like most soldiers, a small shopkeeper, or something else? What did that person know that you do not know today? How did he walk, talk, and think? What did he wear, and why did he wear it? Why would a member of your regiment have volunteered, been drafted, or deserted? All of these pieces of information will help flesh out the military impression you are trying to convey.

The third area is a knowledge of the WBTS in general, and the campaigns of your regiment in particular. In this area, you will end up knowing more than the soldier you are portraying would have known. You will know how the war ended, whereas the real soldier lived the war day by day. This knowledge will help you realize the significance of the actions of the individuals and the regiment.

If your unit was known to have worn ragged uniforms, then you should know why. If you knew that many Confederate troops did not receive frequent issues of uniforms or that Sherman's men were far in advance of their lines of uniform resupply, then the significance of ragged uniforms becomes clear. You can then explain this to spectators, to whom the reason for ragged uniforms is not obvious (they may just think you are a sloppy reenactor).

One of the most influential men in interpretation was Freeman Tilden, of the National Park Service. In *Interpreting Our Heritage,* Tilden defines interpretation as "an educational activity which aims to reveal meanings and relationships through the use of original objects, firsthand experience and by illustrative media, rather than simply to communicate factual information."[8]

He states six principles for interpretation:

1. Any interpretation that does not somehow relate what is being displayed, described (or performed) to something within the personality or experience of the visitor will be sterile.

2. Information, as such, is not interpretation. Interpretation is revelation based upon information. But they are entirely different things. However, all interpretation includes information.

3. Interpretation is an art that combines many arts, whether the materials presented are scientific, historical, or architectural. Any art is to some degree teachable.

4. The chief aim of interpretation is not instruction, but provocation.

5. Interpretation should aim to present a whole rather than a part, and must address itself to the whole rather than to any phase.

6. Interpretation addressed to children, say up to the age of twelve, should not be a dilution of the presentation to adults, but should follow a fundamentally different approach. To be at its best, it should require a separate program.[9]

Although the first statement should be self-explanatory, it is important to understand it fully. Trying to explain something totally outside the realm of someone's experience is counterproductive. What is necessary is to connect, or interpret, the information with the knowledge and experience of the observer.

It is hard for many people, having grown up in lighted, heated, and cooled home environments, to fully understand what it was like to live without those benefits. Having a nightcap on a bedpost for the spectators to see is not enough. It becomes clearer when the interpreter explains that the nighttime temperature in the room would be only about twenty or so degrees above the outside winter temperature.

As the second principle states, information, in itself, is not interpretation. Far too often, people give information only and do not explain the context of the information. Any fact must be brought into relevancy for the audience. For example, saying that the Civil War began in 1861 and ended in 1865 is not as helpful as explaining that the Civil War began 135 years ago and lasted four years, or about as long as most students are in high school.

Interpretation is an art that depends on the talents and ingenuity of the individual, as well as knowledge and experience. There are no set rules for interpretation, since every audience will be different. Everyone will have a different age and background, and what is impressive to some may not be to others.

The fourth principle states that "the chief aim of interpretation is not instruction, but provocation." What the interpreter wants to provoke in the visitor is the desire to learn more. If you can inspire the audience with your enthusiasm and interest, then you have been successful. Many National Park Service historical sites have bookstores to provide further information about the site for visitors.

The fifth principle points out the importance of portraying a way of life, and not just a single aspect of that life. It is far too easy for the interpreter to concentrate on one aspect of an artifact or fact. As an interpreter, you want to portray not only a soldier, but also a person of the nineteenth century. The Civil War had many causes, and people had lives before the war began. Show not only the military side, but also the human side of the period.

When addressing interpretation to children, keep in mind the sixth principle. Children see and understand things differently from adults. They are interested in how and why. Why are you dressed funny? Are you hot in those wool clothes? Is that heavy? Is that real?

Children want to know about the restrictions and behavior of people. By learning what is considered grotesque and outrageous, they learn the limits of behavior in society. Regretfully, this often leads to an emphasis on the less savory details of life in the nineteenth century. Adults should not concentrate on what it looks like to see an amputation, or a description of weevils in bread, but rather the honest, accurate portrayal of typical life in that era.

These six rules of interpretation should be applied to any reenactment or living-history effort. In any interpretation, the goals should be directed toward educating the public with information and by provocation.

Part of the reenactment or living history is the interpretation of what you feel and think as you play the part—explaining these experiences to others. For instance, the kepi was a cheap hat, and not a very good one. It was worn mainly because it looked military, not for practicality. It gave no protection from the sun to the ears and cheeks and did nothing to keep the rain from coming down the back of the neck. Explaining this from personal experience (sunburned cheeks and ears and a wet neck) means more to visitors than saying that many Confederates preferred a slouch hat.

The period clothing, accoutrements, and artifacts are the tools of interpretation. The interpreter should be familiar not only with what they do, but also with how they are used. The visitors will surely ask about the very thing you are most uncertain about. The audience will find all the holes in your knowledge, and you will often find yourself looking up information you were asked about at a reenactment.

You should have a purpose in your interpretation, and a theme or point in your talk. You cannot cover the full range of your area, such as nineteenth-century clothing, in a few minutes, so narrow the area down to what people wore to parties, or how women dressed for housework, or how to dye homespun fabrics. If you try to cover too much in a talk, you end up saying too little that is useful.

The National Park Service and most museums and historic sites want reenactors to concentrate their presentations on the life and events at their particular sites. A uniform talk given at Gettysburg should be aimed at describing uniforms worn at the 1863 Battle of Gettysburg rather than what the soldiers wore during the entire war. The aim of the historic site (which is sometimes different from the aims of the reenactors) is to keep the talk focused on that site.

The audience is the most important part of your talk. Often your talk will be given to passersby at reenactments, who will form small groups, listen to what you say, and pass on while another group forms. Each of these audiences will differ dramatically from the others, so don't fall into the rut of repeating the same information. Keep it new for new audiences, and for yourself. Repeating the same spiel over and over is really boring.

This brings us to one of the biggest points about living history and reenactment. Historians repeatedly state how important living history is for teaching and learning. There are serious purposes to living history; however, the one thing that has made it so popular is that it is fun. It is enjoyable to wear different clothing, and to learn and talk about what you feel and find out when you live another lifestyle. It gives zip to your experience to talk about something you enjoy with people who sometimes know very little about the WBTS but want to learn more.

Living history has several aspects in addition to the knowledge of history. In one sense, you are an actor in costume and on stage. It is exciting and thrilling. Another aspect is the little kid in each of us who wants to dress up, and now we have real toys to dress up with. And part of it satisfies the curiosity about how other people lived. You learn firsthand what it is like to waltz in a hoop skirt, and how to sit down in a chair without having the hoops fly up, hit you in the face, and display your bloomers to the room.

By expressing these aspects of living history, you are giving history a dimension and personal experience that makes it come alive. This enthusiasm will show itself to the spectators, who will be drawn into your living history.

The attraction of reenacting and living history for teaching and reaching out also has a commercial side. In March 1969 the Commonwealth of Virginia launched its tourism campaign by placing an advertisement in *Modern Bride* magazine. The advertisement showed a reenactment of the 1608 wedding of John Laydon and Anne Burass at the Jamestown Colony. The advertisement also introduced the tourism slogan, "Virginia is for Lovers," which is still commercially effective and has been emulated and parodied for thirty years. The clever placement of the ad, the intriguing living-history theme, and the catchy slogan all worked together to impress the reader with the romance and history of Virginia. This impression remained for sometime long after the forgotten advertisement. Many other states, local governments, and historic sites also now use photographs of reenactments and living history to help sell their messages.

Reenactment

Reenactment is a re-creation of an actual historical event that is both representative and historically correct. It is an educational method of combining the skills of historical interpretation and acting for educational purposes. Actors are chosen for their resemblance to actual historical figures and are given speeches to recite, taken from historical sources and delivered in the style of mid-nineteenth-century oratory. The use of actors by the National Park Service to portray Abraham Lincoln's Gettysburg Address every year at the Gettysburg National Cemetery is an example of a reenactment. Every effort is made to give the observers and spectators the impression that they were there when the event occurred. Sometimes the spectators participate by wearing period clothes or even participating with the actors.

The best-known interpretation of this kind is done in America at Plimoth Plantation in Massachusetts and at Colonial Williamsburg in Virginia. Here actors and historians are hired to reproduce the actions and life of early American communities. They do this by sometimes acting out set scripts and sometimes just having fun speaking to the visitors and ad-libbing. An excellent example of this is in Jay Anderson's book, *Time Machines*. A reenactor is asked why there is a fence around the 1630s period garden. Instead of simply giving out the information, the reenactor asked the visitor why he didn't have a fence around *his* garden. By gently challenging the visitor to examine his own actions, the reenactor was able to do much more than give a history lesson.

Plimoth Plantation is known for its first-person impressions. In a first-person impression, the actor studies the life of a particular individual and reproduces it as accurately as possible, down to the use of a specific accent and a knowledge of his trade.

Colonial Williamsburg is known for its craftsmen who manufacture period furniture and artifacts in accurate ways. They explain their crafts and show the spectators how work was done in early Virginia. The craftsmen wear period clothing, but it is not always accurate, and they often wear modern glasses. There is little attempt at the first-person approach, and the spectators rarely participate except to ask questions.

Most Civil War reenactments with interpretations are not as long-lived as Plimoth and Williamsburg. They are usually one-time events, such as the 135th Anniversary reenactment in 1998 of the battle of Gettysburg. There, more than fifteen thousand people gathered together for a weekend to accurately portray the life of Civil War soldiers and their experiences.

Living History

Living history is the art and technology of making the past seem alive by attempting to re-create selected segments. Thus, all reenactors are in some way living historians. This technique is used for both research and education.

Interpreting for Park Visitors, by William J. Lewis, is one of the major works in living history, and I strongly recommend it to every reenactor.

Lewis, an interpreter and instructor for the National Park Service, describes living history in his work on role-playing interpretation as a form of game. The interpreter tries to know as much about the times portrayed as possible, and to express this without coming out of character. In one case, a Civil War soldier was asked, "Was Grant drunk here, too?" by a park visitor. The interpreter answered quickly, "I don't know, Sir. I'm only a corporal, and he doesn't invite me to his parties."[10]

Lewis further states that living history is a lot of work. But this portrayal shows that history was made by everyday people as well as famous people. As a living historian, you must know how you fit into the role, and how your character fit into his or her community and home.[11]

A woman playing the part of a soldier's wife must learn a whole new social system, very rigid and very different from today's social relations. Every part of the day's life was ordered from officers' row, and a soldier's wife was tolerated only as a laundress. An officer's wife had to make do on an inadequate salary and still try to maintain a semblance of middle-class life. All of this should be known by the living historian, questions anticipated, and a ready answer given to park visitors.[12]

Be a Living Example

Living history and role playing use several techniques to be effective. The most widely used technique is to be a living example. The living historian, as a chosen persona, wears the clothing and uses the equipment and technology of a historical period, and talks and interacts with others, bringing history to life to help make historic events and past lifestyles more comprehensible.

There are two different approaches to this technique: first person and third person. The first-person living historian uses the first-person form of address: "I did this" or "I saw that." The third-person historian uses the third-person form of address: "He (or she or they) did this then."

The first-person historian acts, talks, and looks as though he or she came from the period being reenacted. All information given is period-related; none is from contemporary knowledge. Another term for this approach is "time traveler," giving a sense that this person has come through time.

To be done effectively, the first-person historian must have a great deal of knowledge about the persona and time period, including the kind of work the person did, his or her relationships, and why he or she is performing a particular task or activity. This is most effective when there is a scripted scenario between two or more first-person players that can be watched by the spectators.

These small plays, sometimes called "snapshots of history," can be very effectively done at historic sites and homes. Here, guided groups of spectators can pass by open doors to rooms in a historic house and hear and see conversations in one or more rooms, allowing them to feel like they have passed through a house in another time period. An effective thread of conversation might start among the men in the dining room, and a different slant on the same subject could be given by the women down the hall in the parlor. A third perspective could be given by the servants in the kitchen, and a fourth by the grooms in the stable. All the reenactors would have set scripts, accurate dialects, and rehearsed lines.

At historical sites, it has been commented that the less light, the more effective the "snapshot." With low lighting levels in the rooms, the living history portrayal is more focused. The furnishings of the room are seen only faintly, and most of the attention is thus given to the living historians. This focused attention and intimacy are missing from outdoor events.[13]

At Civil War reenactments, the troops talk of WBTS-period subjects as the visitors pass by. In the more open stage of the larger reenactment, visitors might attempt to join in the discussion or argue with the points of view expressed by the reenactors. A loss of control over the situation leads to more expansive roles and true "theater in the round."

When there are interactions between spectators and the first-person historian, there can be a few problems. To be effective, the character has to remain in the first person. By asking the first-person character to answer a modern question, the visitor disrupts the mood and atmosphere of the presentation. A request by a mother with a small child for directions to the bathroom can be answered in several ways. An answer in character, such as "There's a tree over yonder," can lead to frustration, anger, and misunderstanding. The woman no longer wants to learn; she has an emergency on her hands and doesn't want to play games. A modern answer, such as "Port-a-Johns are over by the sutler camp, fifty feet behind you," causes the interpreter to break character. The best solution for this type of problem is for the first-person interpreter to refer the person to someone who can answer the modern question ("I hear the sutlers have something for ladies. If you ask over in that area behind you, they can help you out") or by giving clues alluding to the answer ("There's been some talk about fancified facilities used by the ladies, over by the sutlers, about fifty feet behind you, Ma'am").

People in an audience will sometimes ask for comparative information to aid their understanding, such as how the rate of fire of a Civil War infantry unit compares with the rate of fire of infantry troops in Vietnam or in Desert

Storm. A first-person response in character can only be a blank look, since a man from 1863 would never have heard of Vietnam or Desert Storm and couldn't answer such a question. This can lead to frustration on the part of the spectator, who may not understand why his question was not answered.

Another problem with interaction between the audience and the first-person reenactor is that it requires him or her to ad-lib responses. This can lead to incorrect information and is really a difficult and poor way to show history. The reenactor is likely to answer in a way he or she thinks the person would have answered, rather than presenting what is known, documented, and historically correct.

Role playing is frequently used in living history instead of first person. Role playing is a method of acting where one person takes on a persona of another person. This was popular in the 1970s as a psychological tool and was a technique coming out of the game "Dungeons and Dragons" and other mythological role-playing games. It is very popular among other organizations, such as the Society for Creative Anachronism or the Renaissance Historical Society. By taking on another character, the actor can respond to stimuli and questions as if they were happening to someone else. Most of the time this is harmless fun.

The benefits of a written script are shown, however, when the first person interacts with the public. Unless the actor has a solid understanding of the nineteenth century, the actor moves in and out of historical authority to respond to questions. Actors must depend on their wit, rather than historical fact, to answer back. Few people can respond with historically correct answers to all the questions put forth by the public. A recent reenactment had a man portraying an Irish-Catholic immigrant soldier from the Shenandoah. His presentation was excellent about life in the Confederate army, and his accent wasn't bad at all. His portrayal remained realistic until he began to take questions in the first person, and someone in the audience asked who the Pope was in 1863. The honest question caused an embarrassing moment in an otherwise outstanding performance.

Many questions can be anticipated, though, and correct answers can be formulated beforehand and memorized as part of the script. Certainly the obvious questions of age, gender, race, politics, and religion can be anticipated and should be prepared for. Unfortunately, spectators may not always understand role playing and what is involved, and they may respond from prejudices, vindictiveness, or wanting to cause a "scene."

In the play by Edward Albee, *Who's Afraid of Virginia Woolf?,* the characters in the dark drama played psychological games called "Get the Host" and "Get the Guest." A similar game is played when spectators call out to the role player, "What's that big silver thing up there?" and pointing to an airplane going overhead. The point of this game is to catch the first-person role player in an out-of-character statement and disrupt the presentation. At this point, the teaching of history is out the window, and a game of one-upmanship ensues. A recent example of this was reported at Colonial Williamsburg, where a teenager asked a first-person interpreter what the helicopter flying overhead was. His response was clever, "My Goodness, the dragonflies are big this year!" But this was not teaching history. The first-person interpreter was able to defuse the confrontation through humor, however, and get back to role playing.

When the living historian represents an actual person, his or her interpretation may be challenged by a knowledgeable person in the audience. By portraying someone who had a documented or well-known life, the reenactor is vulnerable to criticism. This criticism is sometimes justified by people in the audience who know more, but someone may have an ax to grind or may even be an actual descendant of that person. This can be embarrassing, to say the least. At the worst, this can degenerate into a verbal competition that is undignified.

So first-person reenactors often do not interact with the spectators. Often they portray "snapshots of history" or "windows on history," where they act out a scene, often scripted and rehearsed, that the spectators merely observe. This is frequently performed in historic sites, such as houses, where the spectators move from room to room and can see period characters talking about current events from the past. This is best where there are controlled circumstances and the visitors don't stand next to or between the reenactors but are somewhat separated or cordoned off.

A good example of this is at the Jamestown glass factory in Virginia. Guides in modern dress lead tours through the factory. These guides explain the processes and methods used by the glassblowers, who are in the costumes of early-seventeenth-century craftsmen. This allows the craftsmen, who act in the first person in a "snapshot" scene from history, to concentrate on creating materials in the style of the early colony. Should anyone in the tour group ask a technical question, the tour guide relays the question to the craftsmen, who will then explain the method or process. These craftsmen usually answer questions about their craft in the first person. Infrequently they may have to break out of the first-person interpretation to answer a question, "I do it this way today, but the colonists did it this way." The tourists leave satisfied that they saw how it was actually done "back then."

In this environment, the visitors use all of their senses. The smell of burning charcoal, the roar and heat of the furnace, the touch of a finished glass sample, the taste of the atmosphere filled with smoke and pine—all add subtle and emphatic definition to the experience. Later, when reading about the early colony, memories of the smells, sounds, and sights from the glass factory are invoked and give added dimensions and feeling to the reading experience.

Living history in the third person gives more flexibility, since the reenactor can wear the correct clothes and use authentic equipment but can answer modern or comparative questions. Talking in the third person reduces the stress of acting a role, since the interpreter does not have to answer questions in character and can use modern terms and concepts to help interpretation. Third-person reenactors seem more approachable to spectators.

To avoid misunderstanding and confusion, always introduce or explain any first-person reenactment, or be sure that there is someone else around who can assist by answering questions. An effective example is a soldier at a particular station, such as a sentry or cook, who lets spectators know he or she can answer their questions. Another is a third-person guide, sometimes called the "translator, or "dodo" (see Glossary), who can answer questions for the first-person reenactor. This person also can act as a go-between, repeating the question of the spectator to the reenactor and allowing the free exchange of information.

Participate with Observers

A second technique of living history is participative, an educational tool whereby people can both observe and take part in activities from past lifestyles. Observers get to act out with the docent or reenactor by either helping with "chores" or doing other structured activities to experience the life of the period or culture portrayed. At its simplest, children can be allowed to lie on a bed and feel (and hear!) how a corn husk mattress differs from a modern one, help card a hunk of wool, or use a butter churn. They can learn for themselves how much energy was required to do a typical chore.

Indeed, having the visitors participate in doing some work or drill is very beneficial for learning. Of all that we learn, handling and doing helps us retain the most information. Lewis states that we retain only about 10 percent of what we hear and about 30 percent of what we read. In contrast, we retain about 50 percent of what we see and an astonishing 90 percent of what we do.[14]

In my classes, I demonstrate how seeing is more important than hearing. I hold up my hand and make an "OK" sign with my thumb and forefinger and ask everyone to copy this sign. Then I tell them to place those fingers on their cheek. As I say this, I place mine on the end of my chin. In a few seconds, everyone starts to laugh when they realize that almost everyone has followed my visual cue rather than my verbal instruction, and placed their fingers on their chins.

Children (and adults, too) have an innate desire to handle, touch, and use objects. Any interpretation should make use of this desire to enhance the teaming process. At a small reenactment recently, we "swept" the spectators for children, "drafted" them into the army, and "drilled" them in formation with wooden muskets. The children enjoyed it, and the parents got a lot of nice pictures.

Several historical farms and sites have expanded on this technique, and it has been especially successful at Old Economy in Ambridge, Pennsylvania. There, children can come for a "live-in" for a full day, dress in period clothes (bonnet and cloth apron for girls, hat and leather apron for boys), and experience the life and chores of children their age two hundred years ago. Adult reenactors teach them techniques that they immediately apply to their living-history experience. For children raised in cities, this kind of environmental living experiment on a farm can be enlightening. The experience brings to life a whole new interest in history. Patricia Black, a historian at Old Economy, comments on the experience:

> Costuming plays a vital function in the role playing of the Live-in. We have discovered that the instant the costume is shed, the spell is broken. Conversely, we have found that the costume provides an avenue for being transported into the past. Youngsters accustomed to the briefest of modern costume find even a long apron and bonnet or carpenter's apron and broad brimmed hat a new and confining experience. They begin to wonder "How did the boys and girls who dressed this way think and act?"
>
> The necessity of the hat is no longer a part of the social scene. Instead of ignoring the hair by tucking it up under a bonnet, a multimillion dollar industry thrives on the glorification, care and tending of ladies' hair. It would be unthinkable to hide it under a prim bonnet. The girls begin to think of a day when water was heated on a wood stove and the only aid to flowing locks was home-made lye soap. There is a psychological confinement to wearing a hat that the modern man, woman and child find quite difficult.

Mechanized food preparation and housecleaning have begun to make the apron suitable only for grandmothers brought up in another era. Little girls simply do not come equipped with aprons [today]. Why?—Because they do not churn butter, bake bread and perform chores of yesteryear which required that their clothes be covered up for cleanliness and modesty. Boys no longer carry water from the well and wood for the fires. They no longer work with hand tools with a carpenter's apron protecting them from flying sawdust. They study an engineering text rather than having the knowledge transmitted from the hands of a master craftsman. The ubiquitous apron performed the additional task of being a paper bag or box, carrying such items as vegetables from the root cellar or apples from the cider cellar.

The girls have seen a multitude of pictures of children wearing bonnets and aprons, but they will glance at them with new insight after having done it themselves. The boys in their broad brimmed hats learn quickly, as do the girls, that the hats feel "weird" and are hot. They also learn that children were just miniature adults and dressed accordingly.

The life of an age is a composite of many factors. How people dressed is a social commentary on an era. People dressed in a certain manner at any given time for a reason. Costume plays a valid role in the understanding of a time period.[15]

Lewis called this approach "environmental living," since the participants have an opportunity to experience the full environment of another time period. The participants, mostly school children, come to the site and spend some time there, sleeping over, eating, working, and playing—experiencing life in another era and another environment. The experience is not complete until the teachers have a chance to discuss it with the children and get them to think about it. What did they learn about life in the past, and how did it change the way they see life today? What did they learn about other cultures? What did they learn about the environment that was re-created, and how do they see their environment today?[16]

A third form of living history is used in historical research as a method of historical experimentation and presentation. Life in a particular culture or time is re-created so that the researchers can learn what problems people faced in that era and how they solved them by using period tools, methods, and technology. Great historical accuracy is required to effectively re-create the environment of a particular time period. In consequence, such living-history research does not readily lend itself to interpretation, education, or interaction with spectators.

An example of this can be found in Europe, where researchers live in medieval and Viking-style settlements. These settlements are not open to tourists. They are serious attempts by historians to re-create the lives of Europeans hundreds of years ago. Actually experiencing what life was like rather than just reading about it has provided greater depth of insight and new information about how people actually lived in other eras.

> Much of this experimental archaeology has taken place in England, Denmark, and other European countries, but Americans have tried similar experiments. At Old Sturbridge Village, for example, documentary research and archaeological excavation supervised by Director of Research John Worrell uncovered information on nineteenth century potter Harvey Brooks's kiln and other aspects of his pottery operation. But such traditional research neither revealed the kiln's effectiveness nor showed how its operation shaped Brooks's economic role or relations. When a reproduction kiln was built and then used, it produced new information that could be learned in no other way.[17]

In Civil War reenacting, "tacticals" are used as a training mechanism. These are tactical, nonhistorical reenactments or war games using the tactics, methods, and supplies of the period. They do not follow a script or plan outside of a vague outline of intent or goals. They frequently have judges or referees.

tacticals

Tacticals usually start on a Friday evening and continue straight through to Sunday afternoon. During this time, the reenactors will eat, sleep, and use only those items they brought with them. The purpose of these events, which are usually closed to the public, is to give the reenactors a chance to experience as nearly as possible the life of the soldiers. By living like the soldiers did, even for just a short time, the reenactors gain better understanding of how to wear the uniform and use the equipment. Tacticals are great fun as well.

Living History at Historic Sites
Living history or reenactments at historic sites may best be done by relying on the historical knowledge of the trained staff and docent volunteers, who can wear period clothing in an attempt to re-create life as lived during a

particular period. The clothing can serve as a starting point for discussion or questions from visitors.

The hosts can use reproductions of artifacts for demonstrations, which makes the presentation more interesting for visitors, and also allows the hosts to have some fun. With the number of antiques and small rooms in many historic sites, however, any attempt at participatory use of artifacts can easily lead to injury, breakage, or pilferage.

In all living-history re-creations, the items used should be either reconstructed or reproductions. Wear and strain on historical or antique items destroy their historical and informational value, especially if used incorrectly. Also, practical reproductions are more reliable, less expensive, and not as likely to break during demonstrations.

At Plimoth Plantation, for instance, antiques were replaced with accurate, museum-quality reproductions so that the reenactors can use the tools and equipment as the original settlers did without having to take great pains to protect or preserve them as they would artifacts.

An example of living history, where facts are given along with a demonstration, can be far more effective than a description in words alone. For example, modern sewing machines have cabinets with skirting that encloses the legs; older machines had fancy open iron grillwork instead. One reason for this is that ladies wore longer skirts in the nineteenth century and did not need an enclosure for modesty. A docent in a long dress can demonstrate this by sitting down at the machine.

The use of observations of specific facts to draw general conclusions about them is called "inductive logic." In the book *The Interpretation of Historic Sites,* William T. Alderson and Shirley Payne Lowe give an example with children.

> This is the kitchen. It has been restored to its appearance in 1890. Now, let's see what we can learn from this kitchen about the differences in the way people lived then and now. Look around for a few minutes and then we'll discuss it.
>
> Alright, now that you've had time to examine the room, who wants to start? Dorothy does. That's right, Dorothy, there's no refrigerator. What else can we observe about food storage, back then? No freezer, either. Now, what difference would that make in what people ate? Jim says that things we eat today that have to be kept cold would not have been in their diet. Do you all agree? Barbara has a question. Yes Barbara, that's an icebox. The block of ice went up here. All right, Barbara, how does this change your ideas about

their food? Right! They could keep things cold, but not frozen. So fruit juice, meat, and vegetables that we get frozen would have been stored in other forms. Yes, they had tinned food that they bought, and they canned a lot of food themselves.

Now, what about preparing food? Yes, that's the stove. Yes, that's the woodbox beside it. You're right, Jim. Cooking was harder for the housewife, having to handle that heavy wood. It was also harder for children your age, who had to help, learn to split kindling and bring in wood to keep the box full.

Yes! The thing that's shaped like an iron is an iron. That's right, Danny, it had to be heated on the stove.[18]

This is also an outstanding example of the use of the affirmative to let children know they have guessed correctly, or at least partially correctly. This encourages children to guess and to apply inductive logic.

A "time traveler" can be asked to spark discussions with the visitors, along with a docent to introduce the time traveler and to field or translate modern questions. This can be enormously effective in imparting not only historical information, but also the look and feel of another era.

All of these methods are teaming tools. They take much of the mustiness out of history and allow people to use their imagination and intuition in their exploration of history. They give the participants the chance to experience the differences in historical periods and the way people lived in those times.

There are many kinds of historic sites. Some are living-history farms, where the farm crops are authentically grown, harvested, and stored. Much work goes into these farms. The crops are grown as much as possible as they were in the period re-created, and often the former varieties of crops are used rather than modern hybrids.

There are compromises with history, however, as tubercular cows and crop pests, which were common in the past, are not tolerated today. Also, many kinds of authentic crops are no longer available. Farm machinery of the past can be deadly, and life on a farm was often dangerous, as is the attempt to re-create such aspects of farm life.[19]

The social life on a farm can be difficult to re-create today. Farms often have difficulty in interpreting the lives of slaves, indentured servants, and women, and it is often difficult to find people willing to play these roles.

Animals used on living-history farms must be very patient with children. Some adults complain about animal rights and abuse when they see horses plowing or oxen yoked together. They aren't interested in learning about differences in past and present uses of animals—they want them liberated *now!*

Another form of living history is to bring together a whole series of homes and businesses to create a living-history village, such as Plimoth Plantation, Williamsburg, or Old Sturbridge Village. All of the surroundings have the essence of a past era, so even after visitors leave a shop or home, they remain in the former era's surroundings.

In such a setting, the interrelationships and interdependency of a small village can be demonstrated. After visiting the garden of a house, the visitor can see how reeds from the garden were made into brooms inside the house. From there, the visitor can go to the store that traded manufactured goods for the brooms, and then sold the brooms to other villagers. One of the brooms would be found inside the schoolhouse, and another in the small church. This is quite an eye-opener for children, and adults as well, who are used to thinking of items as being mass-produced in factories.

TEACHING

How to Give a Haversack Talk

A haversack talk is a formal or informal talk addressed to a group of people, in which items of equipment or clothing are worn or placed on a blanket for display. It can be done in the classroom or in the field.

A uniform talk is a constant part of being a living historian or reenactor. At a reenactment, it is usual to talk to spectators about the WBTS, and sometimes to give short lectures. Often a reenactor will be invited to a class to give a demonstration or talk as well.

The construction of the talk will be extemporaneous instead of a lecture format. Because you are wearing or displaying clothes that are unusual, people will ask you about them. You can expect to be interrupted by questions, by follow-up questions, and by silly questions, and they will often leap ahead to points you want to make later in the talk or go down paths you don't want to tread. Be friendly to the questioners, as they are showing an interest in what interests you. Remember that when you got started, you asked similar questions.

Keep a sense of humor. Children often ask frank questions that may be embarrassing to answer in public. Realize, however, that the audience will be sympathetic to you and will appreciate a good and honest reply.

Lewis cautions that the talk should have a short and simple theme. The theme should be stated as a short, simple, and complete sentence; contain only one idea; reveal the overall purpose of the presentation; be specific; and be interesting and motivatingly worded when possible. "What a Typical Soldier Wore," "How to Load and Fire a Musket," "What Was in the Typical Haversack," "How to Pitch a Tent," and "What Soldiers Ate During the Civil War" are all good examples of talks that reenactors can give. The themes are short and to the point, and leave room for questions and further learning.[20]

A common practice among public speakers is the "preacher's pause." This is a short pause taken by the speaker before beginning the talk. During this time, the speaker can look over the audience and make eye contact, and take time to gather his or her thoughts. The pause relieves stress in the speaker and increases anticipation in the audience, which will quiet down, become still, and wait for what is to be said. Though the "preacher's pause" works well in organized talks, such as lectures given to a class, it doesn't work so well in informal talks like those given to spectators at reenactments.

To keep track of where you are and where you are going, it is good to have a mental outline of the discussion. There are several forms a discussion may take. It can be topical, where it is not necessarily important which topic is talked about first. It may be given in chronological order, in which things are discussed in the order in which they happened; in climactical order, where things lead to a climax, such as the assassination of Lincoln; or in spatial order, where the talk might start with the impressions of a village, then move to state and national politics. Or the talk might be given in process order, where things are done step by step, such as how to grow cotton or load a rifle. By having an organized structure, it is simpler to remember what you have said and what remains to be said, and it is easier for the audience to follow as well.

For a uniform talk, I find it helpful to follow a logical order, starting at the feet and working up, talking first about the shoes, then the stockings, the trousers, the underwear, the shirt, the vest, the coat, and last, the hat. Or, conversely, I may start with the hat and work down. If I am asked a question, it is easy to remember where I left off.

When speaking about the contents of the haversack, I may begin by discussing the eating implements of knife, fork, spoon, plate, and dipper; then move on to foods, such as hardtack, beans, desiccated vegetables, fatback, and salt pork; then personal gear, such as letters, cards, and jackknife; and then armaments, leather works, bayonet, cartridges, percussion caps, the rifle, and loading and firing sequences.

Point directly to the object you are speaking about or, better still, hold it up. With a dozen strange objects on the blanket, referring to an object without indicating which one it is can quickly confuse an audience. Stand to the side of the blanket or quilt holding the accoutrements so that you can remain facing the audience; by simply turning your head, you can locate any object on display. Do not turn your head away from the audience and toward the objects more than necessary; remember, you are speaking to the audience, not the accoutrements.

Keep the front of the object you are discussing toward the audience, and hold the object so that it can be seen. Don't, for example, hold a cap box up with your thumb over the front; hold it from the straps behind, or in the fold between the thumb and first finger.

Anything that the audience can touch or hold will be appreciated. Handling some minié balls or hardtack will give people a more lasting impression of what they are learning. Be sure to count the number of items you pass around and how many come back. If there are small children in the audience, caution parents that the children shouldn't try to eat the hardtack or put other things in their mouths.

It's easy to make your own hardtack for this purpose. You'll need 5 cups of flour, 1 teaspoon of salt, 1 tablespoon of baking soda (optional), and 1 to 1¼ cups of water. In a mixing bowl, combine the flour, baking soda, and salt. Slowly add the water and knead into a medium-firm dough. Roll the dough out on a greased rectangular cookie sheet and shape into a long rectangle. (Use a cookie sheet without edges; if the sides of the hardtack touch a greased edge, they will become discolored.) With a knife, cut the hardtack into pieces about 3 by 3 inches. Then use a tenpenny nail, a punch, or the tines of a fork to mark either a 3-by-3 or 4-by-4 pattern of holes in the hardtack. Place in a preheated 450-degree oven for fifteen to twenty minutes, or until the tops are lightly browned. The hardtack will come out solid but not hard. It will harden over the next couple of days, so it is good to do this on Wednesday for a Friday night reenactment. Basically, hardtack is flour turned into dough, then dehydrated; there is little to spoil or to taste good.

Never let spectators handle weapons, especially edged ones. People often do unwise things with weapons. I handed a bayonet to one young boy, who turned around unexpectedly to show it to his father just as the father was bending down to take a picture of his son. The socket of the bayonet went right into the camera lens, knocking the camera back into his father's eye.

No one was hurt, but the camera lens was cracked and I learned an important lesson.

There is one important basic rule of speaking: KISS (Keep it Short and Simple). Keep your talk fast-paced, short, and to the point. Don't try to say everything; it is better to say too little than too much. Refer the audience to some sources, such as the library, for further information.

If you make a mistake in your talk, admit it and go on. Spectators can appreciate the human qualities of the speaker. Also, if you don't know the answer to a question, say so rather than trying to think up a probable answer. No one can know everything.

Remember that while you are in uniform in front of a group, you are considered an authority on the subject. The audience will believe what you say, even if you give them incorrect information, so it is very important to be sure that what you say is correct or to admit that you don't know. You have an ethical responsibility to tell only the truth.

Don't preach. You may have strong partisan feelings on a subject, but the spectators will not understand them and will feel uneasy if you express them too forcibly. As much as possible, keep your talks unbiased and emotionally level. Many reenactors have "pet peeves," such as how to wear the kepi correctly or the color of canteen covers. If you preach on this type of subject, the audience will not understand the reasons behind your emphatic views. To explain your feelings would take time away from the important points of your talk. So keep your personal opinions to yourself when addressing the public.

Speak naturally and informally. Make eye contact and smile. Try to make each spectator feel that you are talking to him or her individually. Not only does this make the audience more attentive, it also relieves you of a feeling of talking to a big group. Stage fright affects most people, but if you feel comfortable with your subject and you make eye contact with the people you are talking to, most of the nervousness will go away.

If the spectators seem bored, restless, or inattentive, evaluate your presentation. Maybe you are giving out too many facts and not enough interpretation or are not allowing enough room for questions.

If you give talks often, have a friend videotape you giving a talk at a reenactment or school. The next time you give the talk, have him film the audience. By watching these tapes, you will be able to evaluate your mistakes and correct them.

You may want to consider handing out small pads of plain paper and period pencils (scrape the yellow paint off number 2 pencils, remove the erasers, and sharpen them with a small knife) so that spectators can write down questions to ask at the end of the talk. This makes them feel that they are participating as well. Make sure all the pads are returned at the end of the talk.

Don't say that you will answer questions at the end of the talk; say that you will stay to talk to anyone who wants to know more. When people ask for more information, give them names of resources available at public libraries. Geoffrey Ward and Ken Burns's *The Civil War* (shown recently on public TV), James McPherson's *Battle Cry of Freedom,* and Bruce Catton's *The Civil War* series are good general books for adults. Excellent children's books on the WBTS are the *Golden Book of the Civil War,* put out by American Heritage magazine, and Neil Johnson's *The Battle of Gettysburg,* which has excellent photographs of reenactors. Both adults and children enjoy the Time-Life series of books on the Civil War. Let audience members write down these titles (and any others you like) so that they have something to follow up with. Printed bibliographies handed out to spectators, on the other hand, usually end up as litter.

The National Park Service manual states that any interpretive talk should conclude with a statement on the need for conservation and preservation of historic sites. I heartily agree with this; everyone interested in preserving and interpreting our nation's history should end any talk with such a statement. It is not always in the best taste, however, to pass a hat around for donations after making such a statement. Keep the statement general and as a short concluding remark.

How to Give a Civilian Impression Talk

A civilian impression talk is much like the uniform talk. There is generally less gear or accoutrements to talk about, so most civilian impressions are limited to clothing talks but sometimes include the customs, occupations, manners, and mores of the mid-nineteenth century.

Start at the head or toe and work up or down. Describe each article, explaining how it was made and how and why it was used. People in civilian clothes do not seem as intimidating to spectators as men in uniform, and frank questions can be expected, especially from children. Ladies will be asked about underwear, corsets, hoops, bustles, snoods, and so forth. "Does the bustle hurt when you sit down?" "How do you go to the bathroom wearing hoops?" "Why are your shoes all funny?" "Why are you wearing a bonnet?"

Don't simply recite information about the clothing, but interpret what you wear. Describe how it feels, whether it is hot or comfortable. When would you wear it—to a ball, to church, for work at home, around a fire-place? Ladies should be able to explain such things as why women wore hoops. Since many women kept busy (or kept up the pretense of being busy) with one task or another, talk about hand occupations such as sewing, knit-ting, darning, or other domestic or fine arts of the period. Interesting talks can be given about professions for women, from schoolteacher to Quaker minister to professional mourner to shopowner to seamstress to herb doctor or mid-wife. Even cursory reading in Victorian history will reveal an eye-opening range of occupations for women outside the home, especially on or near the frontier.

Men and women doing civilian talks should be prepared to answer ques-tions about their trades or professions. A man in a business suit will likely be asked what he would be doing in that outfit a hundred years ago. If the reen-actor states a profession, it is guaranteed he or she will be asked questions about it. For example, if he says he is a banker, he will certainly be asked about banking a hundred years ago. If she says she is a teacher, surely there will be one in the audience who is not only a teacher, but a specialist on the history of teaching. So do some research on your persona.

The only reenactor I have ever seen who stumped an audience was one who said he was a hog farmer from North Carolina. When he began to talk about using a hog cane to herd swine, the questions came pouring out. You will learn a great deal from an audience. "As you teach, so by your pupils you will be taught."

Team Teaching

Many reenactors give talks as a team. One reenactor might do the Federal side while the other does the Confederate, or each might do a short talk on one branch of the armed forces, such as artillery, cavalry, and infantry. This form of talk is shorter for each participant, allows for a gathering of greater expertise, and can be more enjoyable for spectators.

At one reenactment, a participant brought a Federal uniform in addition to his Confederate gear, threw both uniforms on a blanket, and began a presenta-tion comparing the two uniforms. Soon one of the Union fellows came over and started to uphold the honor of the North. Within a few minutes, a good team approach developed. The two reenactors presented not only two different uniforms, but two different points of view. It was a real crowd pleaser.

Another type of team teaching utilizes the "time traveler" technique described earlier, where one person adopts a first-person persona and another acts as a translator. The first-person reenactor stays in character, and the audience has to ask any questions through the translator, who can then expand upon the answer.

QUESTIONS SPECTATORS ASK

Spectators will often ask leading questions to get the reenactor to begin a conversation. This is called a "conversational gambit." The spectator wants to ask a question but does not want to reveal his lack of knowledge. This leads to the most silly questions imaginable. These questions aren't always based on ignorance (though ignorance plays a big part), but for some reason I don't understand, many spectators leave their common sense behind when they go to a reenactment.

I believe that many spectators view a reenactment as though they were watching television: passively and as nonparticipatory observers. Spectators have sometimes rudely, and even crudely, talked about me and what I was doing in the third person, just as though I weren't really there in front of them. They don't mean to be rude; part of it is that people have grown accustomed to television, where what they are watching is not real. In addition, many people have never been to a live performance where they can interact with the performers, so they really don't know what to say or how to act in such a situation. The most natural of the spectators are the very young and the very old. The youngest know how to ask questions, while the older folks know and remember how to converse.

An adult spectator looks slowly around the Gettysburg National Battlefield Park at all the monuments, places a finger pensively to his lips, and seriously says, "You know, it just occurred to me—why did all the Civil War soldiers only fight their battles in National Parks?"

Another visitor to the same park, which has the largest collection of marble, bronze, and granite statuary in the nation, looks slowly around and asks, "Did the soldiers hide behind all these monuments to shoot at the enemy? Where are the bullet holes?"

After an hour's talk in the blazing summer sun about the uniforms of the Civil War soldier, a spectator asks, "Where'd you get the German uniforms?"

"My granddaddy fought in the Civil War and had a uniform just like yours, too. Only he called it Vetsnom or something."

It is 105 degrees when we come back from a spirited reenactment. We are dripping with sweat, our shirts are sopping wet, and a spectator calls out, "Are those wool uniforms hot?"

"Gee, who buys you all this neat stuff?"

"Don't some of you people dress up like Indians sometimes for the Boston Tea Party?"

"Are those guns real?" (I have never really understood this, the most commonly asked question from children. The question means more than "Are those antique rifles?" It means "Can they shoot real bullets and hurt people?" I have never answered this with a plain yes or no, but always explain that they are accurate reproductions and can also be used for hunting and target practice.)

"Do you use real bullets?" (This is perhaps the oldest of all questions documented about reenactments. See Harriet Beecher Stowe's account on page 3.)

A young child pulls on his mother's dress as they see a cavalryman ride by. "Look, Mommy! Is that a real horse?"

"Did you really sleep in those tents last night? In the rain?"

"Which side are the good guys?"

"Which side won?" (This was a serious question. I thought he was kidding, but he wasn't.)

"Which side were the Americans?" (This spectator was also dead serious.)

In summation, although many of these questions may seem silly or elementary to reenactors, they are asked honestly by people who want to learn more. As educators and interpreters, we should welcome such openings for dialogue and understanding and treat all of them seriously.

2

Reenactment for Infantrymen

The most common form of reenactment is a small, local event. Local events are often hosted by a historic site, state museum, or community group. Here a few regiments come together for a living-history weekend. Other events are large national gatherings, where units from all over the United States and other countries participate. National events are planned at least a year in advance and make provisions for reenacting a specific battle. There are usually only one or two national events each year, and they draw thousands of spectators and reenactors. Authenticity of dress is required at all events, but the rules are sometimes more relaxed at local events.

AUTHENTICITY

To accurately portray the life of the common soldier 130 years ago, it is important to use authentic period clothing and equipment. Modern materials may be used but should always be covered and hidden by period items. Though anathema to a truly authentic unit, some reenactors use a modern sleeping bag at night, and either roll it up and take it back to the car before the spectators are allowed into the camp, or cover it with a period blanket so that camp visitors will see only authentic items. Modern beverages should be carried around in authentic cups and not in commercial aluminum cans.

Try to go "period" as much as possible, however. Doing without modern food, clothing, and incidentals will teach you more about the time period than any books. It is an excellent break from modern stress, too. I am not suggesting that you be uncomfortable, but that you take a weekend to learn how people stayed comfortable and healthy 130 years ago.

The importance of authenticity can be seen in a letter published in *National Geographic* concerning the Cherokee Indians of North Carolina, the subject of a previous article in the magazine. This letter refers to a tribal member who wore a Plains Indian costume rather than traditional Cherokee garb, since this is what the tourists wanted and expected. "Yet how is the public to gain an understanding . . . if individuals do not put forward an accurate description? . . . Perpetuating stereotypes . . . is damaging . . . and misleading to us all." (Quotation from Elizabeth McJanet, letter to *National Geographic,* Forum section, Vol. 188, No. 3, 1995.)

In another article, reenactor Chris Roberts explained the importance of authenticity not only for the spectators and as an educational medium, but also as a personal experience. The actor tries to fool the audience into thinking he is the person he is portraying; the reenactor tries to fool himself. There are moments when the reenactor loses track of the time period. At that moment he has gone beyond fooling others and is fooling himself. Reenactors live for moments like this. But this cannot be accomplished without authenticity. If you look down the field and see modern glasses or a wristwatch, the modern world crashes in and ruins the moment. Roberts says, "A committed reenactor is an authentic one."[1]

Authenticity can be a confusing concept for new reenactors. Some may feel that authenticity keeps you from wearing and doing what you want. This is not what authenticity is all about. Authenticity liberates you to do anything and be anyone in a simpler world that existed 130 years ago. Rather than keeping you from using modern fabrics, it lets you pick and choose from any of the fabrics that were available four generations ago. By learning which fabrics, styles, and fashions were worn in the past, the reenactor learns a whole new way of life. Some things, like wool uniforms, are uncomfortable on hot days. Other things, like courtly manners, are so charming and attractive that they remain with you and become a part of you, even when you take off the clothing of a bygone day.

In a talk at Antietam National Battlefield, Ross Kimmel stated that there were six rules to authentic gear and clothing. First, it is important to look like the actual soldier, and not just like other reenactors. Too often, reenactors get a "club mentality" and try to dress like each other, instead of striving to look like the soldiers did 130 years ago. Second, the reenactor often must use primary written sources for information. Many units do not have access to a complete uniform that can be copied, so to be authentic, the reenactor must do research. He or she must look at drawings and photographs of soldiers from the period, read descriptions in diaries and regimental histories, and study accounts in letters or official records. Third, many other reenactors are also seeking authenticity; consult with them and share information. Fourth, many authorities are currently publishing the results of their research. Although this is secondary information, be sure to use good modern sources for your interpretation. Fifth, avoid stereotypes, and be aware that many things once thought true are found to be untrue in history. For example, one Confederate regiment was thought to have worn slouch hats during the last two years of the war. Research has found several verbal accounts, and some contemporary drawings, indicating that most of the men continued to wear their kepis throughout the war. Finally, be willing to use your imagination, but don't let it run away from you. If you can reasonably assume something was not only possible, but probable, then you can use your imagination. But don't rationalize to fit what really happened into a modern need.[2]

The rewards of authenticity outweigh the costs of time and money. Research and study will show you what types of clothing were worn, and how, during the nineteenth century. Then, when you wear these clothes, they will have much more significance than anything else you have ever worn.

CIVIL WAR UNIFORMS

Militia Uniforms

The early-war period included prewar militia uniforms. These came in all styles, some so eccentric as to be almost unbelievable today. These are referred to as Class A or dress uniforms by reenactors.[3]

Militia companies were very popular in America before the WBTS. Local units trained to preserve civil order; they also served as a social club for men, who would meet once a month or so, drill a bit, and then head for the nearest tavern. Militias hosted frequent dress balls so that the men could show off their fancy uniforms, which were designed to attract ladies and new recruits, rather than being practical. Regular army troops often referred to them as "bandbox" uniforms.

The militia was called out whenever there was a local emergency or a political parade. After the 1859 raid on Harpers Ferry, many militia regiments were formed in the South in preparation for insurrection or the coming conflict. Many were also formed in the North, most notably Col. E. Elmer Ellsworth's Zouave company from Chicago, which was known for its elaborate drill performed at double-quick pace with clockwork perfection. The Zouaves claimed national championships and challenged other militia units to drill contests. Once, on a dare, the Chicago Zouave regiment tied scarves around their eyes and then ran through the drill blindfolded without a hitch.

The militia uniforms were imitations of uniforms from other times and places. For instance, the Zouave uniforms were fashioned after the clothing originally worn by the Zouaves of northern Africa, who were French Algerian tribesmen noted for their fierce loyalty and courage and their precision drills. These uniforms usually included baggy pants, often gaiters, a sash, a short jacket, and a fez with a tassel, or sometimes a turban.

Other regiments imitated uniforms from the Napoleonic period, including the frogged jackets and brimless caps of dragoons and grenadiers. Some militia regiments, such as the Philadelphia Fencibles, sported the uniform of the eighteenth-century British Army, including red tunic, white cross belt, and bearskin "greathat." Fire companies would often form their own company of militia, and one New York fire company regiment went into battle wearing red shirts and carrying a silk flag showing crossed ladders.

Confederate Uniforms

Confederate uniforms were of two types: early-war period (prewar through the spring of 1862) and late-war period (after the spring of 1862). During the early-war period, supplies were plentiful and uniforms were consistent within each regiment or at least each company. During the late period, Confederate military supplies became more difficult to acquire, and there was an increase in the amount of captured or "make-do" equipment to compensate. This is when the butternut colors, civilian clothing items, and captured Union accoutrements were used. There is a great deal of controversy over this, so check with your regiment's guidelines for correct uniforms.

Standard Confederate army uniforms were gray jackets or frock coats with either light blue or gray kersey wool trousers. This was the ideal, but many of the uniforms that were issued fell far short. Defining colors is tricky at best, and the grays used by Confederate troops varied quite a bit and had different names. Some were more colorfast than others. One manufacturer of reproduction clothing gives the colors these names: "Confederate Gray," a clear, medium gray; "Steel Gray," with a light blue cast to the color; "Tuscaloosa Gray," a brownish gray; "Richmond Gray," a dark gray; and "Cadet Gray," a light-colored gray.

In the North, factories under contract to the state or Federal government made the uniforms. Confederate uniforms, on the other hand, were often made at home and by hand, and often showed differences in style and in the skill of the women who made them. One account from North Carolina states that the Ladies' Aid Society sewed nearly 120 uniforms for the men from their county:

> The company had to be equipped, the uniforms for nearly one hundred and twenty men to be made; the tents that were to shelter them, the haversacks that were to hold their rations. All this was done by our society of ladies, and more, such as military blouses and covering the canteens for the men; this was all done by the ladies lovingly and cheerfully with their own fingers, for there was not a sewing machine at that time in all this county; all the heavy stitching of military suits, tents and canteens was done by our fingers. . . . In the fall of 1861, we made nearly all the overcoats for the company.[4]

During the rest of the war, states, homes, and counties supplied their men as best they could. Uniform cloth, materials, and patterns were likely similar among companies, at least until near the end of the war. Uniform style and quality often varied from company to company in a regiment, however. The uniformity the Federal government achieved in outfitting its soldiers was never accomplished by the South.

Trousers were of heavy wool or of a wool and cotton blend, sometimes called "jeans cloth," although it was not denim. There were no summer uniform pants of a lighter material. During the 1860s, all trousers, both civilian and military, were similar. The pants were high-waisted, coming up almost to the navel or the lowest rib, and reached down to the instep of the boot. The area covering the fly buttons was narrow and as inconspicuous as possible. The pants were not worn snug or tight, since that would mean pulling out the suspender buttons every time the soldier leaned over or sat down, but were loosely worn and had a lot of give when sitting or squatting. For reasons of modesty, the male form, like the female, was to be draped, not outlined, in public. Loose trousers also acted as wicks by absorbing sweat from the legs and allowed the legs to be cooled by evaporation. Also, they left enough room for the long underwear that was worn year-round.

The trousers did not have deep or sharp military-style creases in them. The sharp crease style is the result of steam-ironing uniforms, which came out of the Navy laundries of World Wars I and II. Civil War-era pants, if ironed at all, were ironed flat and folded on the seam, so no crease would be obvious. The irons of the WBTS period were heated on a stove, and then hand-pressed on the fabric. Ironing was reserved for lighter cloth, such as shirts, blouses, and other linens, rather than the heavier materials of pants and jackets. So although razor-sharp creases in trousers are a common twentieth-century clothing custom, they show a lack of awareness about nineteenth-century dress customs and are an obvious mistake to most other reenactors.

No creased ironed uniforms!

Darts and tucks were often sewn in pants, especially for boys, whose wise mothers used them to allow room for growth. Signs of individual tailoring and repair also were common.

The army had four sizes of uniforms. Many soldiers wrote that there were really only two sizes: too big or too small. A common joke was to say the army had put a number one man in a number four suit. Anyone who was not one of these standard sizes had to do some sewing to make the uniform fit.

Late-war Confederate gear included civilian items, captured Yankee equipment, worn or make-do clothing and equipment, and the butternut uniform, which was civilian clothing dyed with shells from butternuts. This process was far from consistent, and colors ranged from a light beige to dark, rich brown. Previously dyed materials dumped in the butternut dye kettle had results that were sometimes amazing. Bright plaids dyed butternut came out with mixed results, to say the least.

butternut

New reenactors often wonder which items to purchase first. The musket and boots are the most important, as they are the most difficult to borrow. After buying these items, some of the other uniform and equipment items should be purchased or made. The following are the recommended minimal purchases for a Confederate military reenactor: a uniform coat or jacket, pants and braces, boots, socks, musket, bayonet, belt, cap box, cartridge box, bayonet scabbard, kepi or slouch hat, shirt, and canteen (a rice bag or haversack is helpful). Much of the leather gear, the canteen, and the haversack can be of "captured" Yankee manufacture. When in doubt, check with another knowledgeable reenactor in your unit.

In almost any unit, there are members who have extra uniform jackets and leather gear to loan. Standard ethics among reenactors require that if any item borrowed from another reenactor is lost, broken, or stolen (whatever the reason), it must be satisfactorily replaced by the person borrowing the item—no excuses!

When I first started reenacting, I borrowed a coat from another reenactor and promptly ripped its sleeve at an event. I was horrified at being so careless, and I offered to pay for it or get it fixed. The other guy told me to remember that these were toys and not to be so hard on myself. Hard use is expected, and some wear is inevitable. He also told me that this was the only hobby he knew where the older and more worn the materials are, the more authentic they become. However, it is always a good practice to offer to repair or replace anything you borrow from another member.

It is important to get as much of your equipment as possible quickly. Do not depend on others to help supply you. The person you depend on may not make it to the next event, or there may be another new recruit who needs to be outfitted. All in all, it's best to have your own stuff.

There are two main types of rifles used: the Enfield and the Springfield. These rifles are made by different manufacturers, and have different prices, depending on the quality and country of origin. As with most things, you get what you pay for. Since many of these weapons are made overseas, the value of the dollar will have a large effect on the cost.

New rifles are being manufactured for the reenactment community. In recent years there has been more choice than between simply the 1861 Springfield and the Enfield mentioned above. These muskets vary in price and quality, however, and you need to check with your regiment's historian before you purchase such a big-ticket item. Also, some of these muskets have individual quirks, such as protruding ramrods, stuck hammers, loose triggers, or scratches. It is always a good idea to buy either from a trusted sutler who will stand behind the piece or have someone knowledgeable with you when you choose your weapon.

Remember, if you get a Confederate-made reproduction musket, you wouldn't want to use it in a Federal impression. However, a U.S.-made weapon can be used by Confederates as well. So get the best advice from your unit historian and your pards before you buy.

Several companies make three-banded Enfields:

Armi Sport (Italy) $350
Euro Arms/EOA (Italy) $385
Navy Arms (EOA-Italy) $480

Several companies make Springfield rifles:

Armi Sport (Italy) $395
Euro Arms (Italy) $465
Dixie Gun Works (Japan) $525
CS Richmond Armory musket:
    Armi Sport (Italy) $445
    Euro Arms of America (Italy) $465
1842 Smoothbore Springfield, .69 caliber:
    Armi Sport (Italy) $450
1842 Rifled Springfield:
    Armi Sport (Italy) $495

A Confederate copy of the Springfield is very popular with Southern troops. It's manufactured in Richmond, using Springfield templates captured at Harpers Ferry.

CS Richmond Musket (Italy) $410

The following is a list of essential equipment and estimated prices for 1999. This is a generic list, suitable for both sides.

Equipment	Low Price	High Price
3-banded musket	$400	$500
Bayonet	30	95
Bayonet scabbard	15	30
Uniform coat	70	105
Uniform pants	60	105
Shirt	30	65
Belt with buckle	25	40
Brogans or bootees	80	125
Canteen	30	60
Rice bag or haversack	20	45
Cap box	20	35
Cartridge box	50	95
Cartridge box sling	15	25
Slouch hat or kepi	30	65
Brass insignia	15	25
Totals	**$890**	**$1,415**

The prices given here are estimates for new items and are only a guide. Prices and quality vary greatly among suppliers. You can get most of these items from sutlers at large events. Though prices tend to be slightly higher at larger reenactments, you can buy the whole kit and caboodle all at once. Be sure to compare prices and comparison-shop with several different sutlers, and have someone knowledgeable with you when you make your purchases.

Many items can be made less expensively by someone handy with leather or needle and thread. Used items can be purchased at reduced prices, or by trade or exchange. Any transaction between members of the same regiment should be witnessed by a neutral member to avoid misunderstandings.

Many larger units have an auction at the beginning of the year to help new recruits buy uniform items. Several units will come together, and used equipment will be auctioned. The purpose is not to make a profit for the seller so much as to give a new recruit a break on the prices.

A "mule collar," or blanket roll, can be made from a woolen blanket or quilt with period materials and dyes. It is worn rolled up and doubled over one shoulder down to the hip and is a convenient way to carry your sleeping gear. It can also carry your gum blanket/poncho rolled up inside. Both sides used the "mule collar," although Union soldiers most often carried a knapsack. Made of stiff leather and tarred canvas, a knapsack is heavy and uncomfortable and therefore not recommended as a first item of purchase for either side. Use the "mule collar" instead.

Obtain the essential items before you think of additional items such as D-guard knives, boot pistols, or camp gear. At tacticals, what is taken in is what you eat and sleep and shoot with for the weekend. Too much poundage makes the hobby almost like work and takes away the fun. The Confederate light infantry soldier carried a load of about 40 pounds of uniform, rifle, and equipment. More than that, as any modern soldier can tell you, is heavy.

Union Uniforms

Equipment for Union troops is almost the same as for Confederate, but with the following exceptions:

Union gear was more standardized. There were fewer individual cuts and styles, and there were fewer civilian items. Be sure you know what your unit will permit.

Units received flannel or wool shirts of dark blue, light blue, gray, or white. As with the Confederate army, many men preferred to wear civilian shirts, often made at home by loved ones and worn for sentimental reasons. Also, a temporary lack of army supplies would mean bought or foraged civilian shirts.

Most of the Union troops wore light blue trousers of kersey wool, a tightly woven cloth of pure wool that was long-lasting and fairly comfortable. A few regiments issued dark blue pants, so check with your regimental guidelines. (The generic Union soldier would have light blue pants.) U.S. Army regulations allowed three pairs of trousers for the first year, and then two pairs the next year, indicating that the pants lasted from four to six months each, but doubtless they often required repair.

When they needed repair, Union pants were patched with blue cloth that matched the prefaded color of the issued pants, unlike the Confederates' multi-hued patches.

Be sure to carry spare buttons; you will soon find out why fly buttons are the most commonly dug items from Civil War sites. When sewing buttons on the braces, it is a good idea to sew the inside button to a tin "fly" button on the outside. This will keep the button from pulling at the cloth of the pants when you sit down and will keep the buttons sewn on longer. Civil War soldiers invariably used cotton thread. I use dental floss. Though it is an anachronism, it keeps the buttons on longer. Use cotton thread if you want to be more authentic.

There are many styles of Union coats. According to army regulations, the Union army issued a frock coat and Hardee hat for dress uniforms, and a sackcoat and bummer cap for fatigue details. The sack coat and bummer were more often worn by the troops, and were more easily and cheaply replaced. The four-button fatigue jacket or sack coat was the one used by the troops during fatigue details, and most often worn around the camps. It was common to both eastern and western U.S. troops.

The shell jacket, also called a "roundabout," was a dress coat common to the cavalry and artillery branches. The shell was a shorter coat, reaching only to the waist. It sometimes had as many as fifteen buttons, some only ornamental. Many troops liked them because of the style, but they weren't practical in keeping the men warm or protected from the weather. A version of this shell jacket, with light blue piping, was issued to the New York State infantry and was known as the "Excelsior jacket."

The frock coat was the dress coat for the Union troops. A single-breasted jacket that reached almost to the knees, it sometimes had light blue trim or piping. This coat was issued to the regular army and state militia at the beginning of the war, but most active troops wore only the four-button fatigue coat at the end of the war.

The Army Regulations stated:

1482. The uniform for all enlisted foot men, shall be a single breasted frock of dark blue cloth, made without plaits [pleats], with a skirt extending one-half the distance from the top of the hip to the bend of the knee; one row of nine buttons on the breast, placed at equal distances, stand up collar to rise no higher than to permit the chin to move freely over it, to hook in front . . . cuffs pointed according to pattern, and to button with two small buttons at the under seam collar and cuffs edged with a cord or welt of cloth . . . of sky-blue for infantry.[5]

During the winter, issued greatcoats or overcoats covered the uniform jacket. The greatcoat came down over the knees and had a cape over the shoulders that helped provide extra warmth and protection from rain and snow. The Union-issue greatcoat had a cape that came down over the sleeve, all the way to the elbow; a stand-up collar; and rarely, a rolled cuff. The cavalry overcoat had a split up the back to the waist. For the reenactor, a greatcoat should be at the bottom of the list of purchases, but it is mighty toasty during cold reenactments.

The Army Regulations stated of the greatcoat:

1596. All other Enlisted men—of sky blue cloth stand-up collar single breasted cape to reach down to the elbows when the arm is extended, and to button all the way up.[6]

The Union forces used canvas haversacks, in which were carried the regulation tin plate, knife, fork, and spoon. Early-war units and militia regiments used plain, untarred canvas haversacks, but later these were tarred to make them weatherproof. The haversack had a cloth lining that formed an inside pocket, so there could be a separation between the ration issue and the personal effects. Grease from the rations smeared the cloth, which also helped make it as waterproof as was possible in those days. Reenactors usually carry period or reproduction plates and utensils from which to eat meals.

Regarding haversacks, the Army Regulations stated:

112. Haversacks will be marked upon the flap with the number and name of the regiment, the letter of the company, and number of the soldier, in black

letters and figures. And each soldier must, at all times, be provided with a haversack and canteen, and will exhibit them at all inspections. It will be worn on the left side on marches, guard and when paraded for detached service—the canteen outside the haversack.[7]

Some units have special requirements. Some reenactment regiments use only the Union sack coat, while others use only frock coats or shell jackets. Berdan sharpshooters wore green uniforms. The Iron Brigade regiments wore Hardee hats with plumes. Zouave regiments wore either fezes or kepis. Check your regimental guidelines before you buy any item. Use these guidelines while shopping at the sutlers. If you are purchasing by mail, give the sutler a telephone call first. Sutlers are willing to offer advice and help over the phone. Let the sutler know what regiment you are with; sutlers very often are familiar with the uniform requirements and will have just what you need. Good sutlers keep records of uniform requirements of reenactment regiments. They are often history buffs themselves and will research clothing from the period, and they sometimes turn up facts not known to the reenactment units. As with the Confederate uniform, obtain the essential items first.

STANDARD EQUIPMENT FOR BOTH UNION AND CONFEDERATE TROOPS

Headgear

Soldiers wore a wide variety of hats, caps, helmets, and other headgear. Hats expressed the personality of the wearer, and some of them were very odd personalities. Of the types of headwear, two types stand out: the kepi and the slouch hat.

Kepis

The most common cap among both Confederate and Union troops was the kepi. Two types of kepis evolved during the war. The older style, called a "forage cap," had a high cloth crown. Before the war, the hat had a crown sticking straight up, with a cardboard brace. With wear, the crown leaned over toward the front of the head or off to one side. Later, the Union copy became known as a "bummer." Near the conclusion of the war, a similar cap with a shorter crown evolved, although this one is often confused with the 1872-model kepi.

The kepi was very popular and often (but not always) matched the color of the uniform coat. Kepi trim was usually sky blue or a darker blue, called

"French blue." The brim of the kepi was kept straight and was rarely creased. The custom of folding the hat brim came from twentieth-century baseball players who would fold the brim in two, and then jam the hat in a back pocket when coming in from the field. This is a no-no among reenactors.

The kepi was very fashionable and looked good, but it was not an efficient cover. The cap did not keep the sun or rain off the back of the neck, and it provided no protection for the ears or cheeks. A havelock, a piece of cloth or canvas (usually white) that buttoned onto or fitted over the kepi, was used to keep the sun and rain off the soldier's neck. The havelock lay over the back of the cap and hung down over the neck and ears. It is as uncomfortable and silly looking as it sounds.

Even after the Civil War, many troops wore the kepi, the great-grandfather of the baseball cap we are familiar with today. It has always been a symbol of belonging to a unit. Even today, people with no association with reenactors wear "farb" copies in leather, felt, and cloth.

Slouch Hats

Especially toward the end of the war, both Union and Confederate troops often wore a slouch hat with a broad brim instead of a kepi. The slouch hat gave more protection from the sun and rain and was more comfortable than the kepi or forage cap. There were several types, but the most popular was the Hardee hat, named after Gen. William Hardee. This was a black hat with a wide brim, usually with one side turned up and pinned with a brass eagle pin. The famous "Iron Brigade" of the Union army wore this distinctive hat, as did many other regiments. The hat came into being during the period when Jefferson Davis was the U.S. Secretary of War and thus is also known as the Jeff Davis hat.

The general rule was that the left side was pinned up for enlisted personnel, and the right side for officers. Photographs show many exceptions to this rule, however, so follow your regimental guidelines.

When wearing the slouch hat, don't roll up the brim like *Bonanza's* Hoss Cartwright. This style comes from the 1870s and 1880s—the cowboy days. During the Civil War, the brim was pinned up on one side, left straight out, or had the very edge tipped up, forming a "bowl."

Soldiers wore both slouch hats and kepis flat or straight on the head during drill. In camp, the hat rules were relaxed, and they could be worn on the back of the head or to one side. In the North-South Skirmish Association, any hat that is blown downrange by the wind is a fair target, so keep the slouch hat square on the head while in formation. It looked more military to the nineteenth-century mind, and it somewhat prevented the wind from blowing off the hats.

Wheel, Straw, and Other Hats

Another hat, less often worn, was a wheel hat. This hat, worn by American troops during the war with Mexico, had many civilian copies in use before that war and well into the 1860s. The wheel hat had a stiff leather brim and a round top, and looks similar to a modern policeman's hat or a World War II Navy officer's hat. National troops that were fitted out with Mexican War surplus clothing (such as the 20th Pennsylvania Volunteer Infantry) were issued the wheel.

Several types of straw hats were worn by the troops. On the Union side, they showed individuality. On the Southern side, they showed that soldiers wore what they could get. The straw hat protected the head from sun and rain. Be aware that there are some cheap imitations made of plastic instead of straw; buy only the ones that are made with natural fibers and have a tight weave.

The skimmer, or boating straw hat, has a flat brim and crown. These were only summer hats and, as in the nineteenth century, should not be worn during fall or winter. Keep these to a minimum, or your unit will look like a Gay Nineties barbershop quartet.

Panamas were popular in the South before the war and are known today as "plantation hats." Modern ones are blocked with a frontal crease, decorative open-lattice straw work, or vents. Stay away from these; they are not authentic.

Amish straw hats became popular at reenactments a few years ago. These are more flexible than the straw skimmers and have a wider brim. They are worn today by Amish farmers in Pennsylvania and Ohio and are readily available and inexpensive. These hats are not authentic, however, as their looser weave is not typical of the nineteenth century.

Some people swear that helmets were worn during the WBTS, but I haven't seen an authentic example. Several Northern units, including one New Hampshire regiment, supposedly wore them during 1861. They were very rarely worn, however, if at all, and I do not advise wearing one unless it is thoroughly documented for your regiment.

Troops on both sides wore civilian hats and caps of many different styles, ranging from soft workmen's caps to student caps to wool stocking caps. Do some careful research before wearing nonuniform headgear, however. Stovepipe hats and derbies were both worn during the war, but each had particular styles, and it is easy to get the wrong one, or one from another time period. Beginning reenactors should stick with a known uniform hat.

One last note about caps: If you are at a winter reenactment, pull on a wool stocking cap before going to sleep. This will help keep you warm at night and is easy to carry balled up in your haversack or blanket roll.

Hat Decorations and Trim

Hat cords were color coded for branch of service: blue for infantry, yellow for cavalry, and red for artillery. They were made of wool and had tassels. Rain and summer sun caused the cords to fade in color and stretch, so that the tassels would fall over the front brim of the hat. Reenactors call these floppy tassels "fly chasers." Some reenactors regard them with the same approval as pink fuzzy dice hanging from a rearview mirror. I recommend shortening one side of the hat cord so that the cords do not drape over the front of the hat brim. For the Hardee hat, prewar usage had the tassels loop over the side, rather than the front. Some reenactors therefore have the tassels dangling off to one side, and there are authentic Civil War-era photographs to support this idiosyncrasy, but not many.

When removed and placed on a table or other surface, a common nineteenth-century practice was to place the hat upside down so that the top of the hat would pick up any dust or dirt, instead of the more easily seen bottom rim. Sewing a single loop of thread around the cords at both sides of the hat will prevent the cords from falling off when the hat is removed.

Insignia should be kept to a minimum on slouch hats, at the most an infantry horn, regimental numbers, and company letter. From the spring of 1863 on, Union troops often wore corps badges as well. Gold metallic bullion hat cords tied with metallic acorns are not typical period items and should not be worn. They are officers' insignia and don't belong in the ranks anyway.

Hardee hats had an eagle pin to hold up one side. Informal hat trim includes harp insignia (used by Irish troops), flat bugle (used by mounted infantry), and Masonic trim. Keep this to a minimum. Postwar pins, such as GAR, do not belong on serious reenactment hats.

Cavalry and officers wore plumes on their hats. For infantry, some individual units, such as the Iron Brigade, also wore plumes. Again, follow your regimental guidelines. Civil War plumes ordinarily were black, although there were some rare examples of red plumes. Other colors and dyes were available but were worn only by the ladies. Modern dye colors such as electric blue or acid yellow are not authentic.

Other hat trim was used as well. Some North Carolina regiments, and some Northern units, placed small swatches of pine needles in their hats before going into battle. Other units and individuals wore fur pieces. Several

Pennsylvania regiments, known as the "Bucktails," wore white deer tails in their hats. Some South Carolina troops wore fox tails in imitation of Revolutionary War hero Francis Marion, the "Swamp Fox." Dandies wore raccoon tails, squirrel tails, and such in their hats to make them look fancy. Keep fancy trim to a minimum unless it is documented by photographs for your troop.

Shirts and Ties

Shirts were about the same on both sides. Almost all were pullovers. State troops received shirts of white, gray, or dark blue flannel.

Troops also had store-bought or homemade shirts, and here the variety is endless. Most were of the same general pullover pattern with a wide neck and collar, made of gingham or calico. They fit more loosely than today's shirts, and the throat and collar were much looser than today's.

At the time of the Civil War, most cloth collars were lightly sewn on so that when dirty or frayed, they could be removed and turned over. Shirts had a stump collar, to which a falling collar may or may not be attached. Top buttons in front and back were used to attach a removable stiff collar. During this period, about half the shirts had a stump collar and half had a falling collar. A stump collar was typical of working men's clothing and indicated that they did not wear a tie or cravat. Within a decade of the Civil War, fashion decreed a stiff collar that would button onto this stump. Garrison troops or fancy regiments were derided as "paper collar" regiments by other soldiers.

The cuffs buttoned with only one button, usually at the center of the cuff rather than the end. Typical civilian shirts buttoned tightly over the wrist and had extra cloth that poufed at the cuff.

Another popular shirt style was the "fireman's shirt," which had a cloth shield, sometimes known as a "plastron," in front that buttoned up on two sides. This shirt later became popular as the "singing cowboy" style of the 1930s.

Battle shirts are a bit controversial. Some troops, especially early-war Southern troops, had a tunic or heavy shirt instead of a wool uniform coat. It would fit over a regular shirt but was not as heavy or bulky as the wool jacket. Before you get a battle shirt, make sure one is documented for your regiment's history, since they were not typical and are controversial.

Pockets were not sewn on most shirts, and not at all on the army-issued shirts. Rarely, heavier shirts have a breast pocket or two. The pockets were generally lower on the shirt and larger than breast pockets on shirts today. Using breast pockets to store cigarette packs or modern lighters is a real no-no.

Buttons were metal, wooden, or bone, or sometimes commercially made from other products, such as glass or ceramic materials. For Southern troops, different styles of buttons can be used, including bits of wood, bone, or even acorns. You can use dental floss to tie them on, but make sure the modern materials are not visible.

Buttonholes should be hand-sewn, or at least hand-sewn over the machine stitching. Some surviving Union sack coats have brown thread sewn over the buttonholes. This thread was originally blue, but faded to brown over the years.

On formal occasions, men wore ties or cravats, which, like today, fit under the collar and were tied in front. Pre-tied cravats, with a hook in the back, can be purchased. Ties should not be tied too tight, since a tight collar is uncomfortable.

Vests

Vests were popular on both sides but apparently never were issued as part of a uniform. Vests helped keep the men warm and provided an extra set of pockets. There were a number of styles, some military and many civilian. One form of military vest buttoned up all the way to the throat and had a stand-up French collar and two or four pockets on either side of the front. Civilian styles buttoned up only up to the sternum, with lapels that lay flat against the breast and had from one to five pockets.

Vests of the 1860s did not have points at the bottom front. Both sides met flush against each other at the bottom button and slightly below the belt line. The habit of leaving the bottom button undone was not fashionable until Edward, Prince of Wales, made this necessity a fashion statement some thirty years after the WBTS.

The upper pockets of the nineteenth-century vest were not so deep as our modern ones. Civil War soldiers rarely placed pens or pencils in their vest pockets, so they didn't need to be as deep. Cigars held in upper vest pockets without cigar cases were often crushed by uniform cross belts and slings. The bottom vest pockets were deeper than today's, however, and held a variety of objects, such as knife, matches, and watch. With the deeper bottom pockets, things rarely fell out when the soldier bent over.

The vests were lined with an extra layer of cloth for added warmth. Better vests had a small strip of leather sewn against the inside bottom of the lower vest pockets to prevent wear and fraying from a watch, suspenders, or belt buckle.

When worn with a coat or jacket, the vest should always be buttoned up, even if only the top button of the coat is buttoned. Civilians wearing vests are exempt from this rule, unless they are in formal clothing, such as that worn by a governor or president.

Corps badges or other insignia should not be placed or pinned on the vest, but only on the coat.

Underwear

There was little difference in style between Union and Confederate underwear. The soldiers' underwear, also known as "bishops," looked like two-piece longjohns and covered both arms and legs. Underwear was worn for warmth, modesty, as an under layer of clothes to help keep the body clean, and to protect the outer clothing from the body dirt and odors that cause us to wash our clothes so frequently.

The Victorians wore more underwear than we do today. The women, in particular, piled layer upon layer in the form of assorted bodices and petticoats. For women, an equally important function of underwear was that it provided the means of converting the natural body to any fashionable shape.[8]

Underwear was cotton or wool, most commonly Canton cotton or flannel. Red and white were the most popular colors, although the red quickly faded to pink. It is a good idea to wash red underwear several times before wearing it on the field, as it can stain clothing when wet with perspiration.

The single set of woolen longjohns, complete with a "thunder flap" over the behind, is not authentic WBTS underwear. This style, made famous by character actors in B-grade westerns, is more common to the 1880s.

There are several accounts in which some of the midwestern recruits in the Union army did not know what the issued cotton drawers were for. One soldier's account said that a quick-thinking old-timer told the recruits that the underpants were part of the dress uniform and were to be worn on the outside of the pants during parades. New recruits often found that old-timers had a wicked sense of humor.

Manly Wade Wellman estimated that only a third of Lee's army wore any type of underwear on the march to Gettysburg. Those men "basically attired" wore clothing looted from Yankee stores during the spring campaign.

Modern underwear, if worn, should be hidden below the button line of the shirt and under the collar. If thermal underwear is worn, be sure the sleeves do not poke out from under the shirt cuff or show through any "authentic" holes in the outer clothing.

Leather Gear

Typical infantry leather gear was a cartridge box with shoulder straps, a belt, cap box, bayonet scabbard, and frog. Leather gear during the Civil War came in russet or black. Russet is a rich brown color, similar to rawhide, which is a cheaper way of treating leather. Black leather was sometimes simply painted black. Almost all Union leather gear was black. Much of the Confederate gear was black, but much was also russet.

Union troops had a black leather cartridge box on a shoulder strap, and a leather strap across the chest fit into the straps and buckles on the cartridge box. In the center of the leather band was a "breastplate," figuratively over the heart. Many Confederates had a strap or sling made of linen, and sewed the breastplate directly onto the strap. The strap went over the left shoulder and down to the right hip, and the belt would go over the strap and above the cartridge box. The belt would then keep the cartridge box from bouncing around when the soldier marched or ran.[9]

The large flap of the cartridge box kept moisture and stray sparks out, and there was usually an inner flap as well. The outside flap also had a box plate that worked as a pendant weight to keep the flap down over the box. This box plate was usually a brass oval with "US," "CS," or state insignia, and it was one of the few safety items available. A small pocket in the cartridge box held tools for the musket, such as a nipple wrench. Many times the Confederate cartridge box was slipped on the belt instead of the sling. The Union boxes also had belt loops, but the majority of soldiers in photographs wore them on the leather sling.[10]

Inside the cartridge box are two tin holders. Each holder had a compartment on top and another compartment hollowed out of the lower side. These four sections each held a package of ten paper-wrapped cartridges, for a total of forty cartridges. The hollowed-out hole goes on the top, and the hole on the bottom side should face outward. The tin holders were designed to channel any explosion of the powder away from the body. Don't depend on it, however; keep the flap down and secured. The cartridge box collects loose powder from the paper cartridges. It's a good idea to shake it out now and then, and keep it clean.

The Union belts were one piece of leather, usually 2 to 2$\frac{1}{2}$ inches wide, with a one-piece belt buckle. There was sometimes a brass "keeper" to prevent the excess strap from straying out from underneath the belt. Many Union regiments had state or militia buckles instead of the U.S. insignia, so check with your unit for accuracy before buying.

Confederate belts sometimes were russet leather, but most often they were black. Just before the Pennsylvania campaign of 1863, some Confederate units were issued canvas belts painted black. Civilian belt buckles were frequently used by troops, a common one being a forked-tongue buckle, where the buckle was split in two like a sideways letter *y* and matched two holes in the leather. Perhaps most common were the frame buckle, with a simple rectangular frame around the buckle, and the roller buckle.

Both sides wore a bayonet scabbard that had a loop for the belt and stuck out at an angle behind the soldier's left hip. This was a Gaylord scabbard, the one most commonly associated with the WBTS uniform.

Less frequently used were the Enfield bayonet scabbards. These were purchased from England by both the Confederate and Union troops. The Enfield bayonet had a separate scabbard that fit over the blade, and then the scabbard fit into a leather frog. The bayonet hung straight down alongside the left leg of the soldier.

Reenactors may use either scabbard; get whichever one feels right to you and is agreeable to your regiment. Those with Enfields should have Enfield leather, and those with Springfields should have Gaylord sheaths. Either scabbard should always have a brass tip to prevent an accident with the tip of the bayonet. As long as your scabbard covers the bayonet tip, you should be safe.

The cap box held the percussion caps for the rifle. Union regulations required them to hold at least fifty caps, with a strip of lamb's wool across the top to keep the caps from falling out unexpectedly. Many soldiers stuck the nipple pick, a thin piece of wire used to clean out the nipple or fire hole in the rifle, in the lamb's wool to keep it safe, while others stuck it in their hats. Union cap boxes were made of black leather, with a shield-shaped front flap and sometimes an inner flap as well.

Some Confederate cap boxes were as elaborate as Union ones; others were basic and simple. In any case, have someone with you from your unit to advise you in purchasing. They were sometimes made of black canvas or russet leather.

Socks, Mittens, and Gaiters

Socks were almost the same as they are today, although they were heavier and had less stretch in the fabric. Made of wool, cotton, or linen, they were knitted, woven, or sewn. They were worn until they wore out, and even the best-dressed people wore darned socks.

Women and children in both the North and the South spent much of their home life knitting socks, mufflers, havelocks, and other wearables. Women's knitting societies sprang up quickly after the first few letters started coming home telling of the lack of good socks. Prodigious efforts were made to keep the men supplied with socks and mittens. Many comments in Southern diaries were like these: "I became such an expert knitter I could easily knit a pair of socks in a day" and "Everybody knitted socks. Ladies, negro women, girls and even little boys learned to knit. Each tried to get ahead in number and quality."[11]

The ladies often knitted "shooting mittens" for the soldiers; these had a separate thumb and forefinger. One soldier from Connecticut wrote of the mittens: "We gave three rousing cheers to the ladies of the Hartford Soldier's Aid Society. In this bleak December snowstorm, their hands and hearts are warmer for what you sent them."[12]

Heavy wool socks helped prevent blisters from forming on feet unused to marching, and are sometimes called "blister-proofs." Many experienced reenactors place Band-Aids over parts of the foot prone to blisters, such as the heel or toes. There will still be rubbing of the skin where the Band-Aid ends, however, so blisters can form between Band-Aids. Be careful, since hurting feet can take all the fun out of an event.

A common custom was to pull the sock tops up over the pant legs, sometimes tying them with a bit of string. This custom had several purposes. It kept chiggers and other pests from crawling up the inside of the leg, a common occurrence in the field. When the grass was high and wet, it helped keep the legs drier, and if they did get wet, it helped the clothes dry out faster. Also, many soldiers liked the look; it provided a cheap set of "gaiters." Although soldiers could wear their socks like this in the field, it was not allowed on dress parade, where the soldiers had to look sharp.

Gaiters made of leather or canvas were sometimes used during the Civil War to create a smart appearance. Most Union and Confederate regiments did not use them, however, and very few if any Confederate regiments wore them after the first few months of the war. Gaiters had a strap under the instep just before the heel of the boot. They were similar to modern dress uniform gaiters, except that they had leather laces or straps and buckle tabs instead of hooks or buttons. If worn at all, they would have been part of the regimental uniform. Check with your regiment before buying them.

Boots and Shoes

Boots were something everyone wore. They were essential for walking around areas where there were large numbers of animals, deep mud, and unpaved streets. The most common style of boot or brogan used by soldiers was the "Jefferson bootee," approved by Jefferson Davis while he was U.S. Secretary of War. It is a black boot of thick leather that fits over the ankle, with squared toes. Confederates often wore the leather with the rough side out, and Union troops often wore it with the smooth side out. There were so many exceptions, however, that probably either form would be correct.

Except for the cavalry, only officers wore high-topped boots with the pant legs stuffed inside. If you must wear high boots and you are not an officer, wear your pant legs over the boots. For all infantry, the bootee was the general-issue footwear. There are some exceptions. Check with your regiment's historian for accuracy.

As an infantryman, your boots are one of your most important purchases. Shop around and compare quality and prices. It is worth the extra money to buy a really good pair. If you are buying by mail, the best time is in the winter, since stocks have been replenished and all sizes are available. By spring, many pairs have been bought up, and common shoe sizes are hard to find.

It's best not to buy a pair of boots without trying them both on. Sometimes the size on the box doesn't match the size of the boot inside, especially after several dozen people have been through the sutler's shop trying them on. When you try on boots, make sure you are wearing the kind of socks you would normally use during a reenactment. Street socks are often made of thin nylon, whereas reenactor's socks are wool and quite thick. The difference in sock thickness could make the boots uncomfortable during a march.

Modern shoes are designed to get on and off easily. Nineteenth-century boots, which were tight around the instep and looser in the toe box, were not. You may need a shoehorn to get the ball of your foot through the instep area. This can be uncomfortable for a while, until you get used to it.

During this period, shoe styles in this country were evolving from a straight-last or single-last shoe, which would fit either foot, to a double-last shoe, which was separately shaped for each foot. A last was an iron tool shaped like a foot that a cobbler used to make shoes. Single-last shoes gradually shaped themselves to the foot with wear. By 1861, these were worn only by the very poor or very backward people. An artifact of the single-last shoe was the squared toe of the 1860s boot—it would fit either foot. As the double-last shoe became more common, the toe box was shaped to fit the left or the right foot only.

The soles were attached to the shoes by either sewing or pegging. This was done on the outside of the shoes, so it didn't affect the feel of the boots.

The wooden pegs, often oak, would wear down at the same rate as the leather sole. I prefer the sewn soles, since they are easier to have resoled at a local shoe shop. When pegged shoes are taken in to be repaired, the craftsman often spends more time studying the differences in shoes than he does in repairing them. Many shoe repair shops will not repair pegged shoes at all.

The army-issued Jefferson bootees needed to be resoled every two or three months, and replaced after a year's worth of service, if they lasted that long. The boots got an awful lot of wear, since the soldiers walked or marched everywhere. I read a few years ago that the average American walks about two miles a day, whereas the 1860s American walked an average of ten miles a day.

Shoe soles were oak-tanned leather and would generally last only a few months. The army as a whole needed new boots every six to nine months. For the Confederate army, this became a preoccupation, and a raid to grab military supplies and boots was a reason leading to the Battle of Gettysburg. On more than one occasion, unscrupulous civilian contractors supplied boots to the Union army with cardboard soles.

The nineteenth-century boots had leather heels. Leather heels are slick on wet grass, so to get more traction, many reenactors nail metal, U-shaped devices, called "horseshoes," to the heels. Though they do give traction in charging downhill, these devices can mar wooden floors. This is one area where I stray from authenticity and wear rubber heels on my boots. There is less slipping and sliding, and I don't have to worry about scarring our hardwood floors. A word of common sense: Don't nail horseshoes to rubber heels; you don't need them.

Many soldiers, both Northern and Southern, went barefoot. In part this was because many people habitually went barefoot except during the coldest months, and their feet splayed and made shoes uncomfortable. For Confederate soldiers, bare feet indicated a lack of supplies. For safety's sake, most reenactors don't go barefoot, and all event organizers forbid bare feet on the field. In this case, authentic reenactment is unsafe.

ARMS AND WEAPONS

Firearms

The arms and weapons used by both sides were most commonly the Enfield and the Springfield rifle muskets. Many other types of rifles were used by different troops, but these two were by far the most common.

The official name of the Springfield was the rifle musket, Model 1861, but the soldiers just called it the Springfield, since most of them were manufactured in Springfield, Massachusetts. The Springfield was a muzzle-loading percussion cap rifle weighing about 9³/₄ pounds. It was a caliber .58, which means the muzzle opening was a little more than half an inch across. It had an effective range of about 500 yards, though it could throw a ball twice that distance. During the war, 670,000 Springfields were manufactured, and they cost the government about $19 each, about seven weeks' pay for the average private.

Also popular was the Enfield musket, Model 1853, imported from England. The Enfield was also a muzzle-loading musket, weighing about 9 pounds, 3 ounces. The caliber of the Enfield musket was a little less than the Springfield, about .577. The Enfield was deadly up to about 900 yards, and most soldiers thought it was more accurate than the Springfield. About 920,000 Enfields were imported by both the North and the South during the war.[13]

In reenacting, all muskets must have three bands for infantry. Carbines or musketoons, muskets with two bands and a shorter barrel, were also issued. Most of these shorter rifles went to the cavalry, artillery, or naval units, although this is debated. Many two-banded rifles were issued to infantry troops throughout the war, both North and South, but a recent calculation showed that in the infantry, only 1 man in 125 had a carbine. Many Confederate troops had only shotguns and civilian sporting rifles during the first years of the war. So the argument can be made that having a two-banded rifle as a military weapon is historically correct. Nevertheless, to portray the common soldier, who was issued a three-banded musket, the reenactor should use a three-banded musket. Three-banded muskets should also be used for safety reasons. When standing in two ranks and firing over the shoulders of other reenactors, two-banded muskets are not long enough to keep the flash and smoke of the muzzle away from the front-rank soldiers' eyes and ears. So unless you are with a special unit, such as Berdan's Sharpshooters, who had Sharps' rifles, get the three-banded musket. If your unit later switches to another form of musket, such as a carbine, you can always trade down.

Do not use an antique musket on the field. It may have a damaged barrel, lock mechanism, or nipple, which can cause the musket to misfire or explode, possibly damaging the eyes or ears of the front-rank soldier or your own. A reproduction musket can be faulty, but there is less chance of that. A reenactor knows how well he has taken care of his reproduction musket, since he bought it. The history of the care of an antique musket is always unknown.

There are a few exceptions to the use of antique muskets. Regiments often have a rule, for safety and insurance reasons, that members under sixteen can't carry weapons, and those under eighteen can't fire weapons. Those who fall between these ages can carry a nonfiring antique musket. In line, they can follow all the commands, fix bayonets, shoulder arms, and so on. Also, many new members carry nonfiring antique weapons on their first event so that they won't have to worry about loading and firing but can just relax and have fun. Antiques also can be used in uniform talks to show the differences in weapons to an audience.

The drawback to using antique weapons is that they can easily be damaged in the field, so don't use a family heirloom or an expensive antique for this purpose.

A rifle that is used must be kept clean for safety reasons. After each shot, some residue from the powder coats the barrel and nipple. The sulfur in the black powder combines with the humidity in the atmosphere to form sulfuric acid, which can etch the metal in the rifle muzzle. Left in the rifle for even a short time, powder residue acids pit in the metal, which will result in gas leaks or pressure breaks.

Therefore, after each use, clean the musket with warm water and use plenty of cloth patches to scrub out the powder residue. Take the barrel all the way off to clean it; if the barrel remains on the stock while being cleaned, water will flow into the lock mechanism through the lock or wooden stock and rust out the metal parts. Be sure to dry off all metal parts, and coat them with some light oil. During the WBTS, soldiers did not take the barrel off to clean the muskets. Reenactors should do so, however, as it is safer than the original cleaning methods.

The tools needed for the maintenance of the musket include a nipple wrench to remove the nipple, a nipple pick to clean the nipple and the spark-hole, and small screwdrivers to take out the screws. Several specialty tools are available, including a brace to hold the spring so that you won't need three hands to replace the lock. On Enfields, the square screw opening in the center of the hammer is the same size as the square head of the nipple, so the hammer can be removed and then used as a nipple wrench in emergencies.

Cleaning the lock mechanism is tricky on muskets. Be sure you have a good book showing how to take the rifle apart and put it back together, or have someone experienced on hand to help.

The wooden rifle stock will look better after some rubbing with wood furniture polish. Wood polishes cover scratches so that they don't show so brightly.

A sling is important to prevent fatigue from carrying the rifle. Confederates used linen slings as well as leather. They can be purchased from most sutlers who sell weapons and supplies, or they can be easily made. Leather slings should be black, natural, or russet colored.

Some NCOs and color bearers carried pistols, but most common soldiers did not. Many WBTS-period photographs taken of infantry soldiers show them with pistols stuck in their belts, but these pistols, as well as knives, flags, and swords, were often props supplied by the photographer. The army discouraged the use or ownership of pistols by enlisted infantrymen. In North Carolina, for instance, all pistols carried by infantrymen in 1861 were confiscated and turned over to the cavalry or artillery. Most reenactment regiments have rules against soldiers carrying pistols. They are heavy to carry in addition to a rifle, and they need different ammunition, maintenance tools, caps, bullets, and so on, which add to the load of the soldier.

Gunpowder

Gunpowder can be purchased in 1-pound cans from many sporting-goods stores. Check to see if there are any local or special state laws that regulate the sale of black powder. Don't try to store too much powder, since it is dangerous. Be sure to store it in a cool, dry place, out of the reach of children, and don't store the percussion caps and powder together.

To be authentic, many reenactors store their cartridges and powder in wooden boxes with period markings, such as "Selma Arsenal" or "Frankfurt Arsenal." For safety reasons, however, powder should not be kept in wooden boxes. The risk from fires, candles, and lanterns, prevalent around the camps, should not be disregarded. A steel container with a tight lid is better. I use an army surplus machine-gun ammo box, which has a good seal on it and is almost watertight. This I keep inside another box or hide under a blanket. It is also more difficult for kids to get into.

Static electricity is something to watch out for as well. At a recent event, a handful of paper cartridges were placed on a cotton bale used by the Federals as breastworks. As soon as the cartridges touched the cotton bale, a spark went off, and so did the powder, burning the hand of the Union soldier and giving a heart-stopping scare to those nearby. So keep cartridges in the cartridge box, and watch for loose powder, static, and sparks.

Black powder comes in several forms with different F ratings, between 4F (ffffg) and 1F (fg), which refers to the size of the powder grain, not to the explosiveness of the powder. The 4F rating is very fine grained for priming flintlock muskets. The 3F (fffg) powder grain is recommended for revolvers, single-shot pistols, and rifles under .45 caliber. For muskets above .45 caliber, use 2F (ffg) powder. Most Civil War muskets are .58 or .577, so use the ffg gunpowder. Cannon and large-bore shotguns use 1F, the coarsest-grained form of black powder available.

There are two main commercial brands of powder: GOEX and PYRODEX. PYRODEX is a black powder substitute and is not recommended for reenactments. It is difficult to fire and requires a hotter percussion cap (magnums). PYRODEX powder is good with live ammo, since it burns more slowly and requires compression to fire effectively. With blanks, it goes *poof!* instead of *BANG!* It also fouls the barrel more than GOEX does. I recommend the GOEX black powder.

Musket Cartridges

Cartridges for the musket can be purchased at some large events, but most reenactors roll their own. It is certainly cheaper to roll your own, and sometimes at large events the sutlers will all run out of cartridges early.

During the late winter or early spring, many regiments have a cartridge-rolling party. Everyone comes and rolls cartridges, usually having a unit meeting and potluck supper as well. This can be a lot of fun, and even a small number of people working together can roll an enormous number of cartridges.

Some units roll cartridges that are then "sold" or "issued" to members when they come to particular events. I have seen this done in a few regiments, but seldom happily or successfully.

The paper for the cartridges should be of medium weight, and newsprint or paper slightly heavier is often used. It is usually cut in a trapezoid shape, as shown. You can cut it yourself, or it can be purchased precut from many sutlers.

There are two methods of rolling cartridges. The first is the authentic knotted method, which was used by both sides. Here, the paper is rolled into a tube on a ¹/₂-inch wooden dowel that has a tapered head shaped like the minié ball. Four inches from the tip, mark a solid line around the dowel. Roll the paper on the dowel so that about ¹/₄ inch remains over the cone-shaped edge. The longer end of the trapezoid will be at the tip you tie off, and the bottom of the paper should be along the line marked on the wooden dowel.

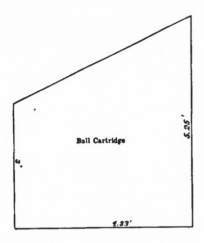

Finished cartridge

Place the dowel with rolled paper into a stand that will hold the dowel firmly upright, and tie a thread or kite string around the excess paper, forcing the tip into the shape of the cone, and held tight by the thread. Loop the edge a few times, and tie off with a square knot. Many people rub the excess paper a bit to make it flare out.

Slide the tube off the dowel, and pour the measured powder into the opening. The correct charge is 60 grains of 2F black powder. Some use 65 grains, but it is best not to go over that amount. Any more than 60 to 65 grains is wasted and does not make a louder report. Some people first put a little cotton or Kleenex at the tip where the bullet would normally go, but it isn't necessary. If you do this, push the cotton down with the dowel, then pour in the powder, and tamp the cartridge on the table to settle it.

Fold the paper flat from the edge of the powder to the end of the tube. Fold the flattened tail at right angles to the cartridge and then back again, so that the tail sticks up from the center of the powder-filled cartridge.

Fold the two sides of the flattened tail in toward the center until the edges meet, then fold down tight to make a crease. The bottom of the folds should be tight against the powder so that it won't leak out. Now bend the tail back against the cartridge so that the tip of the tail is near the tied end.

A simpler way to make a cartridge is to roll it on a dowel made from the cardboard tube of a coat hanger, with 1/4 inch projecting over the end of the tube. When finished, twist the projecting paper and insert it back into the dowel, making a folded end to the tube. Remove the dowel, insert the powder, then flatten the tail against the powder charge. Insert the end of the tail in one of the overlays. When ready for use, thumb the end out from the overlay.

Gun cotton (nitrated paper) was available during the WBTS, but the only use I have found for it was in carbine cartridges, where the exploding of the paper added impetus to the bullet. The paper was soaked in a nitrate solution that would make it burn quickly (sometimes mistaken for an explosion) and add energy to the cartridge. Don't use gun cotton or try this unless you are an expert in explosives.

Do not use penny wrappers or other heavy paper tubes for cartridges, and never use glue, staples, or paper clips on your finished cartridges. If you can't bring yourself to roll cartridges, boxes of prerolled (but not filled) cartridges are available at many sutlers. Those from the Paper Lady are the best. These are empty tubes, usually about 100 to 125 per box. All you need to do is measure the powder, fill them up, and close the tube with a tail. It's more expensive than rolling them yourself, but it's still an easy way to make cartridges.

Edged Weapons

Swords were carried by officers, cavalrymen, some NCOs, and musicians. If you are not one of the above, don't get one. The infantry soldier used the rifle and bayonet and was more than a match for any fool with a sword.

Bayonets were carried by soldiers on both sides throughout the war. Issued bayonets were the socket type that fit over the end of the barrel and locked over the front sight of the musket. The bayonet was triangular, with dull edges and a moderately sharp point. It penetrated, rather than slashed, the enemy.

As a penetrating weapon, the triangular shape caused air to enter the wound, which invariably caused sepsis, or infection. Even a small, deep wound caused by one of these weapons was often fatal, if not from loss of blood, then by the subsequent infection. Bayonets were not effective as a weapon, however; there were less than a hundred Union casualties caused by bayonets at the Battle of Gettysburg. Rather, the Civil War-era bayonet inhibited and frightened the foe as a psychological weapon. Most troops would break and run rather than face an overwhelming foe with bayonets.

One estimate stated that of the bayonet wounds reported in the Union army, only half were caused by the enemy. One-quarter were accidents, mostly on the bottom of the right hand as soldiers cut their hands when they tried to ram the cartridge home on the bayoneted rifle. Another estimated one-quarter of the wounds were caused by fighting in camps. Although the

Confederates did not keep accurate records, the figures were probably about the same.

Around camp, the bayonet had other uses, such as to serve as a spit for cooking over the campfire, as a candleholder, or as a back scratcher.

There were a few sword bayonets made to fit the two-banded rifles and carbines, but there were even fewer issued. Unfortunately, when the reenactment hobby started growing in popularity about fifteen years ago, these two-banded rifles and sword bayonets were available. Many reenactors purchased them instead of the more expensive three-banded Enfields or Springfields. As a result, there are still too many of these two-banded "Zouave" or "Mississippi" rifles around. The sword bayonet is attractive, since it is long and looks like a sword privates can wear.

Knives were carried by many Southern boys, especially at the beginning of the war. A commonly used style had a knuckle guard shaped like the letter *d* and was called a "D-guard knife." This was a popular heavy knife that could be used for chopping wood but little else. If you are just starting as a Confederate, you may want to wait to get a knife until after you have made your initial purchases. There are an enormous number of poor-quality knives sold at ridiculously high prices, so be sure to have someone knowledgeable with you when you buy.

Union infantry occasionally wore knives, but not as often as Confederates, and not as promiscuously. For Union soldiers, especially for beginners, it's best to get a small reproduction jackknife and keep it in your pocket.

BRASS ITEMS

The common soldier had several pieces of brass used to designate his arm of service and country. These were used on the hat, leather gear, and uniform.

Government-issued hats or caps usually held a brass horn, the symbol for infantry. Sometimes they would have the company letter and regiment number as well. The variations of this are endless. Photographs from the period show insignia worn in just about every way possible, with the company letter and regiment number on the inside of the horn, above it, or below it, to the left or right. In one photo, two numbers bracket the horn. The only rule is not to have too much brass on the hat. It should be kept to a minimum, especially for units representing Confederate or Union soldiers after 1861.

Remember that you are impersonating someone who had to take care of all this brass. The less brass insignia, the fewer holes in the hat and the less to polish at the end of the day. Many times the insignia would be lost. Confederates could not get replacements if they lost their hat insignia, and Union soldiers far from supply resources, such as Sherman's men, could not replace lost items either.

For those interested in strict U.S. Army regulations, only metal company letters were to be worn on the forage cap, and these were worn on the front of the cap.[14]

On the leather gear, the most common brass was a belt buckle with the simple "US" or state insignia. If you get something else, check with someone knowledgeable to make sure it is authentic; there is a lot of inauthentic brass out there.

Next most common was the cartridge box plate, used on the flap. Usually this was a simple oval brass state, "US," or "CS" plate, often exactly like the belt buckles. Other types were also worn, so follow your regimental guidelines. By the end of the war, most Confederates had lost their box plates and they could not be replaced. Confederates often used an upsidedown US box plate or belt plate, insisting that the upsidedown "US" looked like "SN" and stood for "Southern Nation."

A breastplate was centered on the shoulder strap sling holding the cartridge box. On the U.S. pattern, this was most commonly an eagle holding arrows, though other types are available. Again, check with your unit.

The breastplate, box plate, and hat brass are kept on by brass loops. A few reenactors cut the loops and bend the metal to brace the brass fittings on the leather or cloth. Others wedge in pieces of cloth or leather to hold the loops in place. Many sew the loops on or run thread between the loops on the back of the material. "Farbs" use very small cotter pins made of metal or plastic to keep them on. The most common method during the war was to use a leather thong between loops, tied off with a square knot. Use whatever is convenient, but keep in mind that you may want to remove the brass to shine it up without getting polish on the leather or cloth.

The buttons on the uniform also were made of brass. When sewing buttons on the coat or vest, be sure they are upright when buttoned. An upside-down eagle would not have passed inspection. A tip for attaching shank buttons is to sew them to another flat button behind the cloth to hold the thread.

CARE AND CLEANING OF UNIFORMS AND EQUIPMENT

The cloth uniform should not be washed too often, but should always be put on a clothesline to air out after an event. Washing wool after each event is

unwise. Wool has natural water-repellent features that are destroyed by deter-
gents. A careful airing and drying will prevent damage from insects and
mildew and will somewhat reduce any odor. It is best to hang the uniform out
in the sunlight as soon after a reenactment as possible. Many reenactors hang
them out in the morning turned inside out, so that the inside of the coat is
toward the sun, and in the afternoon the outside is aired out.

When you do wash the uniform, use the same special care you would for
any wool fabric to prevent shrinkage. Use cold water and do not dry in a
dryer. Rather than wash the wool clothes, it is better to have them dry-
cleaned, which is cheaper when done by the pound. If you have the uniform
dry-cleaned, ask that it not be steam-ironed. If the iron is not covered with a
cloth, it will scorch and sear the wool and make it shiny. Also, sharp creases
in the uniform are not authentic. Before any cleaning, remove all items, such
as the braces from the trousers, the watch from the vest pocket, and so on.

To store the uniform, the cloth is best folded along the seams and placed
with cedar chips in a mothproof area, rather than hung in a closet. Avoid moth-
balls, which can be smelled from a great distance, especially when wool has
been stored all winter. Check all the pockets before putting the uniform away.

If the coat has a linen lining, it may need to be spot washed with a damp
cloth to remove stains from leather suspender tips or salt streaks from perspiration. If the lining gets too stiff from salt, it will collect moisture and wear
out faster.

For slouch hats, fold out the sweatband and stand the hat on the stiff
leather. If the hatband is missing or can't be pulled down, place the hat on a
peg so that air can circulate around it. Do not store a hat or cloth cap in front
of a sunny window, or it will fade unevenly.

Leather gear should be cleaned and polished or rubbed with saddle soap
after each event to prevent drying out and cracking. During the WBTS, mineral and animal oils were more commonly used to care for the leather, rather
than polish. Oiling the shoes will help keep them drier, but oil leaves a dull
appearance rather than a sharp shine. This dull appearance is more authentic,
however. If you use black polish, rub it in well or wipe it off before wearing
the leather, since polish can leave stains along the shoulder straps and belt
lines. Keep the shoes cleaned and cared for; they will wear out more quickly
with improper care. Don't forget the leather sling, or the leather tips of a cloth
sling, on your musket.

The accoutrements take only a little cleaning. Most brass is allowed to tarnish by troops on both sides, except for specialty troops, such as bands,

Regular army units, or Zouaves. Oil the bayonet to prevent rust, especially during storage. Don't store metal objects next to leather gear, or the metal will corrode or tarnish.

To clean the rifle, remove the barrel completely. It should be scrubbed clean after each reenactment, as gunpowder leaves an amazing amount of fouling inside the rifle. Pour soapy warm water down the barrel to clean the musket, shake it around a bit, and then pour the water back out. After the water starts coming out clean, use a cloth wad on the end of the ramrod or cleaning rod to wipe the barrel clean.

A common mistake is to try to clean the rifle with the barrel still on the stock. This is not a good idea, since water always runs down between the barrel and the stock. This causes rust on the barrel and lock and is not good for the wooden stock.

Many reenactment suppliers sell items such as a bristle, a worm, or a pull to help clean the musket. The bristle is very good at cleaning the inside of the barrel. Make sure it is the right size to fit the barrel. A slightly oversize bristle will go down the barrel but not come up. Also, check to make sure that the bristle end screws tightly into the ramrod or cleaning rod and that it has the proper male or female turn for your equipment. The Enfield and the Springfield muskets have different cleaning rods in slightly different sizes, so the same worm or bristle won't always fit both weapons. A bristle designed for a Springfield .58 may become stuck in the slightly smaller Enfield .577 musket.

The worm and bullet pull also screw onto the ramrod or cleaning rod and are used to remove paper wadding, burnt powder, or an unfired ball from the rifle. The worm has two opposing turned wires to catch paper fragments adhering to the barrel. The pull has an inclined screw that will drill into the top of an unfired ball, so when the ramrod is removed, the ball will come with it. Screw these devices on tightly before using, and turn them in a direction that will tighten rather than loosen them on the ramrod.

Black-powder solvent makes the water "wetter" and helps clean the musket. Soap helps dissolve the powder, too. Some people use solvent, and others don't. Experience will teach you what works best. Modern smokeless gunpowder solvent does not work on black powder and will occasionally gum the powder and make it even more difficult to clean out.

Also check to make sure water runs freely out through the touch hole and nipple. If not, take the nipple off and make sure it isn't fouled by the percussion cap residue. Also check the area underneath the nipple, and clean out the pan and touch hole with a nipple pick.

A final wipe with an oily wad will prevent rust and maintain the value of the rifle.

Get an experienced member of your unit to show you how to clean the lock mechanism, or leave it alone. It is complicated to put back together and always seems to take three hands to do it.

If you have a tent, be sure it is dry before you store it. Hang it, as well as the ropes, on a line in the sunlight to kill any fungus or mildew. If a tent becomes mildewed, it will often leak. To store smaller tents, it is best to roll them up. Larger tents need to be folded. Store tents with some materials to repel bugs. Cedar chips or blocks are acidic, and may weaken the fabric of the tent. If you use cedar, wrap it in another cloth before storing for long periods with a tent or clothing.

The less snowy white the tents are, the more authentic they will look. During the WBTS, they were used daily until they wore out, so patches and repairs on the tents are in line with hard use and give you a "veteran" appearance.

HAVERSACKS AND KNAPSACKS

Both sides during the war used a haversack, which carried the soldier's food and some personal effects. Union haversacks were of tarred canvas to make them watertight, or at least water-resistant. They often included an inner bag or liner and were worn by a strap crossing from the right shoulder to the left hip. Confederate soldiers used a similar haversack, or one made of linen, cotton canvas, or carpet. A Confederate bag was sometimes a bit smaller and called a "rice bag." Haversacks closed by either buttons (Confederate) or leather straps and buckles (both Federal and Confederate).

Union troops were always issued haversacks to carry their rations, and were often issued knapsacks as well, which were used to carry extra clothing, supplies, and equipment. Many troops discarded the knapsacks because they were cumbersome and added extra weight, and used the "mule collar" blanket roll instead.

The beginner should wait before purchasing a knapsack. They weren't used that much by Confederate troops after the first year of the war, and there are so many different Federal styles that it would be better to wait until you learn which type you want or need. Knapsacks can also be very uncomfortable. Get a haversack instead.

There is much discussion about whether the haversack was carried beneath the belt or over the belt. I suspect it was merely a matter of personal preference for the soldiers, or at the discretion of the unit commander, and both methods were used. If carried beneath the belt, the soldier left the strap at full or nearly full length, since the belt helped make it secure. When worn over the belt, he knotted the strap so that the bag stayed higher up, under, and a bit behind the left arm. If the strap was too long, the bag would flop around when the soldier ran or stooped over. One wit noted that if the haversack was worn over the belt, it could quickly be discarded so as not to slow the soldier down when running away.

Soldiers with an Enfield bayonet scabbard often placed the belt over the haversack straps but had the leather sheath of the bayonet behind the bag. This prevented the bayonet sheath from migrating along the belt to the front or back.

PERSONAL EFFECTS

A pocketknife was a standard piece of nonissued equipment that everyone used. Though the troops often did without table knives, they almost always had jackknives, which they used to cut the nibs of pens, cut off "chaws" of tobacco, whittle, or play mumblety-peg. The most common type was a simple clasp knife called a Barlow. It was referred to by boys of the time as a "genuine Barlow," as if anyone would make an imitation of this cheap and mostly worthless blade. The case was made of wood, sometimes painted, and it usually had just one blade. Modern Barlow knives and reproductions have two blades. The jackknife would sometimes be used for eating instead of the mess knife. Jackknives with a blade shaped like a hawk's bill were popular at the time. The pocketknife of the period was often carried in the vest pocket, especially the penknife, a smaller knife type used to shape or sharpen the quill for writing.

Watches of this period were of two types: hunter or railroad. Hunter watches had a metal shield over the front of the watch to protect the hour and minute hands and face. The case was opened by pressing down on the stem. Most hunter cases were plain, a few were engraved, and rarely they were deeping incised. The railroad watch, noted for its accuracy, had a crystal front over the watch face.

To change the time, a small pull, usually next to the watch dial, was lifted up, and the stem turned to the correct time. In a railroad watch, this prevented the stem from accidentally turning and changing the time. Older-style watches of this period were wound by a small key instead of winding the stem.

The watches of this period were often on a watch fob, a metal, leather, or cloth tab that attached to a ring over the stem of the watch. As such, the watch could be carried in any pocket and was not dependent on a vest button or buttonhole for the chain. The watch chain was also coming into popularity during this period. Enlisted men's chains were made of plain steel instead of gold or brass. Lucky men carried watch chains fashioned from human hair, a common farewell gift from a wife or sweetheart. These hair chains, braided or woven into various styles, included a favorite style called a "lover's knot." They were also popular and sentimental tokens taken from deceased family members.

Written materials would have been uncommon in the haversack. The jamming of loose rations, such as unwrapped fatback, into the haversack caused an accumulation of grease that would have soon soaked any paper. Any loose papers kept by the troops, such as religious tracts or "firestarters," were kept in the cartridge boxes behind the tins, or in pockets.

Compulsory schooling was not common in the United States until the third decade of the twentieth century, so many people grew up illiterate. One reason soldiers spent so much time on drill was that they could not be expected to get the information from books and had to be shown how to do things manually. In 1863, the U.S. Congress authorized $350,000 for the printing and distribution of books on drill and tactics to the officers, but most folks had to learn by being shown how to stand, move, and march.

One exception to written materials was a small Bible or New Testament. People thought religious books would protect soldiers from chest wounds and heart shots, and they were given to departing soldiers by family members. Even men who couldn't read kept a Bible in the breast pocket. Although many cynics snickered and said a deck of cards or piece of hardtack would do as well, the Bible was often considered extra insurance. Men were openly religious in those days, and gospel sings around campfires were common.

When the men knew a battle was coming, many threw away their decks of cards, but few would toss their Bibles. There were many accounts of the roads leading to battle being strewn with items such as cards and pipes. Part of this was a desire not to tempt fate, and another was not to have "sinful things" sent home with personal effects in case of death.

Missing from many haversacks and knapsacks were items for personal cleanliness, such as soap and razors. Razors used during this time were all straight, or "cutthroat," razors. If you want to take one of these razors along on a reenactment, be sure to try it out at home beforehand. They weren't called "cutthroats" for nothing. They are sharp, dangerous, and give a close shave. If you buy one, take it to a barber for a lesson or two on how to use, sharpen, and store it.

A small strop was used for sharpening the razor, usually leather on one side and rough fabric on the other. Some samples from the period include small strops that would fit over the back of the left hand. The razor also necessitated carrying soap in a rag and a mirror. Since these were just more items to carry, many men wore beards or depended on company barbers. In every company, there would be one soldier entrepreneur or camp follower who made some extra cash as an amateur barber.

Music wasn't heard unless played by a regimental band or the soldiers themselves. A haversack often held a small musical instrument, such as a Jew's harp, mouth organ, or even a pair of spoons, or "bones." A whistle of tin, horn, or wood was also common. Larger instruments, such as banjos, guitars, and fiddles, were common in camp but not in the field, as it was difficult to march with a rifle and such an instrument at the same time. Singing was very popular, and there was less inhibition about singing in public than there is today. Some say that more than ten thousand songs were written during the war. Many of them were unabashedly sentimental by today's standards, but they sure do sound good around a campfire. Hymns were also particularly well loved. Be sure the ones you sing at the reenactment date from that period; you will be amazed at the number of good ones that are still popular today.

MESS GEAR

Both sides used a mess kit, which included a tin cup, tin plate, fork, knife, and spoon. A variety of military-issue and civilian styles are available. The types used by both sides are the same.

The cup came in several styles. The most common was a 2-pint tin cup with a handle, known as a "dipper." It could get a large amount of water out of a stream, bucket, or trough, which could then be poured into the canteen. This was important when there were huge numbers of men trying to get water out of the same small stream or well.

Another style is a smaller cup, about 1 pint, also made of tin. Enamelware materials (patented 1849) existed, but they were very expensive and not commonly used by soldiers. To say white or blue enamelware is "farbish" is not strictly correct, but it was not typical.

A third type of cup is a "mucket." It had about a 2-pint capacity, a bail or hanging hoop by which it could be suspended over the fire, and a handle. It also had a cover on a hinge, important if it was strapped to the haversack and the men marching behind chewed tobacco. Open cups often were considered targets by those men. Reenactors can use any one of these three types of cups.

Tinware is not good for carbonated drinks, because they put stress on the seams and do wicked things to solder. Nevertheless, it is better to use a tin cup for sodas and buy a new one when it starts to leak than it is to walk around the camp with a modern aluminum can. Confederate troops used all types of cups, and late-war soldiers carried clay jars or hollowed gourds for dippers.

The large cup was not conveniently carried inside the haversack. When the haversack was full, the cup sometimes bent and often would spill a little bit of liquid to the bottom of the haversack after use. Most soldiers tied or strapped the dipper to the haversack by either the carrying straps or the closing strap or button. This made it handy and easy to get at on the march but exposed the cup to dust and dirt.

The plate was usually tin, 8 inches or so in diameter, and looked similar to a pie pan. They always started out shiny but quickly dulled from use.

Tin plates and cups conduct heat quickly, and hot coffee or stew can burn your hand while holding the cup or plate if you aren't careful.

Knife, fork, and spoon for reenactors should be of period type. The usual table knife had a rounded end. In the mid-Victorian period, people were just moving to salt shakers from salt cellars. Earlier, they dipped the end of the knife into a small salt bowl, like a sugar bowl, and spread salt on food. At the time of the Civil War, this was a little bit old-fashioned, but not noticeably so.

Forks were changing from a fork with three sharp spikes to the more familiar four-pronged instrument. Either type can be used.

Spoons were usually oversized by today's standards, closer to our soup-spoon or tablespoon. A spoon the size of today's teaspoon was considered a "fancy spoon" for desserts, or was for young children or invalids. Confederates sometimes carved or whittled wooden spoons and forks.

For those who wish to be fancy, matched silverware can be purchased in antique shops. Those who want to "make do" can use a two-pronged, whittled skewer.

CANTEENS

Canteens come in different styles. The most common canteens were two dish-shaped pieces soldered together, suspended by a linen strap. Some early ones were smooth, and some later ones had circular ridges in the sides and are known as "bull's-eye canteens." The canteen spout was sealed with a cork, held by a small chain to the strap band on the side.

Canteen covers come in different colors, usually all made of wool. It was thought that the dark blue wool cover was the most common style for Union troops, but current research challenges this. There is quite an argument about the proper color and cloth style for canteen covers for both Union and Confederate troops. Dark blue cloth was usually left over from the manufacture of the uniform coat and used for canteen covers. Some researchers say the covers were from leftover trouser cloth (light blue) or blankets (gray-brown). Many reenactors state that blanket wool covers were the most durable and hence most popular. Some say that the most common color for the Federal canteen was brown-gray. Arguments can get quite heated over this, so ask your unit historian which kind is correct for your unit, and be prepared to defend your choice.

The wool cover was thought to help keep the canteen cool. The canteen was dunked in water to fill it, and as the water evaporated from the wet wool on the march, it helped keep the water inside the canteen cool, or at least that was the idea. Usually it just made a damp spot on the side of the uniform.

There were several types of Confederate canteens. The most common type was the tin drum canteen, made of heavy tin and suspended by a linen or leather strap. This canteen looks like a round Christmas cookie tin with a spout. There was no cloth cover for this canteen.

Another type was similar to the Union smoothside but had a slightly different spout. When the corks could not be replaced, corncobs, rags, sticks, and other things were used to keep the water in the canteen.

A third kind was a wooden canteen, similar to the drum canteen. These were not as practical to use; if they dried out, the wood would shrink and they could leak until refilled and the wood swelled. They are very popular with reenactors, however.

Be sure to dry out your canteen after each use, and store it upside down so that any condensation will drip out. To fight rust, you might pour in some warm water with baking soda, shake it around, and then rinse it out.

Most canteens were lightly coated on the inside with beeswax to prevent the tinware from rusting. There is some disagreement on this, however. Some say rust still forms under the beeswax. If you want to coat the inside of your canteen, warm some beeswax (not paraffin or petroleum wax) until it is almost runny. Pour it slowly into the canteen, and move the canteen around until the beeswax coats the inside completely. Don't let too much settle at the bottom of the canteen, or you won't have any room for water. Because of the solder and beeswax in the canteen, never keep carbonated drinks or beer in them. These will tear the canteen up.

The canteen strap was very long, so many soldiers tied a knot in the strap just behind the section where it draped over the neck. The canteen rode fairly high, often just under and behind the armpit. At full length, a canteen would flap about and more than likely spill out its contents when the soldier ran. Many antique dealers will say this knot indicates cavalry usage, but cavalry-men tied the canteen strap in two. Examples of infantrymen knotting the strap exist in museum and private collections.

The canteen strap will rub against the metal brackets that hold the strap on the canteen. Every few events, be sure to move the strap a little bit through the brackets so that the wear marks will remain even and the strap won't suddenly break in the field.

A sign of a new recruit is putting the strap of the canteen under the waist belt. Since that would mean taking off the belt while holding on to the cap box, bayonet, and two ends of the belt every time he wanted a drink of water, this shows that he has not had much experience with canteens.

TOBACCO

Though not encouraged, cigarettes are often permitted at reenactments. Cigar-illos predate the Civil War and are often confused with cigarettes. Cigarillos had a tobacco leaf or corn leaf wrapping and in America were known as "shucks." Today's paper-wrapped cigarette comes out of the Bull Durham cigarettes used by cowboys in the 1870s and 1880s. Filters came into use about the turn of the century.[15]

There are two concerns with the use of cigarettes at reenactments, besides the health considerations. First, it is dangerous to have lighted smoking materi-als (cigarettes, pipes, or cigars) around gunpowder. There should be no smok-ing on the march, where a flicked ash can ignite a cartridge box filled with gunpowder. While on a march, an unlit pipe or stogie can be chewed. Smoking should be confined to breaks or when the troops are not standing in formation. When in doubt, ask the noncom or officer. There also should be no smoking inside tents, which is a fire hazard, especially when they are filled with straw.

Second, modern cigarettes are "farbish." Cigarette smoking should not interfere with the ambiance of the camp. Keep cigarette packs and lighters out of sight. When in view of spectators, cup the modern cigarette in your hand so that it is not visible. Also, spectators should not see twentieth-century cigarette butts on the ground of a nineteenth-century camp. "Field-strip" the butts by first tearing the filter off the extinguished cigarette, then tearing the paper and filter to bits and releasing the tobacco shreds. Or toss butts into the fire pit when finished.

Civil War soldiers enjoyed a great variety of carved pipes, some quite artistic. Cigars also were smoked extensively. Many cigar smokers had carrying cases for their stogies and often would put a couple through the hat cord. Modern cigars with plastic on the end are not encouraged at reenactments. Chewing tobacco and snuff were widely used during the Civil War as well. If you chew, learn to hit what you aim at, and don't aim at anything (or anyone) unless you intend to hit it.

INSPECTIONS

There are two types of inspections: camp and regimental. The camp inspection is usually early in the morning. A group of officers and representatives from several regiments walk through the camp looking for anachronisms or "farb" items. Items spotted should be either covered up or removed from camp. All members of the regiment are responsible for keeping the area free of modern trash and non-period ("farbish") items.

Next is the regimental inspection. The regiment will fall in for inspection. After lining up, they will be told to "open the ranks" so that there is room for the inspectors to walk between the two ranks. Then the troops will pull out the ramrods and drop them down their musket barrels. Next they will undo the flaps on their cartridge boxes. The inspectors will come down the rows, pulling the ramrods slightly out and then dropping them back down the barrel to see if they "ring." If the ramrod lands with a dull thud or no sound at all, it means that the rifle either is dirty or has a powder charge in it, both of which are safety hazards to other people.

Reenactors always discuss whether the ramrod "tulip" should go down the barrel first or should remain sticking slightly out. One argument for putting the tulip down first is that it will not scratch the bottom of the barrel when dropped down by the inspector. On the other hand, with the tulip up it is easier for the inspector to grasp. If the barrel is dirty, the ramrod may become stuck and will have to be pulled out with pliers. I have never seen a ramrod get stuck during an inspection, but I have seen ramrods get stuck in dirty rifles.

The question is actually moot. An experienced inspector should not bounce the ramrod hard enough to cause any damage; it is a sign of ignorance about muskets to snap the ramrod too hard. It is more important to be standardized. One way or the other, all members of a regiment should present their rifles the same way. Finally, with many events requiring the troops to leave their ramrods in the camp, many officers will go down the line with just one ramrod that they will use in each rifle, thus relieving the soldier from having to think or make another important decision.

The rifle also will be checked to make sure the half cock of the hammer is working. Since this is the only "safety" your rifle has, it is important that it is working properly.

The inspectors will then go down the back of the regiment, checking the cartridge boxes. They will look in each cartridge box to make sure there are no penny wrappers or stapled cartridges. Those constructed improperly, or with staples, paper clips, or glue to hold them together, will be removed. Illegal loads (those with more than 85 grains of powder) also will be removed. No live rounds (those with a real bullet at the end) will ever be allowed.

After checking your rifle, the inspecting officer will order the unit to place a percussion cap on the nipple and point the barrel at the ground. He will then go down the line asking each soldier one by one to fire his cap. The inspector will make sure that the ground has been disturbed by the discharge of the cap. This shows that the nipple is clean and the barrel is clear of obstructions.

During the inspection, uniforms will be checked to make sure they are of proper fabric and cut. "Farb" items and nonperiod clothing (such as modern glasses) may be grounds for removing the soldier from the reenactment. Since the inspectors are not from your regiment, you may find them stricter regarding modern accessories. Nevertheless, most inspectors are lenient if they know you have been in the hobby for less than a year and are still getting your basic equipment together.

Safety is the highest priority of each regiment. There will always be an inspection at the beginning of an event, often by an officer from another (sometimes opposing) unit. No one who fails the safety inspection or uniform inspection will be allowed on the field.

It is a matter of honor and pride to reenactors that the arms of their regiment are clean and correct. Rusty, faulty, or dirty rifles are an embarrassment to the entire unit. Most regiments conduct a preinspection to correct any deficiencies. If you are new, ask for assistance or advice; experienced reenactors are always willing to show new members how to clean and take care of their rifles.

Many regiments have a "proof book" that has copies of any exceptions from the standard uniform, armaments, or banners. This is usually a loose-leaf note-book with a copy of the regiment's history, uniform descriptions, photographs of members and equipment, and anything else that would justify any variation from the norm. If the inspector disagrees with an article of clothing or part of the drill, the proof book can be pulled out as evidence. It is possible, however, that an inspector may feel that exceptions and variations, although documented, will distract from the purpose of the reenactment. This is up to the inspector's discretion.

RANK

Officially there are four grades of rank: noncommissioned officers (corporals and sergeants), line officers (ensigns, first and second lieutenants, and captains), field and staff officers (majors, lieutenant colonels, and colonels), and generals. Extra ranks are given to specialists, such as surgeons, blacksmiths, and topographers. In living history, people often portray historical personas and assume their ranks. Civilian authorities, such as President Lincoln or the state governor, may also be portrayed by reenactors. In camp, troops should render passing respects to these authorities—come to attention, present arms, salute, and so forth. Officers cannot give orders or command troops other than their home units, however.

Regiments can band together to form brigades and can have extra positions, such as brigade sergeant major. Individuals can have several ranks, depending on their affiliation. For example, the captain of one unit, the 24th Regiment, Michigan Infantry, is also a sergeant in the Iron Brigade Association. So when the 24th does local events, he is in an officer's uniform, but when the 24th is participating in larger events, the 24th Michigan falls in with the Iron Brigade and he becomes a company sergeant. In such cases, the

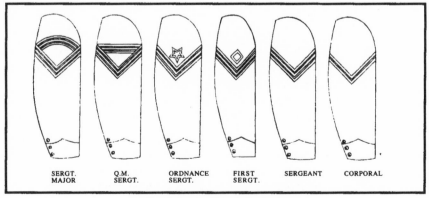

Confederate Rank Insignia

Reliving the Civil War

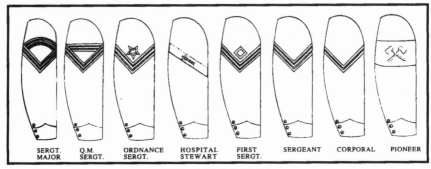

Union Rank Insignia

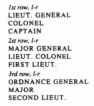

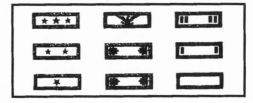

Union Officers' Shoulder Straps

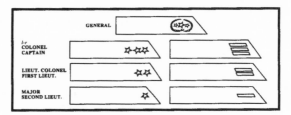

Confederate Collar Badges

individual must have the appropriate uniforms and arms for both ranks. When such an individual is an "orphan" at a local event, he usually falls in with the ranks as a private. He is an officer in his home regiment only. When he is in another regiment as an orphan, he must abide by its rules.

Rank is earned within your own organization. Outside your home regiment, it must also be earned by experience and merit. Since you must have permission to perform as an officer or noncom, ranks are not dependent simply on who can afford the uniform. One of the worst offenses is for an officer of one regiment to give orders directly to the men of another regiment. Orders must go down through the regiment's chain of command to the men. This prevents confusion of orders and counterorders, and also prevents self-appointed officers with no experience from messing up an event by doing something stupid or dangerous.

To Confederate reenactors, the worst are the self-appointed cavalry officers who try to look handsome and dashing while waving a sword around and giving orders from horseback to infantry units, often from other states. This is a common mistake in television shows and movies.

One last note about officers. Becoming an officer in reenactment events or living history does not make you a "real" officer. Do not let it go to your head; you are only acting the part of an officer, just as the other reenactors are acting their parts. Anyone who forgets his part and tries to give direct orders inappropriate to the event is likely to be either laughed at or otherwise surprised at the response of his troops.

MILITARY COURTESY

At least minimal courtesy should be shown to military and civilian officers of your side while in camp. This is part of the authenticity of the nineteenth-century camp. Sutlers, civilian camps, and areas outside of military camps are neutral territory. Salutes are optional in these areas, though encouraged.

Soldiers on guard duty or picket should display proper military courtesy at all times to the public and officers. Spectators often ask for the location of regiments within the camp. Pickets should either know where the regiments are located or be able to refer the spectators to the provost marshal, who can direct them to the proper campfire. This is an often overlooked courtesy to civilians, who may be looking for relatives or friends.

On the march at the route step, many soldiers tip their hats while passing ladies, as was customarily done during the WBTS. Strict military conformity was not required until World War I. On the other hand, soldiers in the ranks should not shout at spectators or make obscene gestures.

Military salutes are required when passing or addressing an officer or high elected official, such as a state governor or president. In standing formation and under arms, salutes are performed by presenting arms. When marching, the troops might be ordered by the ranking officer or noncom to give "eyes right" or "eyes left" as a salute. More often, the salute is rendered by the company commander, who uses his sword. Soldiers do not present arms while moving.

For both the Federal and Confederate armies, the rules for saluting were almost exactly alike, taken from the U.S. Army Regulations:

265. When a soldier without arms, or with sidearms only, meets an officer, he is to raise his hand to the right side of the visor of his cap, palm to the front, elbow raised as high looking at the same time in a respectful and soldier-like manner at the officer, who will return the compliment thus offered.[16]

In passing or addressing an officer while under arms, the soldier will be at or come to shoulder arms. He will then cross the left arm over the body and position the hand over the ramrod of the rifle. When acknowledged, the hand is returned quickly.

Salutes had changed in the nineteenth century from the lifting of the hat in the previous generation to a more formal hand-salute movement, but the change had not truly been codified. There are differences of interpretation in what Hardee said about the salute. He said in the section "Honors to Be Paid by Soldiers": "When a soldier without arms, or with side arms only, meets an officer, he will continue to move on, but he is to raise his hand to his cap, looking at the same time in a respectful and soldier-like manner at the officer, who will make a suitable acknowledgment to the compliment thus received."[17] Some officers acknowledged the salute by returning it; others responded with only a nod of the head.

The salute is a courtesy and an honor. The soldier is not required to salute a member of the opposing force unless he is acting as a representative, such as a picket or delivering messages under a flag of truce. Among reenactors, however, officers of the opposing forces who are especially well respected and regarded by troops often receive passing compliments.

Reenactors in Confederate uniform outside the Confederate camp area and not on the field should salute the U.S. flag as it passes by. Although you are representing a Confederate soldier, you are also a U.S. citizen and should render honors to passing colors. This has caused some controversy in the past. To avoid saluting Yankee officers when saluting the national banner, many soldiers do not salute the flag until it is directly opposite them and immediately drop the salute when the flag has passed by.

MEDALS AND DECORATIONS

Medals are not worn during a reenactment open to the public. They are sometimes worn in the evenings with a Class A uniform coat at formal occasions such as military balls and regimental dinners. Never wear a medal pinned to your shirt or vest.

Precedence in wearing medals is as follows: At the top right on the left breast should go medals from Civil War veterans societies or auxiliaries, such as Sons of Union Veterans, Sons of Confederate Veterans, Military Order of the Loyal Legion, UDC, or GAR. The order for wearing these is by date of organization.

Next come any medals from any federal, state, or national organizations, such as the Manassas Centennial Reenactment Medal, National Park Service Gettysburg "Badge of the 125th Brigade," Boy Scout Civil War Hiking Trail medals, or medals from national or state preservation associations.

Next in precedence are reenactment medals awarded at special events or as honors by your regiment, Civil War Roundtable, or other organization. These might be Soldier of the Year awards, heritage medals, or medals of appreciation. Last come purchased medals or commemorations.

Common courtesy and ethics demand that you don't wear medals you didn't earn or don't deserve or from organizations of which you are not a member.

Wear collar insignia, such as SUV membership rosettes, when the SUVCW membership medal is not worn as well. Remember, each Civil War organization will have its own guidelines. If there is a military rank insignia, such as captain's bar, on the collar, then no other collar insignia should be worn.

No honorary insignia except regimental brass (infantry horn, corps insignia, regimental numbers, and company letters) may be worn on the kepi or hat. GAR or other badges should not be worn to hold the brim of the hat upright or otherwise decorate the hat in an unusual way.

At funerals or reinterments of Civil War veterans, medals may be worn with the uniform. Only medals from WBTS veterans societies or earned military medals should be worn on these occasions. Reenactment or purchased medals are not appropriate at military funerals. More appropriate is wearing the correct rosette or pin discreetly on the collar, instead of the full medal. At funerals of fellow reenactors where regimental representatives wear their uniforms, the rules are more relaxed, and any appropriate medals may be worn to honor the departed.

Reproductions of the Civil War-period U.S. Congressional Medal of Honor are available for purchase. They should not be worn unless you are representing a known individual who earned the Medal of Honor. Additionally, you should not wear a Medal of Honor unless you are a member of a unit, such as the 27th Regiment of Maine Infantry, that was awarded the medals (later to be acknowledged, erroneously) for reenlisting during the emergency in 1863, or you are a direct or collateral descendant of a Congressional Medal of Honor recipient.

When medals are worn during active events, such as dances, the metal portion may sometimes separate from the ribbon and fall to the floor. To prevent this, pin the ribbon to the coat, and then use a safety pin to affix the metal portion to the uniform coat.

BASIC INFANTRY DRILL

Hardee's Tactics, which has been frequently republished for reenactors, is the best source for infantry drill and is used by most units, North and South. Much of Hardee's Tactics was based on or was similar to Scott's and Casey's books (see Bibliography), so it is good to read them as well. Casey's book is probably better written and easier to understand than the others, and there are only minor differences among them. Exceptions to Hardee's Tactics may be done by a particular regiment that may want to do something different, such as Zouave drill or heavy infantry. Zouave drill was noted for its clockwork precision and fast pace, whereas "heavy infantry" drill was noted for its slower, more deliberate pace. Anyone who is familiar with Hardee's basic drill system is welcomed in almost any regiment, however.

Militia regiments before the war practiced from different drill books. When they joined the army, many of these militia units had to unlearn their methods and learn the common drill. This was a new experience for country farm boys, who had never marched in step or followed orders. In 1863, the U.S. Congress authorized $350,000 to be spent on books of instruction in tactics and drill. Many of these books are still around, with pencil marks showing the notes of any number of new officers and men.

General Hardee divided his book into several parts, called "schools." The first part is the "School of the Soldier," which is what we would call the manual of arms today. It was the set of nonmarching drills that the individual soldier should know. The instructors would place the bodies of the new recruits in the correct positions to teach them how to stand, handle weapons, and march.

The second part is the "School of the Company," which deals with movements of the soldiers as part of a group or company. The "School of the Soldier" mostly deals with the movement of the arms, whereas the "School of the Company" deals with formation, marching, and action commands. The new recruit is often shown the paces by other members of his unit in an "Awkward Squad." New recruits drill with experienced members so that the new recruit will learn the movements by watching experienced soldiers go through the drill. By first seeing a demonstration of the command and then going through it with an experienced soldier beside you, you can easily learn the movements and cadence. An attempt to teach the drill with only new and inexperienced troops, however, is something folks in other units will walk over to watch.

This introductory drill should be done before lining up the regiment for the reenactment or drill demonstration, so that the new recruits won't throw the rest of the regiment off pace. Also, it is a matter of pride for most units to have their members prepared and ready to go.

The WBTS movement of troops was based on linear movement: The troops moved back and forth in straight lines. The lines were in two ranks— front and rear. Each man in the front rank along with the man in the rear rank behind him formed one file. It is from this that the term "rank and file" originated. The movements in the march were designed to get these ranks of men in position and facing the enemy so that the most firepower could be directed against the opponents.

These marching maneuvers will be taught to you by members of your regiment. A copy of Hardee's Tactics will show you the basic methods, and it is unnecessary for me to repeat the instructions here. If you have any questions, ask the more experienced members of your regiment. You will be surprised at how many of them won't know the correct answer, so read up on your Hardee's.

Once these two schools are mastered by you, any other movement is up to the officers to foul up. The private is safe if he stays with his company, even if the officers or NCOs make a mistake. Educating officers and gently setting them right is one of the most exasperating tasks of a private!

Some rules of the road not mentioned in Hardee's books should be noted. When ranks of men are moving, especially shoulder to shoulder, many men in the center will be squeezed when there is some expansion and shrinkage of the line. Particularly with younger recruits, the temptation is to give way to pressure by turning the shoulders slightly out of line. When the company stops, this causes the center to be too crowded. So the soldier is to "demand his place," and if pressured, he must either gently resist or move to the left and pressure the man on his left to give way in turn. In no case should he give up his place by turning his shoulders. On the other hand, this can quickly deteriorate into a shoving match, so keep your temper in check.

The command to "guide right" or "guide left" means that the entire line should give a little in that direction. If the command is to guide right, keep in shoulder contact with the man on your right. If the man on your left then strays away, that is his problem. In line, try to keep your elbows slightly touching the elbows of the men on either side of you. This keeps you in line without having to look. This should also prevent the line from forming a bow when some men march faster or slower than others. By keeping in touch, the pace should be regulated down the line.

Modern men sometimes are uncomfortable about being so close to other men. In line, the command "Forward, march!" means to march shoulder to shoulder (really elbow to elbow) and make physical contact with the men on either side of you. This means maintaining touch with the elbows of the men on either side of you. Since men will move their elbows out of line to keep in touch, rather than look like a bunch of men walking arm in arm, the command is shoulder to shoulder. A space of even a few inches between men in line can cause a bow or a gap in a line. This detracts from the military effect of a moving line of soldiers. Also, when firing in line, this gap can cause the man in the back rank to fire incorrectly in the gap between the men in front.

The front-rank man and rear-rank man in a file need to trust each other. The two men of one file and the two in the next were "comrades in arms" during the Civil War and made a foursome that would forage, mess, and camp together. Today in reenacting, the more experienced three comrades will look after a new recruit and make sure he is doing the movements safely and correctly.

The front-rank men and rear-rank men need to check each other in a modern "buddy system." They need to make sure the other man is not getting too much sun or overexerting himself. On a sunny day, if your buddy or comrade turns pale or stops sweating, make sure he is all right. Many men will not speak up or volunteer to fall out, but will if asked. When a man is really sick, faint, or has sunstroke, his comrade in arms will stay with him to make sure he gets attention or gets back to camp all right. In one group I was with, a sick man fell out of the ranks. Because his buddy didn't stay with him, the man was alone when he fainted on the way back to camp. When he woke up, he found someone had stolen his musket. So buddy up and watch out for each other.

Because the rear-rank man fires over the shoulder of the front-rank man, he should always say, "Coming over!" when he is about to fire over the right shoulder of the front-rank soldier, except when under orders to fire by company. Though this will not be found in any drill book of the period, it is a reenactment custom for safety reasons. It keeps the man in front alert to what the man in the rear rank is doing so that there will be no surprises and less chance of accidents.

Standardization is another point for each regiment. There is much to interpret in Hardee's drill, and each regiment does one or two things differently from all other regiments. What is important is that each regiment does it consistently. When brigading with other regiments, if the differences are obvious, they can be reconciled for that one event.

There are no exceptions for left-handed soldiers or officers. Although there were as many left-handed men in 1861 as there are today, all drill was designed for righties. Left-handed people had to learn how to do everything right-handed. Officers did not reverse swords, and all soldiers carried their rifles as if they were right-handed. As a southpaw myself, I know how annoying this can be, but to do it right, you must do it right.

"Muzzles up" is a rule of the road when marching at the route step. It is comfortable to carry the musket by the sling, with the butt of the musket behind and above your shoulder. Don't do this during formations and marching, however, for several reasons: Powder in a loaded musket will fall out, dust and dirt will foul the barrel, the ramrod might fall out, the angle of the weapon causes it to take more room in the ranks, and it is more likely to hit the fellow behind or in front of you or to swat someone in the face when you try to come back to shoulder arms. Also, if the rifle is loaded and it goes off, with the muzzle down it is generally pointed at the heels and legs of the man in front. So keep your muzzles up for safety in formations.

When waiting in lines, many men rest their hands on the tops of the muzzles. Don't do this. The opening of the muzzle is where the smoke, flame, cartridge paper, and ball come out, and you run the risk of losing some fingers or the center part of your hand. Always treat your rifle with respect.

The modern pace of marching and walking is too fast for Civil War-period drill. Their way of life was slower and more deliberate. So don't "hustle" in marching and drill. Keep marching to a comfortable cadence. A slower pace is sometimes annoying to twentieth-century reenactors, but it is more authentic.

In Appendix F are selected instructions for some of Hardee's drill, modified by the National Park Service for weapons firing demonstrations. Some of the instructions have been modified for safety reasons; others are dependent on interpretation. If you are unsure, you may want to follow the NPS guidelines.

3

Camp Life

At any reenactment where the people stay overnight, there are camps. The authentic camps are always separated into opposing sections: Confederate and Union. These are military camps, with sections for each regiment, horse lines, an artillery park, a provost marshal's office, and so forth. There are also camps for civilians and for sutlers, as well as support camps. Within these camps, it is important to keep everything authentic or have modern equipment hidden under authentic covers, as these camps will be visited by spectators.

TENTS

Comrades in arms each carried a piece of heavy duck canvas, one with a row of buttons, the other with buttonholes. The two pieces buttoned together to make one tent. The canvas was suspended from a center pole or line. There are endless variations, but most are made from two tree branches with Y-shaped forks that serve as uprights, between which is suspended a straight branch that is longer than the length of the tent. From the extended ends, many reenactors drape their accoutrements, jackets, and muskets. This keeps the items off the dirt, but the weight of a musket has knocked down many a tent. Tents also may be tied to two upright poles and then pegged to the ground.

When buying a tent, buy both sides at the same time and make sure the buttons and buttonholes align. If you wish, you can also buy triangular pieces of canvas that fit at each end of the tent. These end pieces were typical of tents made after 1864. Buy these at the same time you purchase the side pieces, and make sure the buttons match up with the buttonholes on the side pieces. Many reenactment tents have shiny brass grommets along the bottom edge for attaching rope loops to the tent pegs. Hand-sewn holes were typical, so try to avoid buying a tent with grommets.

Enlisted tents were usually open at either end and were known as "dog tents," because there was just enough room for two men and a dog. During World War I, the tents were smaller and the doughboys called them "pup tents," as they are still called today. Officers' tents were more ornate and fancy.

Three other kinds of tents were popular during the war: the A-frame, the Sibley, and the wall tent.

An A-frame tent was larger and was used by officers or as a general-purpose tent. It was higher, with a front entrance that closed and secured with flaps. Troops in garrisons or a permanent post usually used the A-frame tent. Many of the heavy artillery in the forts around Washington stayed in these tents.

A Sibley tent was named after Gen. Henry H. Sibley, who fashioned his tent after the Plains Indian tepee. It was round and tall, with a center pole, and looked like a canvas tepee. The Sibley held about a dozen men, but in inclement weather twenty men could pack it. The men slept with their feet to the center and heads out along the walls of the tent. The walls could be raised for ventilation, but when the weather was bad and the apex opening and canvas entrances were shut, the air inside the tent was awful. One Yank stated in his reminiscences that "to enter one of them on a rainy morning . . . and encounter the night's accumulation of nauseating exhalations from the bodies of twelve men (differing widely in habits of personal cleanliness) was an experience which no old soldier has ever been known to recall with any great enthusiasm."

The wall tent had short walls of canvas at the ends for water runoff. These were popular because the walls could be raised during hot weather to allow more air circulation.

Many larger tents have an extra piece of canvas that comes out as a tarp or flap. This permits activities out of the sun or rain. Keep in mind, however, that any tent you purchase will have to be put up in the rain and wind, so get one that is easy to erect.

In a canvas tent, if you touch the canvas when it is raining, it will leak at that spot. To stop such a leak, run your finger gently from the touched spot to the next sewn seam or the ground, so that the water will follow the new trail you have created.

After your first reenactment in the driving rain, you will want to purchase a gum blanket, a stiff piece of canvas covered with gum rubber to make it waterproof. The gum blanket is about 60 inches wide and 70 inches long, with a hole in the center so that it can also be used as a rain poncho. It also often has smaller grommet holes around the edges so that it can be tied down or suspended over a tent as a waterproof tarp. In good weather, it can be laid under the blankets with the gum side down to protect the soldier from damp-ness from the ground. Many soldiers drew checkerboards or other games with pencil and paints on the plain canvas side, to be used when things got dull around camp.

At many reenactments, the host will supply bales of straw. This makes sleeping on the ground a lot more comfortable and a great deal warmer. Put your gum blanket or a waterproof tarp underneath the straw so that moisture won't migrate through the chaff. Seasoned reenactors often own a canvas tick that they fill with straw to make into a mattress at night. When the event is over, they dump out the straw and have only an empty canvas bag to take home. Learn the difference between straw and hay, and do not pick up and carry away hay, which is feed for the horses, for your bedding.

To pitch a dog tent, tie short pieces of rope or twine through the gussets or holes along the bottom, and loop them over the tent pegs. When the tent is snug, you will not need a rope to reinforce the upright poles. Tent pegs can be of many types: old railroad spikes, curved iron spikes turned out by skilled blacksmiths, or even whittled tree branches, which are the best choice. The best are those with enough of a head on the spike to allow two tent ropes. It's a no-no to use modern aluminum spikes in reenactments, except in modern camping areas. When using iron or steel spikes, do not use a steel mallet or hammer to drive them home. The steel mallet can chip and send a sharp piece of metal flying into your face and eyes.

Although Army Regs demanded two paces between tents, many reenac-tors pitch their dog tents so that a tent's pegs can be shared by the tent next to it. It is more important in this case to be consistent with your regiment than to be the one soldier to follow the regulations.

MILITARY CAMPS

The proper setup for a Union army camp is described in the *Revised U.S. Army Regulations*. Generally, these regulations concerning camps and formations were somewhat followed by Confederates too. In addition to the various tents in a military camp—officers', noncommissioned officers', men's, cook's, and supply tents—there should be a "color line," where the flags of the regiment are stored. Make room for a parade street where the troops can fall in or stand to in formation. This should be the place for the stacking of arms.

Camp streets should be at least wide enough that a double rank of men can march between the fire pits and the tents. If a wider street can be fit in, it would be more comfortable for women in hoop skirts, parents with children, and photographers who want to get wide shots of a camp street. Both the *C.S. Army Regs of 1863* and the *Revised U.S. Army Regulations of 1861* called for a street "not less than 5 paces wide."

Try to have some period activity or discussion going on in camp when spectators are passing by so that people will feel as though they have visited a real camp. Soldiers sitting around talking about football or twentieth-century politics don't fit in with a historically accurate camp. Pipe smoking, card playing, reading reproduction magazines or newspapers, sewing and repairing clothes, whittling, and preparing meals are all activities that can be done while waiting for the call to arms. Prepared sketches, such as mail call in a Southern camp, circa 1863, are popular and test the acting ability and historical knowledge of the regiment.

The 6th Ohio of the Cumberland Guard had a clever custom for maintaining a proper nineteenth-century atmosphere in camp. If someone mentioned a subject outside of the time period, such as modern football, computers, or current politics, he had to wear a jawbone of an ass suspended around his neck on a string. This person then wore the jawbone until he caught someone else in the regiment making a similar mistake, at which time he passed it on. This kept the men on their toes.

CIVILIAN CAMPS

Civilian camps were placed so that civilians following the army would have a place with less hustle and bustle and danger of attack. Normally, civilians stayed out of the military camps during the day, unless escorted. Civilian camps allowed the ladies to relax in an area without rough comments or rougher sights.

Civilian camps are neutral territory, so visit them in your full uniform if you want to. Be sure to tip your hat when passing ladies, and watch your manners and language.

Many civilians put as much effort in their impressions as the soldiers do, so respect their authenticity, and don't spoil the effect of their camp by using modern artifacts.

SUTLER CAMPS

Sutlers try to have an authentic camp next to their wares. Their camps are closest to the entrance and get the most traffic from reenactors and the public.

Try to do most of your purchasing and looking just after you register. On Friday evening, most of the customers will be reenactors. This is your best chance to ask questions not only of the sutlers, but of other reenactors as well. If you wait until Sunday afternoon at a large event, the sutlers will be filled with spectators, and there will be no time for questions and in-depth answers. Leave the sutlers free on Saturday and Sunday afternoons so that they can sell to spectators. Friday and Saturday evenings and early Saturday morning are the best times for reenactors to shop at sutlers. When their tents are closed for the night, don't try to wake them up to sell you something—wait until morning.

SUPPORT CAMPS

Next to the civilian camps, or combined with the sutlers' camps, are support camps, with tents for the Soldier's Christian Association, Temperance Union, U.S. Sanitary Commission, and so on. Visit and ask questions. Sometimes these organizations pass out free or inexpensive copies of Bibles, books, and pamphlets to soldiers in uniform.

4

Civilian Reenacting

Reenacting is a fun hobby for individuals and families alike. Children as well as parents can participate in reenactment or living history. More people join WBTS-period military units than those from any other time period. These units often have a civilian camp where spouses and children set up in authentic areas.

There are many civilian roles at WBTS reenactments; only a lack of imagination and knowledge of history limits them. Although the Civil War brought many men into the army, only one man in eight in the United States and only three men in ten in the Confederate States joined up. All the rest, and all of the women, remained civilians. The civilian is and always has been the typical American.

Some reenactors portray military or civilian specialists and come to represent and portray specific skills, such as medicine, cartography, signaling, or blacksmithing. The main disadvantage of this is the enormous amount of money it costs to get authentic tools and contemporary knowledge of a technical specialty. Another disadvantage is carrying around all the specialist equipment, which can get very heavy, especially for blacksmiths or farriers.

If you plan to perform in a military reenactment, you must abide by the rules of the host unit and sponsor. Check first to see whether they will accept your civilian persona or scenario, or if it will conflict with the goals of the reenactment. You will need to pass the same requirements as the military folks for authenticity and correctness of dress.

Consider working up a scenario and script with other reenactors, with different roles that can be easily viewed by the spectators. Although the lines don't have to be memorized, some dialog can be rehearsed so that the performance will flow.

ROLES FOR WOMEN

There has been a burst of new activities for women and civilian men in reenacting, and the sophistication and authencity of civilian presentations continues to grow. More and more events sponsor women's roles as well as separate civilian activities and are educational opportunities in their own right. In addition, new societies and organizations that focus on the civilian aspects of the Civil War now have active events and sponsor their own activities.

Women played many roles during the WBTS era. Women often are considered to have been passive spectators during the Victorian period, but this was far from the truth. They were very active during the Civil War, although they didn't do what was considered "men's work."

The family was very close during that period, with multiple generations living in the same town, if not in the same house, all their lives. When it came time for the men to march away, many women went with them to cook, sew, clean, and help. Women from small farms (the majority) stayed at home to keep the farm in production. But many of the women from lower classes had no other place to go except with their men. Many miners and mill workers lived in houses rented from the company, and their families didn't own homes. When the men left, their families left with them. The families worked where they could and tried to keep up, especially during the first few months of the early war. The War Departments on both sides tried mightily to find work and housing for these women to keep them from following the troops but weren't successful. There were just too many of them.

During this period, women were undergoing a transition in status. A movement had been started during the preceding decades to keep women at home. Working conditions were so severe that women were encouraged to stay home with their children, to become educated and sophisticated and use their talents to improve the world around their families.

Local women often visited the military camps for a variety of purposes. At the Camp of Instruction outside of Bath, Maine, there was a daily scheduled omnibus that took townswomen back and forth to the camps for sightseeing or other reasons. Some went out of curiosity, others to visit male friends and relatives, and still others to sell produce, soft bread, and so forth. The civilians did not camp with the military, but during the daylight hours there were many female visitors to the military camps. During some campaigns there were so many wagons and carts of civilians intermingled with the military train that they held up any movement of the army by a number of hours. On some occasions they seriously held up the advance or retreat of the army.

An unescorted woman was open to insults and unwanted attention during those days. Women visiting the camp alone were considered "loose women." A lady was generally escorted by a male relative or military escort, or stayed with a group of women.

Many women enact elaborate, scripted scenes with other male and female reenactors. These can be used to show the life of women and families while soldiers are demonstrating life in the field. When they are not bound to a scripted and authentic set, these small playlets can create an excellent atmosphere at a reenactment. Most that I have seen have been so ad-libbed, however, that they were no longer historically correct, but only a vague representation of the times. Nevertheless, these playlets can be very effective in giving a taste of history.

Women reenactors can be mothers, wives, sisters, daughters, sweethearts of officers, contractors, or politicians. Sometimes the women, particularly the younger women and girls, wore clothing cut in the regimental style and marched with the men in parades in the hometowns. They were called "vivandièrs" (or "viviandieres") and helped keep up the men's spirits by helping out with the cooking, washing, singing, and dancing. They were sort of an early USO.

Local townswomen (or women from back home) visited the camp to sell produce, jams, and jellies. Other female visitors were tourists, tradeswomen, laundresses,[1] cooks, itinerant seamstresses, sutlers, merchants, letter writers, nurses, or nursing aides. Most nurses were male during this period; women generally took care of convalescents by writing letters, keeping bed linens clean, and conversing with the soldiers. Mothers or wives might come to camp to look for straying husbands, lovers, or sons, and other women to see officers with complaints about soldiers stealing.

Other roles for women reenactors include representatives of the Bible Society, Baptist Sewing Circle, U.S. Sanitary Commission, or the Women's Decent Burial for Soldiers Association; political haranguers or soapbox speechmakers; abolitionists; and wives or pretend wives of politicians on "fact-finding missions."

There was a small but active number of women who worked as professional (paid) mourners at funerals. There were also women who were local shopowners and farmers. Some women were entertainers, such as actresses or singers, although they were thought to be of questionable virtue because they often showed considerable personal freedom.

Bad women were a part of the nineteenth century, as they are today. These women have reenactment roles as spies; gamblers; con artists; insurance foils; aggressive matchmakers (this can be especially good with ethnic regiments such as Irish, Italian, or German Brigades, or with ethnic families in any regiment where matchmaking was a traditional practice); "conjure ladies" who cast spells, foretell the future, and sell charms; and women who carry whiskey illegally into camp (under their dresses or even in their prams) to sell to soldiers, and who are sometimes caught by the pickets or hard-eyed officers. The list is limited only by your imagination and historical accuracy.

One of the most touching, although seldom done, scenes is that of the women coming together to watch their men march off to battle. The women waving handkerchiefs, crying, trying to be cheerful while husbands, sons, and neighbors march away can add drama and pathos to almost any reenactment. Spectators love it, and to be honest, so do the men. It's nice to be missed by people who care, even when it's pretend.

The civilian camp can be very active, with multiple scenarios being played out. While the men are back in camp relaxing and cooling off after a heavy reenactment, activities in the civilian camps can take some pressure off the men and supply a ready diversion for visitors.

ROLES FOR MEN

There are any number of civilian roles for men. Almost any civilian job has a counterpart that can be found in a military camp. Remember that although one man in eight joined the Union army, the other seven remained civilian all through the war. Civilian living history is necessary for an accurate reenactment.

Male civilian reenactors can portray preachers, doctors, lawyers, sutlers, schoolteachers or headmasters, tourists, teamsters or workmen, artisans, spies, telegraph operators, linesmen, railroad engineers, undertakers, slave catchers, dancing instructors, gamblers, con men, politicians, or local farmers with complaints about the soldiers stealing or insulting wives and daughters. Other roles may include fathers, brothers, or sons of soldiers who come to visit or bring new boots; someone who comes to camp to find a runaway son, younger brother, or apprentice, only to get enlisted or drafted; a politically appointed pompous inspector from the governor's office who comes to poke about in that state's regiments and annoy the officers; or an army contractor who comes for payment or to sell something shoddy (sometimes he barely escapes a lynching!).

Many men had specific styles of dress for the type of work they did, and it is amazing how much can be told by the cut of the clothes. With only a little research, the clothing worn by artisans can be re-created.

If you decide to play the part of a carpenter, surveyor, or photographer, be prepared to answer questions about the trade. Many visitors will know something about the skills needed and will ask questions galore. They will be disappointed if you don't know the answers.

An accepted part of military reenactments is a visit from the provost marshal (military police), which can be disconcerting to the civilian man and amusing to everyone else, especially if the civilian reenactor is unfamiliar with Civil War-period reenactment and the authority of the provost marshal.

ROLES FOR CHILDREN

Reenacting is a family hobby, and many children play their own roles. The main problem with this is that many children lack the knowledge of the period to accurately portray children of another era. Treat them in the same way as new recruits in the hobby, who often have little knowledge of the mid-nineteenth-century period. There are a number of youngsters, however, who have a knowledge of the times that many adults would envy.

Adults working with younger reenactors should ensure that the children completely understand why they are to say or do certain things. If there is a particular point in a script to be made, or a difference between children of today and yesterday, the children need to understand this.

Interestingly, if children don't agree with the point being made in the script, they often won't make the point understandable. Even if they really try hard, children who don't agree with the script don't do well. Therefore, it's best to first have the children help with the main points and turns of any script, then go over the script with the children so that they understand what is to be done and what is to be emphasized, and use input from the children to polish and refine the script.

The best scripts for children have only one or two main points that the children can aim for in a variety of ways, can handle a flexible number of children, and allow the children to demonstrate their own knowledge. Don't make the mistake of trying to make children into little adults. And remember, kids in the audience are quick to spot a phony action.

Scripts for children can include schooldays with or without rowdy behavior; lessons from different regions, such as history of the Confederacy or Northern math; schoolchildren hiding wounded or enemy soldiers with or without the knowledge of teachers; and soldiers coming into the schoolroom to look for new recruits, deserters, or wounded. Around a house or historic site, scripts that include children can concentrate on daily life and chores, games, school lessons by parents, or apprenticeship work.

If children can show off a special skill, such as a period game or pastime, adults will be charmed, as will other children. A game that is too active, such as hoop racing, will not keep an audience's attention for long. People won't be able to keep up with children who disappear over the horizon. The children doing the reenactment might invite spectator children to participate. This is best done with noncontact games or games without too many rules, such as baseball.

Children also can participate in giving a uniform or dress talk. They can learn the facts surprisingly quickly and often come up with interesting observations about their clothes.

All events where children are participating must be adequately supervised by adults. Don't let the children use expensive props or toys, or anything that could be easily broken. Keep an eye on any planned demonstration, and help the kids with their presentation. It's a lot of fun, and you'll be amazed by some of the insights children can come up with.

NINETEENTH- AND EARLY TWENTIETH-CENTURY CLOTHING

The whole philosophy about clothing was different in the nineteenth century. Men's clothing was worn much looser, and although belts were used, most men wore suspenders that required trousers to be looser with more movement. Women's clothing was worn close around the body above the waist but in several layers of clothing that accentuated the woman's form without outlining it or revealing it immodestly. The human form was meant to be draped by clothing, and the natural shape of women's bodies was exaggerated and hidden by crinoline. The evolving social concepts behind clothing and apparel were seldom articulated and were often a combination of ideas from widely differing values and philosophies.

One explanation for the looseness of clothing is that it represented the nineteenth-century religious concept that the human body was not important, but the soul of the human was. Therefore, clothing should not attract attention to itself, but to the person wearing it. This is summed up in an old saying from the South: "Don't say that is an attractive dress; say rather that she looks attractive in that dress."

In addition, people were not able to control their environment as we do today, and their clothing reflected the lifestyles they lived. They had no central heat or air conditioning and had to dress accordingly and make do with natural products.

Then, too, there was a revolution of attitudes between the sexes from the 1850s through the 1860s. Women were becoming better educated and slightly more independent. As a result, there was a great deal of uncertainty about relationships between men and women. The dowry went out of fashion during this period, and marriage bonds were beginning to be thought of as old-fashioned. Women began marrying at later ages—eighteen to twenty, instead of fifteen to seventeen.

Affluent men in cities and towns and on large plantations continued to view women as "ornaments" to the home. Meanwhile, most American men on small farms and the frontiers recognized women as needed helpers and treasured them for their skills and worth, a novel concept at the time. Though men could tame a frontier, women were needed for civilization. Dorothea Dix, Harriet Beecher Stowe, Julia Ward Howe, and Florence Nightingale showed that women could influence men directly to effect change for the common good.

Education for women became more widespread, and this era saw the birth of the woman social reformer. This was the "roll-up-your-sleeves" type of woman who could organize a home, hospital, or asylum for the betterment of the community. The 1860s were the formative years for many women political activists and future social reformers. Out of the 1860s would come the Progressive Era of the late 1880s.

Though women had become more independent, they were still trapped in the "Perfect Lady" mystique. They had to be aloof and distant, warm and loving, practical and flighty, and maintain a balancing act on a pedestal. There was a great deal of confusion in the late 1850s; this period wasn't matched for depth of social and gender changes until the late 1960s and early 1970s. The rule books of flirting no longer applied, and new rules of etiquette and relationships had to be worked out. This was more obvious in Europe than in America, because the Civil War consumed so much time and interest and caused much stress and hardship for both women and men. At the end of the war, there were more unmarried women because of the numbers of men killed. Those women who did marry often would have a husband carrying disfiguring scars of battle, or missing an arm, leg, or possibly an eye.

The shape and fashion of women's clothing went through the same radical changes that women's thinking did from 1850 to 1869.

For the reenactor, although clothing may be correct for the period, it may not be correct for the person you are playing. Juanita Leisch discusses a method of choosing appropriate clothing that she calls the "Could, Would, Should Test." She first asks herself, "Could I wear this?" Obviously, if the style or materials are not current to the period, the item could not have been worn. Next she asks, "Would I wear this?" This would depend on "social accuracy"—whether the persona would wear an item of that style. For example, even though a bright, magenta-colored scarf may have been available during the Civil War period, it would not be appropriate for someone playing the part of a Quaker farm girl. Lastly she asks, "Should I wear this?" This also would depend on "economic accuracy"—whether the persona could afford the clothing.[2]

Before the invention of form-clinging zippers in the 1920s, almost everything was buttoned, hooked, tied, or pinned together. Because of this, it took longer to dress and undress. Coupled with the late-nineteenth-century habit of changing clothes for morning and afternoon, this meant that women spent a lot of time putting on, taking off, and adjusting clothes.

Aniline (chemical) dyes were invented in the 1850s as a by-product of medical research into artificial quinine, used to treat malaria. They weren't a common part of printed fabrics by our period. More commonly used were vegetable or mineral dyes. The aniline dyes are brighter and less likely to fade. Women were particularly conscious about their image, and wearing bright colors was thought to be unattractive, attention seeking, and indicative of loose morals. Few ladies were brave enough to wear red, lest they be thought "scarlet women." Even decent women did wear quite flashy high-lights, however, such as accents or brilliant brooches, almost in the style of today's costume jewelry.

On the other hand, drab colors were also not typical. The colors of cloth-ing seen today in museums and private collections have frequently faded. Originally, the clothing from the 1860s was much brighter and more colorful than most people think. Vegetable dyes can give a very deep, rich, or vibrant color, and this should be reflected in period clothing.

Men of the 1860s usually wore light-colored trousers and dark coats. This was typical of the Union uniform as well: sky blue trousers and a dark blue frock or sack coat. Many Confederate uniforms were also darker above and lighter below. Men's suits made from the same piece of cloth, including coat, waistcoat, and trousers, were called "dittos" and were more popular in Europe than in America.

Women wore colors differently from men, usually with darker colors from the waist down and lighter from the waist up. Any two colors of sharp contrast should have a neutral color in between. Darker colors could have bright highlights.

Men's trousers were loose and "broke" at the instep. Civilian coats were not much different from today's. For most of the nineteenth century, gentle-men did not take off their coats in public and show shirt sleeves; Only coun-try folks, trappers, and other persons of the rougher sort did this. When men went to an office or other work, they could take off their dress coats and put on other attire. This change in attire was considered very elegant. Thus, butchers would go to work in suits, but once at the butchery, would take off their coats and put on special aprons and other clothing. Short sleeves were not worn by men during the nineteenth century.

During the 1860s, all infants and children, male and female, wore dresses up until school age. After this, their clothing would mimic adult clothing, so children often looked like miniature adults.

Children's clothing was made for growth, and tucks and pleats were common. Although there were as many differences in minor details as there were mothers who sewed, nineteenth-century children's clothing all had com-mon characteristics. It often included an elongated shoulder, sometimes a quarter of the way down the arm, since it was easier to let out from this than at the shoulder. This was also a stronger seam, and less likely to tear.

Girls wore skirts that spread out from the hips. A common practice was to put in a "growth stripe" at the bottom of the dress, which concealed an extra tuck of fabric. As the dress hem was lengthened for growth, the tucks could be pulled down, and the seams or faded areas were then hidden by stripes, ruffles, or other needle art. These were also helpful with hand-me-downs, since a clever seamstress could hide the new hemline with another stripe. Younger girls wore their skirts just below the knee, older girls wore them midcalf, and preteens just over the ankles. When they became more mature and responsible, the girls lengthened their dresses.

In the country, boys wore trousers like men. In the city, many boys wore knee-length knickerbockers and loose, waist-length jackets. There was a change in men's styles in the 1860s to looser, more comfortable clothing, in marked contrast with the tighter, more restrictive clothing of the 1850s. The looser clothing styles helped children's clothes to wear longer.

For boys and girls of all classes, nothing was so common as hand-me-downs. In those days of large families, few could afford individual clothes for all the children. Sometimes an outgrown girl's calico blouse would be adapted as a shirt for a younger brother. Because girls' blouses were cut in smaller pieces and constructed differently, however, other authorities claim that this practice, in reality, was not a common one.

Women's Clothing

The clothing from the Victorian period has been documented far more for the upper and urban classes than for the lower or rural classes of society. Reenactors attempting to portray middle-class or lower-income women of the period must make do with some conjectures about cheaper variations of upper-class clothing.

Most young women sought to imitate the styles of European ladies and the more cosmopolitan American women. A common frustration of women on farms and the frontier was that black-and-white drawings in magazines with a few color plates and written descriptions were all they had. Rural women needed practical dresses for work on the farm and often had only one or two to their name. These dresses had no hoops or bustles, and they ended just above the ankle on grown women. The dresses were most often one piece, but sometimes were in two pieces for easier dressing, mending, and cleaning.

For the townswoman, however, nothing was so typical of the mid-nineteenth century as the hooped skirt. The hooped skirt was an innovation that freed women from the bustle and its many petticoats. Before the hooped skirt, women wore several layers of petticoats under the dress, sometimes as many as fourteen. These were hot and heavy, and caused many a wrinkle in the skirt. At parties, women wouldn't sit down because the skirt would be crumpled against the layers of petticoats, ruining the shape of the dress until it was ironed again.

The hooped skirt draped over a crinoline, a set of hoops much like a cage, connected to each other by tapes. This allowed the dress to fall away from the body in the accepted form, without the need of so many petticoats. Sometimes a single petticoat was worn under the crinoline for modesty reasons, and another petticoat might be draped over the crinoline to smooth away the lines of the hoops.

A tightly laced and narrow midriff was considered desirable in the mid- to late-nineteenth century. The great advantage of the crinoline was that even a thicker waist looked narrower in the wide skirts. There were two great trials in clothing during this century: tight collars and ties for men, and tight waists for women. During the first part of the 1860s, both sexes got a little relief. The men's stocks and cravats became looser, and the celluloid collar was still to come. Women could relax a bit from the tight corsets in crinoline, since the wide skirts could hide many an extra inch of waistline.

The fashion of wearing the crinoline began around 1854. Over the next ten years, the shape of the skirt changed from a dome shape to a triangle. From about 1863, the crinoline started to become flatter in front, and the skirt was gored so that the bulk of the cloth hung behind. The walking dress of this year and the next revealed both feet and ankles. In 1865, a bit of red flannel petticoat was often seen, along with evidence of female anatomy.[3]

The open fires of the period could pose a hazard to women in hoop skirts. At reenactments, women wearing hoop skirts should beware of open fire pits in camps. In addition to the risk of fire and smoke, soot and ashes can soil the long skirts.

Young girls' dresses had higher hems, but women's dresses came to within a few inches off the ground and often brushed the floor as the woman bent over or walked on uneven ground. The dresses sometimes had special protective bands around the hems, which could be removed and washed or replaced. Women working as nurses during the Civil War often raised their skirts off the floor to keep the bottoms clean. Later, the incidence of tuberculosis among sanitarium nurses grew sharply because of their trailing skirts. When they undressed at night, the raising of their dresses over their heads allowed bacteria to be transmitted from the hems directly to the nurses.

Since bleaches and brighteners were not available in the nineteenth

century, whites were not as "snowy" as they are today. Bluing and cleaning
agents were available, but most women used ordinary soap and scrubbed the
clothes by hand. Clothing was worn until it wore out, so stains, wear, and
repairs accumulated over time. They weren't thought unusual—everybody
had them. To say women were less clean than today is to do them a great
injustice, however. Women would study each stain and run through a whole
arsenal of methods for removing or hiding any spots. Their clothes had to last
a long time, and the women took great pride in the way their families looked
and suffered great shame for any evidence of uncleanliness.[4]

Women tried to protect their clothing as much as possible from the wear
and tear of daily use. Their clothing was protected by many layers of underclothes and suffered very little from body dirt. In *Crinolines and Crimping
Irons,* Christina Walkley and Vanda Foster state: "A dress worn over a
chemise, a camisole and several petticoats, was effectively protected from
contact with the body. Vulnerable points such as neck and wrists were safe-
guarded by detachable collars, cuffs and undersleeves which were removed
for frequent washing."[5]

Bonnets were in fashion between 1861 and 1865, and were the customary headpieces for women. During this period bonnets underwent subtle style
changes. The bonnet fashions changed from low brim to high spoon.

Hats for women were just coming into fashion. Straw hats had been worn
for a number of years, especially in the South, and had developed out of the
straw bonnet. In the larger cities like New York, however, hats for ladies were
just becoming accepted.

During most of this period, a suntan indicated a common woman who
worked outdoors, and ladies sought to protect themselves from the sun. The
sunbonnet, which later underwent many fashion changes, was originally
intended to protect the face from the solar rays. Straw hats with incredibly
wide brims also were worn, particularly in the South and Southwest.

Aprons of all sorts were worn. Most middle- and working-class women
wore aprons to protect their clothing. Working women tied or pinned aprons
to their dresses and would even wear special aprons to church. Not only did
they protect the clothing from stains, but they were in many ways fashion
statements themselves. The aprons were often of materials and colors that
complemented the dresses. Aprons could be as simple as a towel worn over
the hips to elegant, coatlike contraptions that buttoned in the back and covered the whole dress. They were often frilly and sometimes almost baroque in
the use of pleats, layers of cloth, and other frills.

Women of all classes tried to keep their hands soft and milky white, and few went out in public without wearing gloves of some type. These ranged from heavy leather gloves for work in the garden to almost nonexistent gloves of silken threads for evening wear. White kid was the glove for men and women for formal occasions. Fine cotton or linen was acceptable for day wear.

Men's Clothing

Men's clothing was amazingly conservative during the entire Victorian period. Although the cut and fashion changed slightly, essentially the business suit remained the same: a coat, vest, and trousers. Even the colors were basically the same as today—black, dark blue, brown, and green, although the suit pieces did not always match each other. The suit was not complete without a white shirt of cotton or linen.[6]

In America, the middle and the commercial classes were running the country, and the styles of men's dress reflected their values, being both functional and sober. Even though men may not have worn dress clothes to work, when men dressed up they aspired to look like bankers.

Very young boys of the midcentury wore feminine attire in the nursery, sometimes up to the age of six or seven. They were dressed in petticoats and skirts, and sometimes even in frilled drawers and pantalets. Boys were part of the women's world while still in the nursery, until they were grown enough to become separated from the women. This clothing habit of the nineteenth century does not go over well with modern boy reenactors, who understandably are reluctant to wear frilly dresses in public.

Older boys dressed much like grown men. The period from adolescence to adulthood was undefined, and except for scholars at expensive schools, boys dressed pretty much like their fathers. In *Children's Fashions of the Nineteenth Century,* James Laver states: "Both trousers and jacket were reasonably loose. The jacket was made of dark, sack-like material which did not show dirt too easily. Shirt collars were still unstarched, and their headgear was a cap or hat of the straw 'wide awake' variety."[7]

Civilian trousers, like uniform pants, were held up by braces, had effaced button flies, and were fitted around the waist and loose around the legs and seat. During the 1850s and 1860s, it was fashionable for the legs to be pegged, or narrowed at the ankle, especially for younger men. Day trousers were usually made of pale-colored cloth and were often checked or striped. Dark trousers were the norm at night. When a man owned only one pair of pants, it was usually of dark cloth.[8]

Hip pockets were uncommon during the Civil War period, and pants sometimes, but not often, had an extra watch pocket. Pocket watches were bulky at that time, and a pocket watch in the trousers was thought to ruin the fashion line, as well as being difficult to get at. The watch was usually kept in the vest pocket on a chain. If it was worn in the watch pocket of the pants, a watch fob was used instead of a chain (a fob is a short strap of leather or metal used to hold a watch; a fob also is a decorative "doohickey" or seal dangling from a watch chain).

Overcoats worn by men were heavy, because they needed to keep the men warm in an environment where they would come indoors only rarely during the day. When they did come indoors, it was most often to a fairly cold room that was heated only by a fireplace.

Several techniques were used to keep the wearer dry. Capes covering the body from collar to wrist kept rain off the shoulders, the most likely place for water to soak a garment while worn. The shoulder capes were cut to show off the different layers and to prevent the sodden upper capes from soaking onto the coat. As one layer became saturated, the others would keep comparatively dry. Generally, overcoats were made from a tightly spun wool yarn woven into a strong warp and weft.

Oilcloth was developed during the second half of the nineteenth century. It was quite different from today's oilcloth. Originally, wax and various oils were rubbed into the cloth. Waxed fingers were rubbed over the seams before they were sewn, making a tight and fairly water-resistant material. Over time there was a loss of water repellency, however, and sometimes the wax would crack and fall out of the seams. The oilcloth often was dull colored and had the texture of a canvas tent. One of the big disadvantages of an oilcoat was that the coat could not be placed in front of the fire to dry—the oil and wax would melt and run out onto the floor, and sometimes even catch on fire!

Men routinely wore items to protect their clothes. Shirt sleeves were longer, often down to the thumb joint, to help protect jacket cuffs. Businessmen and clerks wore sleeve protectors, cloth tubes worn over the arm from the wrist to just above the elbow, where they were tied. These tubes protected the sleeves and cuffs from ink stains, a real hazard in the days before ballpoint pens and fast-drying inks.

Heavily starched collars and cuffs prevented dirt from adhering to the cloth. Often these were lightly sewn to the shirt and were removable. Collars and cuffs were often turned when they began to show some wear.

Many men also wore aprons. Innkeepers used aprons that covered the chest and came to the knees. These often buttoned onto the third button of the shirt, and could even be worn under a coat or jacket. Tack and stable workers often had leather aprons, while indoor workers had cloth aprons. Carpenters' aprons were fairly short, covering only the area between the belt and the upper thighs. This apron was worn more to keep tools at hand than for protection. Men's aprons were usually plain and unadorned, except for pockets and tool loops.

Workers often wore bandannas tied around their necks. The bandanna was kept under the collar of the coat, and often also under the shirt collar. The bandanna kept dirt, dust, and straw from falling behind the collar, and it also prevented the collar from wear from a heavy beard. During a time when most men did not use umbrellas, the bandanna also kept rain out. These bandannas were either a solid color, usually white, or sometimes a pattern, such as small red checks. Reenactors should not wear modern railroad scarves, which are "farb" items.

Hats were worn outside most of the time. They protected the head from rain and sun, as well as the cold. Hats and caps were taken off when entering a church, house, or other heated area but remained firmly on the head when visiting barns, tents, and other cold and drafty places. Boys were required to take off their hats when speaking to elders, especially "elders in responsibility," such as preachers, doctors, or teachers.

The individual's trade often defined his hat. A hat made of newspaper and shaped much like a World War II campaign hat was indicative of a printer. Machinists and mechanics wore cloth caps made like inexpensive wheel caps. The hats worn by chefs and cooks were the same as today.

Top hats were worn by professionals—such as college professors, doctors, and lawyers—and the more wealthy businessmen and charlatans. In the South, broad-brimmed hats were worn by farmers. In the cheaper hats, the brims and crowns often grew limp and shapeless after only a few rains, earning the term "slouch hat." For the better hats, water or steam was used to shape and mold the hat to fit the head a little better and to shape the crown to a more satisfactory design. Often the hats were made of replaceable materials, such as palmetto or other grasses. Only the very wealthy could afford beaver-felt "plantation-style" hats.

5

Reenacting Etiquette

As with any hobby, there are ethical and polite rules that govern reenacting. These rules are not intended to restrict participation so much as they are designed to channel and enhance the hobby so that it will be enjoyable for everyone. Many, if not all, of these rules are just common sense. Common sense is notoriously lacking when it is most needed, however, so the following are some rules of etiquette, manners, and ethics for reenactors. Your regiment may have a few other particular rules you should learn.

GENERAL RULES

All reenactors are expected to be somewhat familiar with the etiquette and manners of the nineteenth century. While in period clothing and in public view, these manners and customs should be demonstrated and applied. Your actions and speech should reflect the generally accepted social customs and speech patterns of the time period. Never deliberately give out false information, either by speech or in dress or in action. During visitor hours, you will be under observation and should not do anything in dress or conduct to mislead the public. If you don't know the answer to a question, admit that you don't know and direct the spectator to the people or resources where the answer can be found.

Research the proper clothing and equipment or armaments of the persona you will represent (and for military reenactors, the unit), and attempt to honestly portray that person. If you find that the clothing or arms you have purchased are incorrect, obtain the correct dress. Do not wear unauthentic materials ("farb" items) at historical events, although reasonable latitude is given to members new to the hobby.

Also, do not knowingly engage in the sale or trade of incorrect artifacts or reproductions or misrepresent unauthentic items as historically correct.

All exceptions to the norms of dress and arms should be documented. Do not adopt bizarre or eccentric dress unless known examples from the period are noted. A single documented exception to the normal uniform usually is not sufficient justification for a representative soldier.

Do not portray a historic figure in a manner that is inconsistent with that person's lifestyle and biography, and never participate in any performance where historic figures are ridiculed or mocked to communicate contemporary social or political beliefs.

Reenactors should cooperate with one another and share information. Criticisms of uniforms, equipment, or arms should not be made without giving a resource for authoritative information. A newly discovered resource with information about another unit should be shared with members of that reenactment unit.

Do not interrupt another reenactor while he or she is doing a first-person impression. Do not stand with the crowd and disrupt, heckle, or call out corrections during another reenactor's talk. Constructive criticism is sometimes welcome, but don't argue with another reenactor in front of spectators. If there has been a serious lapse of honesty or misinformation has been given, discuss it privately with the reenactor between talks.

Abide by reasonable rules of conduct, especially those relating to safety matters. Do not participate in any reenactment that is dangerous to other reenactors or to the public. Regimental officers and representatives should not allow their units to participate in scenarios that are excessively strenuous or dangerous and should protect their units from abuses by reenactment sponsors or directors.

Safety is everyone's business. When something is unsafe or dangerous to other reenactors or spectators, speak up and say so. Don't let someone get hurt because you are too polite to insist on safety.

The welfare of children is the responsibility of all reenactors. Many spectators are not aware of the dangers to their children from campfires, horses, tent ropes, and arms. Reenactors should try to ensure that children who stray away from their parents do not run into physical danger. Parents should be told of any dangers to their children; if necessary, make announcements such as "Don't let the children run between tents; they may fall over the tent ropes."

A regimental representative, or any member of a unit, should not attempt to recruit an active member of another regiment. This is called "sheep stealing." Although a regiment can make it known that it is accepting new members, to attempt to grow by recruiting from other units is detrimental to the hobby as a whole. Recruit new reenactors, and do not promise new members extra enticements to join, such as unearned rank or special privileges.

Rank should be earned and not awarded. Any unit that raises unqualified people to rank risks being shunned or avoided by other units. Since larger events require regiments to brigade together, unqualified officers and non-coms can be a potential problem. A knowledge of drill and march should be a minimum requirement for any rank higher than private. Those regiments operate best that require progression through ranks. Giving rank to younger members is historically correct but is acceptable only when they are known to be qualified.

No reenactor should show extreme or unwarranted contempt for the other side or for rival regiments. Out-of-character and inappropriate name calling or obscene expressions of contempt can quickly lead to real violence.

This is a family hobby and should be treated as such. Women and children are always around, so speak and act accordingly.

Anything borrowed from another reenactor that is lost, stolen, or damaged should be adequately and quickly replaced.

Do not contribute to the willful destruction of historical property for private gain or by unlawful relic hunting.

Whenever possible, end each talk to spectators with a sentence or two promoting the conservation and protection of historic sites. Far too many historic sites are being bulldozed to make way for new malls and apartments. Don't add to the attitude of apathy toward preservation.

CAMP MANNERS

At all times during the day, keep the camp authentic and cover up or remove nonperiod items, such as plastic coolers and soda cans.

When not in action, if you want to leave camp, tell someone when you plan to return. If your rifle is helping support a stack of arms, the sergeant needs to know whether to store it in a tent or give it away if you aren't there to claim it when the troops form up.

If you are visiting another unit, always ask for and receive permission before you enter a tent or touch someone's rifle or horse.

Don't visit the opposing camp in uniform during public hours; it ruins the impression for spectators. When visiting at night, you may get a ribbing, but wear your "colors" to the enemy camp. You'll be surprised how many friends you can make.

Camp etiquette requires military courtesy to officers and high-ranking civilians, such as state governors. The soldier should stand and salute as reenactors portraying such individuals pass by.

At large reenactments, there are people who travel great distances to attend. Keep the noise down after eleven o'clock or a time otherwise agreed upon. If you arrive late and after dark in a new camp, set up as quietly as possible. Set up only the equipment needed for that night, and unpack or set up other items in the morning. If you cannot locate your unit, don't wake people looking for it. Settle down on the perimeter of the military or civilian area, and locate your unit in the morning.

RULES FOR ACTIVE ENGAGEMENTS

The following rules apply to any active engagement:

There should be no hand-to-hand fighting unless it is prearranged and scripted. It is far too easy to get carried away, and someone might get seriously hurt. If another person insists on attacking, bring your rifle up to port arms (right hand around the neck of the stock, left hand just below the second band, ramrod and sling facing the opponent) and gently cross your rifle against the opposer's. Ask in an undertone that the opponent go down, or volunteer to "take the hit" yourself. Traditionally, the more experienced reenactor should take the hit, allowing the less experienced reenactor to continue the fun of the scenario. When agreed upon, both of you swing to the side as though one of you were hit by a bayonet or stroked with the rifle butt. Never do something unannounced or unexpected to the opposer in such a situation.

If the scenario gets totally out of hand, which happens very rarely, your unit leaders should command your company to stand still at right shoulder shift. A unit standing still at right shoulder shift while under fire is a sign of contempt and should be used only when enemy units are seriously misbehaving. Attention will be drawn to a unit standing still in a sea of action, and this should calm down any hot dogging. Among authentic reenactors, this is a stinging rebuke and is very infrequently done.

Stay with your regiment. Don't wander off on your own or try to be a hero. Don't run out without orders to reinforce another unit making an attack. The units on the field are scripted as regiments and companies, not as individuals or small groups of men. Stay with your unit unless you take a hit or fall out, then make sure your buddies know what is happening and that you aren't hurt.

If you feel the effects of heat or exertion and feel you may get sick, fall out. This isn't the real army, so if you feel faint, take some time out. Just be sure the members of the unit know why you are going down, so that they can come looking for you later. Let them know if you are going back to camp or if you are going to stretch out under nearby trees. Many units have another member stay with someone who gets ill. If you are truly sick or injured, shout "Medic!" The use of the twentieth-century term lets the other reenactors know you are not acting. Most units have one or more members trained in first aid, so don't hesitate to call on them. But be warned, the call for a medic puts a stop to all action, so save it for real emergencies.

If you become separated from your unit and you can't find it, fall in with another nearby company or regiment until you see your home unit. Salute and ask permission of the officer before joining the regiment, and if you see your home regiment and want to rejoin, ask permission to fall out and rejoin your unit. An aggressive officer or sergeant might otherwise shoot you in the back as a coward.

Stay in your rank. The usual formation is two long lines facing the enemy, with a front and rear rank. When firing from the rear rank, be sure to have the muzzle of the rifle positioned between the second and third band next to and over the right shoulder of the man in front. If the muzzle is too far back, the front-rank man will get an earful of smoke and burnt powder. If the muzzle is too far forward, he may get the full sound of the discharge or flying pieces of spent cap.

In the front rank, it is important that the soldiers stand in a straight line, shoulder to shoulder. Unless each man touches the elbow of the man on either side, a correctly positioned shot from the rear rank could injure an incorrectly positioned front-rank man.

It would be a good idea for front-rank men to wear inconspicuous ear protectors. Period ear protectors were cotton balls or pieces of cloth. Modern ear protectors that fit inside the ear are inexpensive and effective. Any ear protector used should protect the ears from loud noises but not interfere with hearing commands.

During skirmishes, the two ranks sometimes combine into one long line. Here again, when moving or firing, it is important for the men to stay in line, shoulder to shoulder. Anyone a few inches out of line can be hurt by the noise and flash of a musket fired over his shoulder incorrectly.

Never try to touch or capture the enemy flag. Correct behavior is to take the flag bearer prisoner. The flag bearer will furl the flag but retain possession of the flag and staff. He will then carry the flag upright and pointing to the front but at a 45-degree angle or less and under the left arm.

There are a couple of reasons for taking the flag bearer prisoner rather than grabbing for the enemy flag. First, most regimental flags are historically correct, expensive, and easily torn or ripped. Second, there is an emotional attachment to the unit's colors, and other soldiers in the unit are not likely to simply stand by and watch it be taken by someone from the other side. An attempt to grab a flag will too often start a real fight.

Don't charge artillery head-on. A common rule with the artillery is that ramrods crossed over the mouth of the cannon means that there is a live round in the barrel. Sometimes the lanyard pull and friction primer do not ignite the cartridge in the cannon, but the spark may still be glowing and can set off the cannon unexpectedly. So when advancing against artillery, look for the ramrods. If they are crossed over the muzzle, advance well to the left or to the right, and not head-on.

If the rammer is upright on the wheel, this means the gun is loaded or is ready to fire. Advance to the left or right—not head-on to the cannon. If you see a rammer upright, either crossed over the muzzle or against the wheel, be careful not to knock it down.

Don't touch a horse without the permission of the rider, even just to pet the horse, and don't grab its halter or reins. Don't discharge a gun over or at a horse. If necessary, fire way over its head. Don't feed a horse apples, carrots, or sugar without permission, since too many handouts can make the horse ill.

Never point your gun at someone. Always aim high, or to the right or left. As a last resort, aim low. The loaded rifle may have pieces of paper from wads, even wads from several shots earlier, lead fouling, dirt, or other debris that can leave the muzzle at tremendous velocity. No hobby is worth losing an eye or getting powder burns. Keep the muzzles up, and pray the other guys do too. If the enemy is within 30 yards, the muzzles should be pointed straight up. The enemy will respond with hits as though you had aimed at them.

When loading the rifle, never insert the paper wad unless on specific orders. The wads fly out of the barrel dangerously and can cause injury. Drop the paper on the ground (it can be picked up later) or place it in your pocket when you prime the rifle. As a good rule, don't use wads at all, even at memorials. When a salute is fired over a grave, the wads can fly out and hit spectators. Also, they often catch fire, and when they fall to the ground, they can catch the grass on fire too.

Don't use glue, staples, or paper clips to hold cartridges together. Left on the paper and then rammed into the barrel, these things become "bullets." Wrappers for rolls of pennies are about the size of cartridges, but don't use them. The powder leaks out too easily, and the paper is too heavy. If wadded, they make a solid projectile, and they easily catch fire and can smolder for a long time.

While on the field, never use the ramrod to ram cartridges home. Often event hosts insist that ramrods be left in camp and not be allowed on the field at all. There are two reasons for this: First, the ramrod can mistakenly be fired from the rifle like a steel arrow. This is deadly. Second, after only a few shots, the ramrods can become stuck in the barrel. The combination of the powder residue and humidity makes a sticky, moist glue. When the ramrod is inserted, this can create a vacuum that binds around the base of the ramrod and holds it in place, rendering the weapon useless.

Bayonets should be drawn or fixed only for parade. Though bayonets are carried in the field, they are never fixed during action, as they are too dangerous, not only to the other side, but to you and your side as well. Wounds can be caused by falling on the rifle, dropping the rifle bayonet-first on your foot, or impaling your hand while loading the rifle. Many reenactors tie the bayonet in the scabbard with string or a piece of rawhide so that it won't fall out.

Do not take antiques on the field. This often creates intense stress and causes wear to these items, which then may fail at the worst possible moment. Antiques are expensive, and it is a tragedy if they are lost or broken. There are also safety considerations. A musket that is 130 years old may have a barrel that is etched or cracked inside. This is dangerous not only to the reenactor, who may be willing to shoulder the risk, but also to other men in line. An inspector will often insist that antique weapons be carried only by noncombatants and not fired at all on the field.

Don't insult the enemy. Though there were often exchanges between pickets from opposite sides during the war, communication between opposing troops on the field was not done. Talking in the ranks was also forbidden while in formation so that orders could be heard. Be positive rather than destructive. If you must talk, instead of disparaging the enemy, encourage your own troops.

Take hits. The enormous toll of dead and wounded in WBTS-period engagements is almost unbelievable to spectators. Casualties of 20 to 50 percent in one regiment in one battle were not unknown.

A common question of new reenactors is when to take a hit. Part of this is common sense. If the fighting is heavy, the unit should take a reasonable number of hits. Units that don't take their share of hits are called "hitless wonders" and are accused of being "ironclads" or "wearing iron underwear." So play fair and take hits. Officers should encourage their troops to take casualties when the fighting becomes intense. There is no shame in taking hits; it is part of the hobby.

Only you can determine whether someone has scored a hit on you. Let your own honor be your guide. If you see an enemy soldier take positive aim at you and fire, take the hit.

When you take a hit and pretend to be wounded, you can make all the noise you want and call for your mother, friends, or sweetheart. Avoid overacting or clowning, however. This is a reenactment of a real event where real men died, and they should not be satirized or mocked. If you are really injured or sick, call for a medic.

If you plan to use makeup to simulate wounds, let your unit know beforehand. This can be very effective and quite disconcerting to other reenactors. Often the makeup is indistinguishable from real wounds, and they may think you are really injured. False arms, legs, and fingers are sometimes scattered around battlefields as well.

When taking a hit, fall forward on your face. This prevents you from falling unexpectedly on your haversack, or worse, your bayonet. Lie face down, with the lock of your rifle underneath you. This permits you to view the battle, and keeps the sun from burning your face or causing sunstroke. It also prevents someone from stepping on your rifle and breaking the lock, sight, or other fragile part or even worse, walking off with your expensive weapon. Lie with your head in the line of march and not at right angles to the oncoming troops. It is easier for regiments to pass by on either side than to step over you.

When down, lie still. Don't lean on your elbow and watch the battle, shout at friends or the enemy, or do things wounded men would be unlikely to do. If you want to act, do something realistic, such as struggle or limp back to the lines, help other wounded, or try to bandage your arm. Sometimes, when

"Order arms"
Stand with your feet at a 45-degree angle, heels together, hold your left little finger along the seam of your pants, and place your musket along the right side of your body.

"Shoulder arms"

Hardee's drill specifies that you place your musket with the trigger guard between your first finger and thumb. Hold the barrel of the rifle along your body at the "Attention" position.

"Right shoulder shift"

Place the musket on your right shoulder with the plate out. Hold the beak of the stock between your first and second fingers, close to your body, and put the bottom of your musket and your hand just above your cap box.

"Load"

Place the musket between your feet and hold it pointing away from you, barrel out, using your left hand at the third band. If you are in the second row, make sure the barrel is not pointing at the back or head of your front-row comrades. With your right hand, reach behind you and unclasp the cartridge box. Keep your hand in that position until you are given the next order.

"Charge cartridge"

Using only two fingers, pour gunpowder into your musket barrel. Never put the paper, or wadding, in the barrel, since it will come out smoldering and could injure someone or cause a fire.

"Ram cartridge"

It has been said that Union troops suffered more wounds in the right hands and forearms than the Confederates did because they held their hands higher over their heads when using the rammer. These photos seem to support that claim, since the Yankee troops, LEFT, do seem to hold their hands higher than the Confederates, BELOW. Both methods are correct, which can cause difficulties for reenactors following different interpretations of a drill.

"Return rammer"

Hardee's drill instructs soldiers to return the rammer using only the little finger. This way, if there is still a spark in the musket and the gun goes off unexpectedly, you'll only lose your little finger. Never place your hand or forearm over the barrel opening.

"Prime"

Hold your rifle at half-cock and raise it over the cap box. Open the cap box and place a percussion cup on the rifle's nipple.

"Aim"

If you're in the rear rank, move your right leg up and to the right. This positions you to fire over the shoulders of the men in front of you. Never aim at anything unless you want to hit it, and never aim to hit anything unless you want to kill it.

Yankee soldiers would have seen similar stalwart North Carolinians aiming their muskets at them as they advanced. At reenactments, however, you must never aim a musket or rifle—whether it's loaded or not—directly at another person. Aim above people or to the side.

"Fire"

If you're in the rear rank, position your rifle so that the ear of the man directly in front of you is between the first and second bands of your musket.

Two common weapons used by reenactors are (A) the Springfield musket and (B) the Enfield musket.

A typical Civil War soldier might have carried a tin plate, eating utensils, salt, hardtack, a toothbrush, a Bible, dice, and a carrying pouch.

Under light marching orders, a Confederate reenactor carries his haversack of supplies, a canteen, and perhaps a coffee boiler.

Specialist reenactors know their personas and can accurately describe how their equipment was used. Some specialists spend quite a bit of money to obtain various items, as did the reenactors who own this quartermaster tent, ABOVE, the telegraph BELOW, and, FOLLOWING PAGE, the medical equipment.

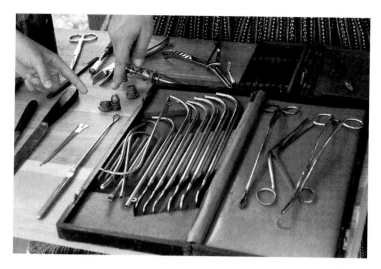

Medical equipment of 1861. A specialist is explaining various types and uses of antique medical equipment, typical of a Civil War surgeon's kit.

Laundresses were authorized in both Union and Confederate regiments. Research into methods, techniques, and equipment will show you how to present an accurate impression.

This working dress, minus the hoops and ornate trim, is more practical when worn around camps, tent stakes, and fire pits. Plain clothes are typical of small farmers, poorer women, and refugees. Aprons of many sorts, pinned or tied, were used to protect the clothes.
PHOTO BY BILL CHRISTEN.

This humble dog tent can be used by two or more comrades. Each section would be carried by one man during the day, then buttoned together at night.

The wall tent is most often used as an officers' tent, but it can also be used as a field hospital or for storing supplies.

The Sibley tent was named after Confederate Gen. Henry H. Sibley. General Sibley was a captain in the 1st U.S. 10Dragoons before the war, and he modeled this tent after the tepees of the Plains Indians. A Sibley tent could hold up to twenty men.

Many small reenactments and living-history encampments take place at historic sites among unhistoric buildings. These reenactors are demonstrating in front of a museum while a reenactor at the podium interprets the action for the audience using a modern public-address system.

A handsome boy, too young to fight battles, poses in his civilian sack coat, vest, and pants. Note the military-style stripe on his leg and the piping on his coat. Military trim was fashionable for those with relatives in the army and also popular among the general public.
FROM THE COLLECTION OF MIMI RAWLINGS

In the nineteenth century, very young girls wore dresses with tucks that could be let down as the girl grew. Stripes, ruffles, and other devices were used to hide the seams. FROM THE COLLECTION OF BILL AND JO CHRISTEN.

This pretty adolescent is wearing a typical nineteenth-century, polka-dotted dress. Her off-the-shoulder sleeves have only moderate trim, and the dress's hem is higher than that of an adult.
FROM THE COLLECTION OF MIMI RAWLINGS

This little boy, wearing skirts, does not look happy about getting his picture taken. In the nineteenth century, many boys wore dresses until school age. Not surprisingly, it is very difficult to get modern boys to dress like this for a reenactment.

FROM THE COLLECTION OF MIMI RAWLINGS

During the Civil War, as they do today, wealthy girls typically wore very ornate clothes. This photograph shows a rich child wearing an off-the-shoulder dress with a fancy belt and holding a basket. Though the stripes on her dress could be used to hide new seams as she grew, most likely this little girl would have had a new dress instead.

FROM THE COLLECTION OF MIMI RAWLINGS

This fairly prosperous family from Maryland wears typical civilian clothing of the late 1850s. The dress of the younger daughter, FAR LEFT, *is gathered at the waist and was most likely a "hand-me-down" from her older sister,* MIDDLE. *The mother's dress shows an intricate pattern on the cloth and a plain jacket. The father and son are wearing plain, but serviceable, suits.*
FROM THE COLLECTION OF MIMI RAWLINGS

the unit marches past, soldiers can be "resurrected" and can rejoin the regiment. Keep resurrections to a minimum, however.

If you face a choice of dying or being taken prisoner, become a POW. Traditionally, raising both hands over your head is the symbol of nonresistance. This is difficult for a reenactor to do, because few want to lay their arms on the ground. To show the opposing force that you want to surrender, raise your musket overhead with both arms. Hold the weapon either straight up with the butt foremost or horizontally overhead with one hand on the neck of the stock and the other hand between the third and second bands. After becoming a prisoner, sling the rifle with the barrel pointed down from the left shoulder. Don't let your rifle or accoutrements out of your sight. If large groups of prisoners are taken, they may be asked to stack arms. Otherwise, lay your arms down on the ground and have a seat and enjoy the show. If you want to act, you can ask the guards questions such as when you'll eat or what it is like in a POW camp. Prisoners remain prisoners only until the end of that phase of the reenactment. So enjoy your incarceration while looking miserable.

If you take prisoners, don't harass them. Don't try to make them sing "Dixie" on their knees or swear allegiance to the Union. But do have fun in the first person, and try to get them to give information about their units and so forth.

DANCE ETIQUETTE

There are many books on dance etiquette from this period. Reenactors at historical balls and dances need to be particularly aware of the following points:

Gentlemen never wear spurs on the dance floor, as they may catch on ladies' dresses. If possible, don't wear riding boots; wear shoes or bootees instead. If you have horseshoes on your heels, cover them with duct tape or masking tape so that they won't scratch the floor.

Sidearms should not be worn at dances.

Ladies and gentlemen both should wear gloves. Men's gloves should be plain white cotton. Ladies can wear what is appropriate for their dress and station.

If the dance is outdoors, men and women can wear their hats and bonnets. If held indoors, men should remove their hats; women may or may not remove their bonnets or head scarves.

Dances are held for fun and relaxation. It is boorish not to participate unless injured. Don't go just to watch others dance with no intention of joining in. Women often go to extraordinary lengths to prepare for dances, with appropriate clothing and jewelry. Officers and regimental representatives should encourage their men to dance with the ladies. There is nothing so silly as a bunch of shy men in uniform lingering on one side of a room, and women wanting to dance waiting on the other. One word of warning to Union troops: Southern men seem to congregate naturally on the side with the women. If you don't invite the women to dance first, you may find that the Southern boys have cut you out.

6

Health and Comfort

Health and comfort in reenacting are very important. Blisters, sunburn, and dehydration can ruin an otherwise good weekend. Few people get sick at reenactments, but those that do often don't follow common-sense rules for health. Most units have someone trained in first aid, so don't be shy about asking for help.

EYES

Smoke from fires and gunfire and being outdoors in the bright sun can make eyes red and sore, so take along some eye drops. When firing into the wind, close your eyes to protect them from the blowing smoke and burnt gunpowder.

Modern eyeglasses should never be worn in a reenactment. If you have only slight vision problems, you may want to go without glasses. If this is not possible, contact lenses are the best solution from a reenactment point of view. Though many styles of glasses were available during the Civil War period, most of the common soldiers didn't have them. In part, there was a feeling that it indicated a weakness, not only of the eyes, but also of character. And they were difficult to take care of, too. So those who didn't badly need glasses went without. A regiment that has many men who wear glasses may want to restrict newer members to contacts, to prevent a "nearsighted brigade" appearance.

Some common soldiers did wear eyeglasses during the WBTS, however, and it is valid to have a pair in frames from the period. Jeffrey Mosser states in an article about period eyeglasses:

> Reenactors who wear glasses sometimes ask themselves whether they are correct in doing so. Many feel that poor eyesight certainly kept one from serving in the army. . . . [Army] Regulations . . . stated that "nearsightedness does not exempt" one from military service. Only in cases of extreme myopia was any exemption granted. When the military draft was instituted in 1863, many draftees, not knowing the regulations, had private eye examinations prior to appearance before the enrollment board. They came to their physical exams armed with documents attesting to their acute nearsightedness. The army surgeons held these men to military service.[1]

There is much argument over the use of glasses by men during this period, however, and there are heated arguments over how many privates and non-coms wore them. Although there are many accounts of men wearing glasses, the accounts are anecdotal, and there is no consensus on this subject. Without a doubt, contact lenses are the best, and period glasses second best.

Contact lenses can be expensive, and facilities at reenactments are usually primitive. There often are few facilities for cleaning your hands properly, and black powder ground into the hands can make the attempt to remove the contacts from your eyes a dirty proposition. Electricity is not always available for contact lenses that need disinfecting. Many reenactors dump the lens case in a can of boiling water, but this is not always a good idea.

Many reenactors buy period glasses, which are amazingly comfortable, and have modern prescription lenses placed in them. This technique is fairly easy to do by most optometrists or ophthalmologists. Antique frames may break during the process of putting in the new lenses, however, and some labs will not accept responsibility for this.

If you decide on reproduction frames, check with other members of the unit for authenticity. Most reproductions sold by optometrists are 1920s styles and are not appropriate for Civil War-period reenactment. The correct style for the mid-1860s has a straight arm (a temple or bow) from the frame, and not one that is curved to fit behind the ear. These arms often had a small hole to accept a ribbon or string. The frames are narrower than the face, and the lens is placed directly in front of the opened eye. The size of the lens should be only slightly larger than the opened eye.

At the time of the WBTS, fashions in glasses were changing. Oval lenses were popular before 1860, but during that year a hexagonal lens became fashionable. Either style would be correct.

When wearing period glasses, you must look directly at whomever you're talking to. This concentration of attention can be a bit disconcerting to twentieth-century people, but it is actually quite charming once you get used to it. Don't wear these glasses while driving, however, because peripheral vision is poor.

Whenever you go on a reenactment, take along a modern pair of glasses in addition to period glasses. During the evening you may want to switch, and it is a good idea to have along an extra pair in case of a mishap.

HEAT AND DEHYDRATION

Heat and dehydration are big problems in reenacting. Heavy wool uniforms and a hot sun can make an afternoon uncomfortable.

The mid-nineteenth-century American thought it beneficial to perspire freely and wore layers of clothing that today seem restrictive and hot. They saw water as a cycle, believing it was healthy to take in a great deal of water, especially mineral water, tonics, or special waters, and then to perspire freely. They also drank fewer prepared drinks and more plain water than we do today. Today people use antiperspirants to prevent wetness and are embarrassed by obvious perspiration. The people of the last century saw perspiration as a natural function, the prevention of which was considered dangerous. A cold dip, for example, would "check the perspiration" and was not considered healthy.

After a few summer afternoons in full wool uniform, the system of free perspiration does not seem so bad. The wool uniform acts like a wick to pull sweat from the body, which then evaporates and cools. Nevertheless, the wool uniform is still hot.

Sunstroke is avoided by drinking plenty of fluids and taking time to rest and cool down. Life was slower 135 years ago, even in the army. Drink water and Gatorade, and plenty of it. If you begin to feel too tired, fall out. Either take a hit or tell someone else in the unit that you are falling out. If you feel really bad, especially if you feel faint or stop perspiring, ask someone to stay with you. If your comrade in arms becomes too red in the face or too pale, ask if he needs to fall out. Many men will not voluntarily fall out of formation, but will if asked.

Drink water slowly; too much water too quickly can cause stomach cramps. Be sure to fill up your canteen before going into the field. The best place to store water is inside you, so drink up before heading out. You can take Gatorade in packets of powder and add it to water in your dipper. Some people put it in their canteens, but this is not a good practice because the acids can eat at the canteen's soldered seams. Don't take carbonated drinks, which play havoc with your canteen and coat the lining of your stomach, preventing water from being absorbed. Don't take beer, either. Take water or Gatorade. Do not take salt tablets unless you've checked with your physician.

Sometimes the host provides cold water and ice on the field on hot days, so always take your dipper along. If ice is provided, put a piece or two under your hat, or put some in a neckerchief and wrap it around your neck. Don't use more than a piece or two, so that you don't shock your system. Don't chew the ice. Suck on a piece slowly and let it melt in your mouth. If you swallow the ice whole, it can shock your system when it reaches your stomach. It can also crack a tooth if you chew on it.

If you are taking a picnic cooler to the event, freezing a plastic milk carton full of water is a good idea. It helps keep things in the cooler cold, and as it melts, it produces cold water.

Another trick is to take a wet washcloth in a plastic sandwich bag. The plastic bag can be placed in the haversack and the washcloth pulled out to wet the face, hands, or neck as needed. Very refreshing, but not at all authentic.

On hot days when dehydration is likely, foods that slowly release water in the intestines are also helpful. These include fruits and vegetables such as apples, melons, and raw onions. One note of caution: Don't carry soft fruits in your haversack or you may end up with a mess. Apples are good period foods to carry along. Especially authentic varieties are the Granny Smith and Mary Baldwin apples, which are like those grown during the Civil War.

Sunburn is usually not a severe problem during reenactments, because so much of the body is covered in heavy clothing. The main areas that become sunburned are the head and hands. Take along some sunscreen, or wear a slouch hat instead of a kepi. Many troops wear bandannas around the neck, but only wear ones authentic to the period, and not railroad scarves.

COLD

The cold can be fought with long underwear and heavy clothes. WBTS troops wore clothes in layers to keep warm. Most wool uniforms can keep a body warm only to about the freezing mark; below freezing, wear either thermal underwear or a greatcoat. A common practice during the WBTS period was to fold a newspaper over the chest between the shirt and undershirt; this kept the cold out and the heat in. If you don't have a pair of authentic gloves, wear a pair of old socks over your hands. Don't pile on too many blankets at night, or you can perspire while sleeping, and then get cold from the evaporation.

If your hands or feet are cold, the rule of thumb is to warm your torso. If it is cold and you stop shivering and begin to feel numb, get help at once. If you are camping out, it is also a good idea to wear a stocking cap on cold nights, as you lose much of your body heat through the head.

BLISTERS

Blisters are the bane of the infantry. When you are used to soft shoes and carpets, spending a weekend marching in brogans can cause blisters. The best protection is to make sure your brogans fit. Shoes or boots even a bit too tight can make you miserable. Before you buy a pair, try them on with the kind of socks you will be wearing on the march. Rather than sending a sutler your size, send him penciled outlines of both feet.

Use Band-Aids to protect the parts of the feet that begin to rub, and do it before blisters form. Wear thick socks, and don't tie your boots too tight. Jeffrey Mosser gives this 1860s remedy from a Connecticut captain: "Soaping the inside of the stocking does some good, by diminishing the friction, and as a consequence, the blistering. It is also advisable to wash the feet before starting. . . . Beware of washing them at night; it cracks the heated skin and increases the misery."[2]

When a blister forms, some people pop it to allow the fluid to drain and relieve the pressure. This does not stop another blister from forming right next to the first, however, and it allows dirt and bacteria to enter the wound.

DIGESTIVE DISORDERS

Period food is great, but it is sometimes upsetting to a stomach used to modern food. Take along some antidiarrheal tablets in your haversack in case of digestive problems. It is also a good idea, especially at big events where toilet supplies sometimes run low, to take along one or two small packets of tissues.

OPTIONS

If your health requires that you not participate fully in an event, but you desire to participate somehow, there are always light-duty things to do around camp. Taking part in a reenactment does not necessarily require excessive physical effort. Sentries are always needed to guard the camp and answer questions. Cooks need help preparing the food, and people are needed to take water to the troops. Civilian reenactors can act as photographers, sutlers, or local farmers looking for runaway children or stolen livestock. Keep in mind, however, that many reenactments take place in the summer, and there will be stress just from being out in the hot sun.

7

Hosting a Civil War Reenactment

A historic site may decide to host a reenactment event. Before you send out invitations, be aware of the different points of view regarding the goals of a reenactment that site directors, museums, and reenactors may hold.

A museum or other site may want reenactors around as props in a history program or to participate in a military ceremony or memorial. The museum or site may want to have a lot of activity and gunfire to attract visitors. Whatever the reason for the reenactment, the site coordinators should keep the goals firmly in mind and should discuss these goals with the representatives of the reenactment units. The ultimate goals are for everyone to be safe, happy, and satisfied.

PLANNING THE EVENT

The first step is to contact a good reenactment regiment and discuss your plan with its representatives. The representatives will have some good advice and can give you the names and addresses of other regiments that may be interested in attending. They will help you organize an event, but they will not do all the work for you. Reenactors are volunteers and have other jobs and responsibilities.

If you want the reenactors to help with anything special, let them know in advance. Find out whether your plan is possible and practical by walking through it with the reenactors. Although a wild charge from the edge of the woods may seem easy enough, no one wants to charge through knee-high brush and vines with loaded guns. A steady schedule of drill may sound good, but men in wool uniforms get hot and tired, and you need to schedule some rest too. So run your ideas by these experienced and knowledgeable people, and change your plans if necessary.

Rules should be carefully thought out and prepared before the event. A short explanation of the rules does wonders for cheerful compliance. For example, if there is to be only one fire per military street, state why: "For archaeological reasons, this ground must remain undisturbed except for a few selected areas for fires," "County fire ordinances restrict the number of fires to one cooking fire per street," or "Insurance regulations require us to limit the number of fires within 200 feet of any building."

Here are some general rules any host and reenactment unit should insist on:

No firing of guns toward crowds.

Ramrods may not be drawn on the field.

Spectators may not handle weapons of any sort. (Edged ones are especially dangerous.)

Before participating, each soldier must pass a weapons inspection to make sure all weapons are safe, clean, and operational. Inspections are best done with a representative of the opposing side.

There will be no extemporaneous fighting, especially hand-to-hand fighting between units.

There should be a minimum of 10 feet, and preferably 15 feet, between campfires and any tents. Ten feet is needed for fire and spark protection and so that two men under arms can pass each other. Fifteen feet allows a "column of twos" to pass between the fire and tents. Also, the wider the streets, the easier it is for spectators to walk around and to take photographs.

Many reenactors wear metal "horseshoes" on the heels of their boots. You may want to add a rule forbidding their wear on polished wooden floors or requiring that they be taped over, as they can mar the surface.Have some heavy tape handy.

There are also some responsibilities that you hold as the organizer of the event.

Spectator control and crowd safety are the responsibility of the host. Rope or tape off special areas for the reenactment or drills to prevent spectators from crossing the field of fire. Alert fire and rescue crews to the scheduled event beforehand, since an emergency could arise, especially on hot summer days. Also alert the police or sheriff's office. Nothing is more alarming to them than to receive reports that armed men are shooting at each other.

Collect the names and addresses of all people participating in the event, including all family members, as well as names and telephone numbers of persons to contact in case of emergency. This is important for safety reasons, and you can also add the names to your mailing list.

At a minimum, the host must provide potable water for drinking and cooking, firewood, and hay for the horses. Bales of straw for sleeping are nice, but not essential. You are also responsible for waste disposal.

Potable water is a necessity, and during reenactments, the participants need it badly. Soda vending machines are not a substitute for water. Often, water is brought in with a "water buffalo," a large container of water hauled behind a truck. Make sure this water has been tested for purity and that the buffalo has not been used to haul water for construction purposes. Fire hydrant water generally is not safe to drink, since the backflow valve is often below the water level inside the hydrant, where bacteria can live. In hot summer months ice is also necessary for health and should be provided.

The reenactors will need firewood for cooking and, in colder weather, for warmth. Provide good, dry wood. Wet wood is more smoky and dangerous than dry wood. Rotted wood won't make good coals for cooking. Cheaper wood in round sections or half rounds that need to be split are often either left burning at the end of a reenactment (and will smolder for another couple of days) or not used at all. If there are any particular requirements regarding fires, such as stone rings, sod retention, or size restrictions, make sure they are understood by everyone before making camp.

Hay is necessary if there will be horses. Even if cavalry is not invited, artillery horses and officers' horses often are brought to camp, not to mention buggies for civilians.

If you can, provide straw for the reenactors. Straw makes for more comfortable sleeping, keeping the bedding dry and off the ground, and the bales are used for sitting. Straw should be provided free of charge; don't try to make a profit by selling it.

Proper arrangements must be made for toilets and sanitary facilities. Portable toilets are necessary not only for the crowds of spectators, but for reenactors and their families as well. Sanitary facilities must not be too far away from the camps and must be cleaned during the reenactment weekend.

Don't place them in direct sunlight; place them under shady trees, and make sure they are level. During a reenactment, people will be using portable toilets at least three times as much as the typical construction crew for which use estimates are generally given, so put out plenty of toilets, and have them emptied and resupplied at least once during the weekend. Have all of them inspected by an event coordinator on Saturday morning and afternoon, and Sunday morning.

Because ladies wear hoop skirts at these outdoor reenactments, dances, or dress balls, it is a good idea to have an extra wheelchair-accessible portable toilet to accommodate their large crinolines. While in the modern world these wheelchair-accessible toilets are reserved for the truly handicapped, I do recommend that additional ones be used to accommodate the unique nineteenth-century women's fashions and that these extra reserved portable toilets be marked for women only. If possible, also provide a room or an extra tent for the ladies to use as a dressing room, and place in it a mirror and stools, chairs, and tables of various heights. Remember also that canvas tents illuminated from the inside can cast silhouettes on the tent walls, much to the amusement of passers-by, who frequently stop to watch a lady's shadow change from modern driving clothes into period dress.

Modern trash containers—and plenty of them—are needed around food or drink vendors. Trash in camp is usually collected in plastic bags hidden out of sight in tents. Place the camps far enough from food vendors that trash from spectators will be kept at a minimum, or line period containers, such as wooden barrels, with plastic trash bags and place them around camp.

All events should be scripted and should be understood by all participants. If reenactment of a real engagement is planned, the main unit commanders and any other interested reenactors should be supplied with photocopies of the accounts in the *Official Records of the War of the Rebellion,* as well as any other pertinent accounts. The more the actual historical event is understood by the reenactors, the better the action is for the spectators.

Also discuss with the regimental representatives any program or special events. Will drilling be done? If so, be sure someone acts as a docent for the event and explains to the crowds the purpose of the drill and what the troops are doing. Make arrangements for a megaphone or loudspeaker system. A drill or action without information, interpretation, and explanation is merely a spectacle and does nothing to teach history.

Will there be guided tours through the camps? If so, how will they be done and by whom—reenactors or museum staff? Will there be set stations on the tour where talks or demonstrations will be given? Be sure everyone knows when and where these will be and that those giving demonstrations are able to do so correctly.

Station a sentry in camp at all times when the area is open to the public. He or she can keep an eye on the equipment, answer questions, and watch out for spectator safety.

Give the reenactors an opportunity to learn about your historical site before the event at an evening lecture or slide show, or with print materials. By sharing your expertise and knowledge with the reenactors, you both will be rewarded. These volunteers will temporarily serve as extra docents to your historic site. After the training, they will be able to not only answer questions about their units and the Civil War in general, but also relate that information to your museum or site.

There are several different types of activities your event might include. A good crowd draw is a Civil War ball, with a reenactor band using antique or reproduction period musical instruments. These bands are often fairly inexpensive, and instruments from 1860 sound different from modern ones. Such events are enjoyable to reenactors and local citizens alike. The dance steps are explained by the bands via a walk-through and are fun to learn, and a ball also gives the ladies a chance to show off their authentic dresses.

At any indoor gathering of reenactors, such as a ball or drill demonstration, the heat from many bodies in wool uniforms can raise the temperature of the room, so be sure that there will be adequate ventilation.

Singing period songs around the campfire with reenactors who play the guitar, banjo, or even the "bones" is a popular activity. Choose songs from the period, and hand out copies of the words so that spectators can join in.

Your event might also include guided tours by costumed interpreters. If your site was a battlefield, consider having reenactors lead groups over the battlefield. Words written by the actual combatants can be read from 3-by-5-inch cards by the reenactors. Candlelight tours through the camps also are effective. Be sure the reenactors agree to the tours and that trash or modern items are removed from the path beforehand. Horse and buggy rides around the camps are also a lot of fun.

The reenactors are volunteers interested in history. They have committed to a weekend or afternoon to help you and have spent money on gas and gunpowder. Therefore, they should be allowed to see the site by special tour or given free admission. As an expression of appreciation, sites often give participants in authentic costume a discount in any museum bookstore or gift shop, as well as free or discounted memberships in "friends of the museum" organizations.

A controversial issue in reenacting is the charging of fees to both spectators and reenactors. Reenactors often pay fees to attend events. A reasonable fee is not unexpected, as the site needs to pay for insurance, portable toilets, advertising, and so on. It is unethical, however, to charge both the reenactors and the spectators. Either charge the reenactors and let the spectators in free, or vice versa. The reenactors, who put out big bucks and big chunks of time, are doing you a great service and should not be taken advantage of. At one reenactment several years ago, the reenactors were charged more in advance fees than the spectators were charged for visiting the camps. Subsequent years saw large drops in attendance by the reenactors.

Consider the possibility of a local documentary about your historical site. TV people often think in terms of visible action, and a reenactment can spark their interest in local history. Consider not only the commercial stations, but also the public and community-access channels. Also be sure to contact the newsrooms of local stations regarding news coverage. If a station plans to shoot footage for a news broadcast, always get the permission of the reenactors. This is usually part of the registration form. The newsroom often will make available a copy of the news feature for a small fee. Let the reenactors know when the footage will be shown and how to get a copy.

INTERPRETATION AND PARK RESOURCES

The following statements from the National Park Service regarding interpretation at national parks apply to almost any historic site. Keep these points in mind when hosting an event.

> The quality of the National Park Service mandate to provide for the enjoyment of scenic, historic, and natural resources and insure their survival for future enjoyment, while posing genuine challenges for park management, still establishes the boundaries and responsibilities of interpretation in relationship to park resources. In summary, interpretation would not exist as an activity were it not for park resources. Interpretation exists, in fact, to "showcase" resources—to make them appropriately available and understandable to visitors. More specifically, the very purposes of the Service dictates that interpretations respect the following principles:
>
> Interpretation is not an end in its own right.

The interpretation of park resources never justifies the abuse of resources, or disruption of experience whose availability is distinctive to the parks' particular resources.

Interpretation of all kinds should encourage and stimulate greater, more varied, more precise visitor interest in the park and receptivity to its resources and values. All interpretive activities or programs should provoke visitors to see or sense something that they haven't previously perceived in the park, or examine with new insight something they haven't seen before— or to reexamine mentally what they had previously experienced in the park. Interpretation is not an educational end in its own right.

All interpretations should directly or subtly convey the primary value of the park resources and the importance of respecting them. That means that interpretive activities of all kinds should not overshadow park resources or be so unrelated to resources that visitors remember the presentation rather than the purpose for the presentation. Nor, in terms of physical actions, should interpreters or interpretive methods be exempted from the standards of resource care that are required of visitors.

All interpreters should strive to increase the visitor's awareness of the intrinsic dangers that may exist in the resource and develop an appreciation of how to cope with those dangers in a way which will not harm the visitor or the resource.

Interpretation should insure that visitors understand clearly the relative integrity and quality of the resources that they are seeing. We cannot mislead visitors about the reconstruction or massive restoration of a historic property or the substitutions of replicas for original items; nor should visitors be encouraged to view as wilderness those areas where human influence is still having a major impact on ecological processes. Conversely, they should understand that wilderness can include areas still showing effects of major human impacts. Such honesty need not lessen the value of the resources where visitors learn about the realities of sustaining historic fabric or natural systems over time.

Interpretation should direct visitors to as wide a range of ways to appreciate and understand park resources as is possible without encouraging abuse or overuse of the resources. It should recognize the need to permit different levels and kinds and focuses of visitor appreciation, including those that are based on what has been described as the "receptive mode," which can depend on freedom from intrusion by "messages" other than those intrinsic to the natural or historic scene. Encouraging visitors to experience in the receptive mode—and assuring them the opportunity to do so without imposing messages upon them can, in many circumstances, be a high form of interpretation.

Historical objects are equal to sites and structures as important components of our park cultural resources. In general, the principles that pertain to the interpretations of major resources apply to the interpretations of historic objects. But in fact, most historic objects are categorically more vulnerable than sites and structures because their importance and the requirements of their care are less well understood in the Service. Historic objects are often perceived as bothersome attic dust collectors or as handy, eye catching props for interpretive programs. We have, in the past, seen the apparent abundance of some kinds of objects as justification for the loss or endangerment of some particular items. The following principles are extensions of the above list, all of which pertain specifically to the treatment of historic objects:

Historic objects should not be viewed or treated as expediently available utensils. They are park resources to which the 1916 National Park Mandate to preserve for future enjoyment applies.

Our treatment of historic objects must be such an example of agency mission and philosophy as in our treatment of historic sites and structures. Decisions regarding placement or use of a historic object revolve not solely around whether we have enough to spare, but what action will best reveal to the public our agency's role as a resource steward.

Many historic objects are singularly fragile. Their long-term value and care must be in accord with professional curatorial and conservation standards.[1]

As a professional historian or historic site administrator, you may see nonperiod items or techniques used by reenactors. It is best to bring this to the attention of the regimental officer, rather than confronting the individual on the site. Often your advice will be taken; occasionally the amateur historians and reenactors will have proof that they are correct.

FOLLOW-UP AND EVALUATION

After an event, the host should send thank-you letters on museum stationery to the leaders of the units that participated. Thank-you letters are always appreciated, and they are often reproduced in the regimental newsletters. Also, they can be used by the participants to justify mileage and other expenses used as income tax deductions. If you have a tax-exemption number, provide it in the letter.

After any living-history event, you should spend some time evaluating the event objectively. Get feedback from the reenactors and participants, the host site staff, and the crowds. While the event is in progress, the host site staff should record their observations, as well as noting comments overheard from the crowds.

The host site should determine whether the event was successful in achieving the stated goals. Ask the following questions:
- Did it increase the number of visitors to the site?
- Did it help interpret the mission of the site to the public?
- Was the information presented to the public specific to the historic site?
- Was it a good historical presentation?
- Was it a learning event for the crowds?
- Did spectators discuss and interpret what they saw among themselves?
- Did they ask questions and seem enthusiastic about the presentation?
- Did they ask many questions of the site staff?
- Did people ask when or where the reenactment would be done again?

The reenactors should always evaluate the presentation as well.
- Were the camp and uniform presentations correct and accurate?
- Did the reenactors interact with the visitors, or were they too involved in their own activities to answer questions or interpret what they were doing?
- Did the members of the regiment learn about the historic site and its relevancy to the regiment?
- Did the host site make the reenactors feel welcome?
- Did the host site director visit the camps and meet the men and women?
- Did the director show an interest in the performance?
- Was there involvement by the site's staff with the reenactors, or were the two groups uninvolved with each other?
- Did they get a chance to learn from each other's presentations?
- Was the event enjoyable, and was it worth the effort?

It's important to learn from mistakes and omissions. Think about what could be done next time to make the event better—to make it more historically accurate or more specific to the site, more enjoyable for the crowds and the reenactors, or safer. Through evaluation, your events will grow better each time, to the enrichment and enjoyment of everyone involved.

8

Trends in Reenactment

VIRTUAL REGIMENTS

Recent changes in technology have led to an explosion in computer communications among reenactors and to the establishment of the "virtual regiment" on-line. This is probably the best form of communication among hobby members across the country, and comments from reenactors in Canada, Europe, Asia, and Australia give a cosmopolitan flavor to the discussions. At some reenacting events afterhours, members sport a discreet "@" sign or banner to identify their membership in the virtual regiment.

Different computer service providers sponsor living history or reenactment discussion groups or live chat rooms. Many others are available on the Internet or the World Wide Web. Chat rooms, which are realtime discussion places where topics are dissected and argued over, are often fun, and sometimes include interviews of authors, park historians, or authorities in many fields. Discussion lists are on-line forums where people write messages to each other, commenting on topics of mutual interest. If you get involved in any these, please follow all "Netiquette" rules.

Discussion lists on reenacting and the Civil War are too numerous to list here, and they often change electronic addresses and locations. However, the

"Widow Barfield," aka Betty Barfield, has replaced Al Ahronson who replaced Wes Clark, and she now runs CW-Reenactors@world.std.com, which has been around for a number of years (although the electronic address has changed a couple of times) and is an excellent list for discussions of reenactment and living history. This is also a "moderated" list, in that the messages are monitored for adherence to list rules, and people violating those rules are kept out for a while to cool off. Many people find this a welcome change from the sometimes too freely spoken opinions in other lists and chat rooms. There are other special discussion lists on particular battles, historical dress, living history, and any particular side of most arguments. A search on a topic on a good search engine or web crawler should result in a few solid hits, and you can go from there.

Web sites for museums, historic sites, and regiments have proliferated beyond counting. Many historic sites have used photographs or film clips of reenactment and living history events to draw attention to their site.

Units, organizations, and regiments are also setting up web sites for themselves. Most include a history of their unit, some photographs, and either a listing of events or other calendar items, as well as contact points and membership information. It is a wonderful recruitment tool for historical organizations. Bob Szabo runs a good list of reenactment units and contacts on his reenacter's web site at www.cwreenactors.com.

One interesting use of the Web can be found in the advertising of small sutlers on their own web sites. Smaller-volume sutlers often run their business as a hobby, and they cannot afford to advertise in the reenactment journals but can advertise cheaply on the Internet. Here they can combine personal computer accounts with their sutlery or manufacturing business at a reasonable cost. As one sutler put it, "Sutlering is what I do after the kids go to bed and before I do." I do urge them, however, to support the hobby by advertising in the reenactment journals. Also, it is a good idea to advertise in the print media since many reenactors are nineteenth-century oriented and are not computer literate.

Computers are also wonderful tools for research. For example, the University of North Carolina Library System has placed full-text copies of many rare Civil War-era books on-line. Other places, such as Louisiana State University, have web sites with primary information on some individual regiments. Be sure to include in your search the full name as well as the numeric designation, such as "Fourth North Carolina" and "4th North Carolina."

Other sources of primary information range from antebellum oil painting images of George Caleb Bingham at several sites such as www2.iinet.com/art/artists/major/b/bingham.htm to the wonderful on-line photograph collections at the Library of Congress (www.loc.gov) or the National Archives and Records Administration (www.nara.gov). All of these sites, and many others, have primary sources on clothing as well as images showing how clothes were worn during this period.

The above are just a few examples; there are literally thousands of other Civil War and reenactment sites on the World Wide Web and the Internet. And because addresses change so often, it would be impossible to list all available sources.

BRIGADE ORGANIZATIONS

A recent trend has been for smaller units to coalesce into brigade organizations. This is done to increase prestige at larger events with larger numbers, or for historical reasons. Within the brigade, the various regiments subordinate their individual roles and act as one unit. They elect officers and NCOs, which may or may not be the same as those in the individual regiments. Examples of brigades formed of different units are the Iron Brigade Association, the Army of the Pacific, the Mifflin Guard, the National Regiment, the First Confederate Brigade, the ANV (Army of Northern Virginia), and Jackson's Division. Some brigades have lasted; others have fallen apart.

The brigade organizations have brought some stability into the reenactment community and help enforce common interests in history, authenticity, and accuracy. "Farb" units outside of the brigade organizations found they had less say in reenactments. They often faced hostility when they fell in with more accurate brigades, and some were not accepted at all.

Some brigade organizations have combined with others to act as umbrella organizations for reenactment groups. The North-South Alliance, the Western Federal Council, and the First Confederate Division form the backbone of the Western brigades. Within these organizations are smaller brigades. For example, the Western Federal Council is composed of the Army of the Pacific, the Cumberland Guard, the Frontier Battalion, and the Western Brigade. Each of these brigades is made up in turn of smaller units.

Within the brigade organization, smaller regiments lose some of their autonomy, but this is more than made up for by increased clout at events and the ability to work with like-minded people on common goals. As with any large organization, politics can often be the cause of disruption. With so many strong-minded people involved in this hobby, it is no wonder that we occasionally disagree.

With the brigade movement, more attention has been paid to the instructions for brigade line evolutions and marching instructions. Dominic Dal Bello of the Army of the Pacific has recently written an instruction book for moving brigades or battalions. Also, more senior officers are acquiring brigade experience.

Brigade organizations have also formed overseas. In Germany, there are three organizations that include both Northern and Southern brigades, and the British also have formed several brigade organizations. Although Civil War reenacting is not a large hobby in Europe, there is a lot of interest and the hobby is growing.

HARD-CORE AUTHENTICS

The hard-core movement is often misunderstood and sometimes maligned. The "progressives," as they like to be known, have a distinct vision of the purpose of reenacting and are experimenting with increased authenticity. They also have different motivations and often don't understand the motivations of other reenactors who don't play by their rules. Unfortunately, this lack of understanding has led to some sharp exchanges and arguments.

The progressives work to make their appearance more accurate, and they try to live as the common soldier would have lived. Thus, their camps often have round-the-clock military discipline. These reenactors drill often, sometimes going without a meal, and when they do eat, it is only army fare or period food. The image the progressives portray is almost invariably that of a soldier on campaign, and their worn appearance and mended clothing is generally a source of pride among them. Many of the hard-core progressives are "appearance defined" in their presentation. They often have a mental picture of their appearance and unit that they desire to portray.

One of the major joys of progressive units are the bonds formed through shared activity and common experience. Like soldiers of the Civil War, progressives experience the same poor conditions that the original soldiers did, camping without tents and sleeping out exposed to the cold and rain. They spend weekends eating bad and insufficient food, and they practice a steady regimen of work, marching, and drill. They suffer the cold, carrying insufficient clothing and blankets as well as sleeping campaign-style by spooning with each other for warmth. As a result, everyone is a full participant in his regiment. Everyone experiences to a higher degree the shared responsibilities and shared accomplishments. Trust and confidence build up quickly in such a unit, as each man sees what his comrades endure and overcome. Bonds formed between men in such situations are unique and sometimes downright mystical. The result is a unit with an excellent esprit de corps.

For those men who want to challenge themselves physically and work as part of a team toward a common goal, this is an excellent opportunity to do so. The shared image of campaign-style soldiers is frequently achieved to a wonderful degree, and the results are impressive, to say the least. The men in these outfits also share their enthusiasm for learning about Civil War-period army life and drill and equipment, and they help each other out extensively, sharing information and research with each other and spending incredible amounts of time helping new recruits learn drills and camp disciplines.

The jarring appearance of non-authentic people and equipment often shatters the serenity of the shared experience and strikes at the common goal. Although spectators are welcome in progressives' camps, and they are happy to show off their equipment and uniforms, they do tend to camp by themselves away from other less authenticity-minded reenactors. Most of their activities are held at smaller events, and at larger reenactments progressives are sometimes overwhelmed by the lack of authenticity around them. In reaction to this stress, and in order to maintain their common goal of authentic appearance, progressives slip off and camp on their own. Regretfully, this tendency to camp with their own like-minded kind results in charges of elitism from other reenactors. And to some extent, this is true. There is a real break between the comradeship of progressives and the other reenactors that extends to social as well as living-history interactions, and this can lead to trouble.

Historic sites often have smaller events that have units participating at special reenactments. When the plans for the event include ordinary reenactors and progressives, some friction may result. It is important to remember that the sponsor of the event, the historic site, is often unaware of the disagreements between these philosophies and may be at a loss for understanding the reasons for the conflict. It is up to us in the reenactment community to work our problems out and to not expect site sponsors to act as referees in arguments about authenticity or intent. Otherwise, the result often will not be better reenactments but an end to them entirely.

Along with the progressive movement has come the recent development of the "generic" regiment. As part of the mental image of the Civil War soldiers, many progressives have taken on the persona of members of an imaginary unit, such as the "Tennessee Valley Rangers" or the "Tupelo Fusileers."

These are companies, regiments, or squads that have no historical existence, but are a representative Union or Confederate outfit. To this end, the rules of the units require their members to wear the clothing appropriate to the Army of the Cumberland in 1863 or the Army of Northern Virginia in 1864.

Because they have separated from the discipline of a historical unit, however, the members are unable to do "real" research. Particularly, they are unable to follow the evolution of equipment and uniforms that happened over months and years, and they are unable to find out what they don't already know or expect. Relying on anecdotal and incidental information from different units, they start out with an image of appearance and work to get that, even though it is not based on an actual unit, actual time, or actual soldiers. The result is that they do not dress like the real soldiers in a real unit but instead begin to look and appear like other progressive reenactors.

Historians in other units often find that letters from the original soldiers, diaries, and other accounts show that expected clothing and materials weren't used or at least, weren't used as intended. For example, after reading the written records of some companies, one might discover that although cotton socks were issued to most units in North Carolina, the soldiers constantly wrote home asking for wool socks to be sent. A generic unit does not have that history or authenticity, nor does it challenge conventional thinking. The number of men wearing kepis versus slouch hats or other types of hats in any unit can be determined only through examining contemporary drawings and written accounts of the historical unit. A generic unit has no such history, and so decisions are often based on "by gosh and by golly!" instead of accurate history and authenticity.

WOMEN IN THE RANKS

The question of whether to allow women in reenactment regiments was raised when the first units were formed. Without a doubt, some women dressed as men during the Civil War and served as soldiers. If a woman can pass as a man and won't be detected by other reenactors or the public, then her persona will remain intact. More of a problem lies with women who dress as men but are easily recognized as being women. Many of these women claim that they are no less authentic than the older men who are over forty and overweight. They point out that there are many men who are not authentic in dress and deportment, but they are not excluded. So why should women be singled out because of their gender? Why not exclude all the "farbs," too?

On one hand, women in the ranks confuses the public, and any explanation of the role women played posing as men takes time and attention away from the main points about the historical setting and reenactment event. It becomes even more bewildering to the public when women advance in rank to more public spots, such as officers, sergeants major, or even file closers.

On the other hand, we live in the twentieth century, and in our times women cannot be excluded based on gender from any public activity. A lawsuit on this principle against Antietam National Battlefield Park was won in 1989 by Lauren Cook Burgess, a university administrator from North Carolina. The court decision shows that if women want to participate in this public activity, the law upholds their right. As a result, obvious women in the ranks are generally ignored by other reenactors.

Should a problem arise, it is up to the event coordinator to handle the confrontation. The park staff or historic site personnel should remain out of the argument as much as possible. The park personnel cannot act as monitors to determine who is right and who is wrong, who is authentic and who is not. They are not referees. By inserting themselves into the argument, park officials can turn an argument over authenticity into an argument over gender rights. A wise manager will try to get the problem handled at the lowest level, perhaps by volunteers or non-employees. Volunteers do not have the power to arrest or order someone off the land, but they do have the ability to persuade or confront the participants or to alter the scenario altogether and hopefully resolve the argument without shouting or the threatening of lawsuits.

Besides, many of the women disguising themselves as men are becoming better at hiding their gender. Aware of their little-known heritage, many women are researching true cases and becoming more careful in their representation, and their search for authenticity leads to increased adeptness at disguises and greater adherence to anonymity in the ranks.

Recently, at a large reenactment, I hitched a ride in a horse-drawn trailer going to the camps. A young man and a drummer boy sitting opposite were having a low-voiced conversation about something that I wasn't paying any attention to, until the boy said, "Yes, Mom." A closer look caused me to smile, since the disguise of Pvt. Mom was so good that I didn't penetrate it until the boy tipped his hand. And she hadn't been more than a few feet away from me for some five minutes.

Appendix A

NPS-6

National Park Service
Servicewide Safety Certification
and Standards Program
for Interpretive Demonstrations
of Reproduction Historic Weapons Firing
and the Storage and Handling
of Black Powder Used
in Those Demonstrations.

Special Note on Historic Battle Reenactments
and Demonstrations

Battle reenactments and/or demonstrations of battle tactics that involve firing at opposing lines, the taking of casualties, or any other form of simulated warfare are absolutely prohibited in all areas administered by the National Park Service.

Although battle reenactments or any other type of simulated warfare are prohibited, there are some situations where the demonstration of historical military tactics, using recreated military groups from outside the Service, might be an appropriate form of interpretation. Such a demonstration can be extremely effective if presented in an authentic, dignified manner. This type of program requires careful planning and control and must be conducted in strict compliance with the official Standards contained in this document. Park managers should not consider this type of activity where such planning and controls are not possible. . . .

STANDARDS

The following section describes the actions and conditions that are fundamental to the operation of an optimum interpretive and visitor services program at the Park level. The purpose of these standards is to serve as a guide, both to the park interpreter and management staffs and to those responsible for evaluating park interpretive and visitors services programs.

It is recognized that individual standards herein are subject to change from time to time and remain valid only so long as they are consistent with current NPS policies.

Servicewide standards for interpretive and visitor services are being met when:

PROGRAM PLANNING

1. The chief park interpreter is an actively participating member of teams involved in formulating the park's statement for management, outline of planning requirements, general management plans, interpretive prospectus, exhibit and audiovisual plans, and other planning activities affecting the park's interpretive and visitor services program.
2. The current annual statement for interpretation and visitor services has been prepared, approved by the superintendent and regional office, and is available to all members of the park staff.
3. A visitor data collecting program designed to assess the park's present and potential visitors is operating in the park. The results are analyzed periodically to identify the ages, social and cultural backgrounds, geographic origin, duration of stay, learning needs, and physical capabilities of the area visitors. These observations are integrated with the existing studies of the park's and region's constituents and used as a basis to update the park's interpretation and visitors services program.

Note: An existing program is available for use in achieving this standard. The Service's "Visitor Observation for Interpretation" developed by Dr. Hanna at Texas A&M for the Division of Interpretation and Visitor Services, WASO. Information on this program is available through your regional office.
4. Servicewide objectives, special emphasis programs, current park operations, and public involvement results are analyzed periodically to identify current directions and possible new trends affecting the area's interpretive and visitor services program.

5. The park's resources management and research programs are analyzed periodically to identify current resource problems, new directions or emphasis in resource management, and the latest information on the resources of the park. This information is used to update the park's interpretive and visitor services programs at least annually.

6. The superintendent and chief park interpreter review annually all planning documents relating to interpretation and visitor services to assure accuracy, current validity, and consistency with park objectives and Service policy.

7. The regional chief of interpretation and visitor services is kept informed by the chief park interpreter and consulted during the planning process as appropriate.

8. All elements of NPS planning and programming documents that relate to interpretation and visitor services (i.e., NPS Form No. 10-237 and 10-238, etc.) are kept current and accurate. The required justifications for interpretation and visitor services activities and facilities are clear, concise, and complete; they relate the request to management objectives, and include the likely negative consequences should the proposal not be implemented.

PROGRAM DEVELOPMENT

General

1. The chief park interpreter and the park's interpretive and visitors services staff are informed about the current state of the art of interpretation, including innovative techniques, environmental/energy education concepts and methods, methods for use in interpretive demonstrations and skill instructions, use of established public transportation systems, techniques for serving special populations, cultural studies, and the interpretive programs of other agencies and organizations, both government and private.

2. Full utilization is made of all the park's potential personnel resources for use in interpretation and visitors services, including (but not limited to) seasonal, volunteers-in-parks, cooperative education program and internship students, and cooperating association and concessioner employees. Interpretive and visitor service contacts with visitors are encouraged on the part of all other park personnel whose jobs normally entail meeting the public (e.g. maintenance, protection, and resource management personnel).

3. Personnel schedules are arranged so as to make interpretive staff available as much as possible for direct visitor contact, especially contact not constrained by scheduled programs.

4. A wide range of activities, techniques, and media, that will aid in meeting the park's interpretive and visitors services objectives within available resources have been identified and analyzed in terms of their environmental impact and energy consumption. Those that have minimum adverse impact (including energy consumption) and set good examples of environmentally sound behavior are selected and emphasized.

5. The content of all interpretive and visitor services programs is based on information obtained from current and highly respected research and has been carefully scrutinized in order to eliminate religious, cultural, and ethnic biases. The staff is prepared to document the validity of all facts, interpretations, and conclusions.

6. . . . each park has systematically identified whether and to the degree to which their park purposes and historic themes are related to contemporary groups and cultures in or near the park. Additionally, the study has outlined how and why information or presentations about minority, regional, or cultural groups should be incorporated into interpretive activities. It has been concerned with the living carriers of local cultural traditions as well as historic personages and materials culture. This information has been integrated into the interpretive program in an accurate manner that insures the park visitors have an opportunity to learn of historic and current local cultural interaction with the resources and themes of the area.

TRAINING

1. A formal, active, on-the-job training program of interpretive and visitors services skills has been implemented for both permanent and seasonal employees, including VIPs, and cooperating associations and concession employees, as appropriate. Incoming new seasonal interpreters are provided with at least 40 hours of intensive training and auditing of ongoing activities. At least 24 hours of this training has been accomplished prior to their beginning public contact work. On-the-job interpretive training includes regularly scheduled time for library research, field observations, area orientation, monitoring of other interpretive presentations, and the regular interchange of information between interpreters and others professionally engaged in the study and management of park resources.

2. Training objectives have been prepared and include:
   - Understanding of the logistics of living and working in the park.
   - Visitor and employee safety considerations.
   - The development of skills in communicating with park visitors.

- An awareness of the park's visitors as individuals with specific backgrounds and needs.
- An understanding of park policy, regulations, and management goals and objectives.
- Thorough understanding of subject matter relative to the park resources and interpretive themes.
- Understanding of the park's environmental/energy programs.
- Familiarity with techniques required to fully serve the needs of special publics.

3. The opportunity for interpretive and visitor services contacts by maintenance, protection, resource management, and other personnel is recognized, and persons performing those functions are invited to participate in, and assist with, the interpretive training program. Assistance is requested from the regional office, if necessary, to assure a professional level of training.

4. A pre-arrival set of publications and other information on the park is sent to new seasonals at least four weeks before they enter on duty. Interpretive training and other informational materials are sent to returning seasonal interpreters during the off season.

5. Interpretive training materials are available at the park for use by all personnel involved in the interpretive and visitor services program. Training publications include "Interpreting Our Heritage" by Freeman Tilden, "Interpreting for Park Visitors" by Bill Lewis, and other NPS produced training publications such as "The Audience and You." Regular use is made of other NPS produced training materials such as the "Interpretive Training Package" (audiotaped examples of interpretive talks and tours with an accompanying manual); "The Fine Art of Interpretive Critiquing" (videotaped examples of supervisors critiquing and evaluating interpretive programs with an accompanying information booklet); and "The Park, the Visitor and the Interpreter: A Personal Training Program for Interpreters" (a communications skills training curriculum package for individual study consisting of a syllabus workbook and accompanying videotape).

SAFETY

1. All interpretive and visitor services programs and activities are designed, and reviewed frequently, to insure staff and public safety; in compliance with the Occupational Safety and Health Act, Executive Order #12196, Federal regulations, and NPS safety management guidelines.

2. Information is available to all park visitors and staff concerning the known

physical, biological, environmental, and climatic hazards existing in the park and emergency preparedness information relevant to the park's environment and recreational activities.

3. Specific, pertinent safety information and/or training is included in all skills training workshops or visitor activity demonstrations.

4. All black powder storage and handling areas, demonstration sites, and all guns used in historic weapons firing interpretive demonstrations are inspected on a regular basis in accordance with the NPS Standards for Historic Black Powder Weapons Firing in Areas Administered by the NPS (see Appendix B of NPS-6 for a copy of these standards).

RESEARCH

1. A list of research needs for the area's interpretive program has been prepared and documented. Research projects from this list are submitted to the Superintendent for inclusion, based on their relative priority, on the park's annual outline of planning requirements.

2. Qualified park interpreters are encouraged to engage in park related research projects (with the exception of archaeological or anthropological field research which must meet the guideline below) provided they meet with the following criteria:

• Projects must be on the park's approved list of research needs.

• Superintendents must approve involvement in the research projects and be satisfied that the park's interpretive and visitor services program will not be adversely affected as a result of the time and effort devoted to the research.

• The project must be coordinated with appropriate regional interpretation and professional offices. Regional offices are responsible for keeping the WASO offices of natural and cultural resources management systematically informed of research in progress.

• Research should be described in the annual park superintendent's reports.

3. Archaeological, anthropological, and ethnological field research undertaken by parks must be approved by the Regional Archaeologist who is responsible for certifying that the individuals carrying out the project are qualified and that the project meets criteria established for all such Service projects. The Servicewide criteria for field research in archaeology involving site survey, surface collection, and/or site excavation require that:

• The individual is a subject matter specialist in the area of study and is a qualified professional principal investigator or is under the supervision of a person who possesses both qualifications.

- Funds have been programmed to properly complete the research, including analysis, synthesis, and publication of findings.
- The park manager agrees in writing to provide sufficient time for the individual to complete the research.

Anthropological and ethnological research that involves acquisition of data from informants must be conducted in accordance with the above criteria and must conform to the Code of Ethics of the American Anthropological Association.

Collection research, library research, or research that does not affect physical resources or involve informants may be conducted by park interpreters without regard to these criteria, but in accordance with statement #2 above.

PROGRAM ORIENTATION

Information and Orientation

1. Information is available to park visitors before, at the beginning of, and during their visit and includes:
   - Orientation to the facilities, resources, and geography of the park.
   - Safety considerations and emergency preparedness information concerning the biologic, physical, climatic, and environmental hazards of the area.
   - Options for recreational activities and interpretive and visitor services programs available in the area.
   - Park policies and regulations governing the use, care, preservation, and protection of park resources.
   - Basic information about the significant natural, cultural, and recreational values of the park's resources.

2. As appropriate, the public is informed of opportunities to participate in park planning, policy making, and management processes.

3. A process exists and is used to provide information in neighboring communities about special park activities and celebrations. Similarly, appropriate community information is provided in the park.

4. Information about services, facilities, and activities which meet the needs of special publics is prominently displayed in the park and made available to the media and organizations that serve these groups in the surrounding region.

PERSONAL SERVICES—GENERAL

1. Face to face interpretation is available, as resources permit, to all visitors who desire it.

2. A variety of interpretive and visitor services programs and activities are offered in which the subjects, locations, durations, physical requirements, and learning behavior correspond to visitor needs and use patterns. Whenever practical, interpretive activities involve visitors as participants rather than merely as spectators.

3. Activities that have minimum adverse environmental impact and energy consumption are emphasized; park employees set examples of environmentally sound behavior, and the public is made aware of these efforts.

4. The ratio between interpreters and the numbers of visitors in an activity is kept at a level that allows an activity to accomplish objectives set for it without adverse impact on park resources.

5. A park's primary program, activities, media, and personal services should be directly related to the park's primary themes—as established by legislation and formal park planning—and to the resource management and protection strategies of the park. Programs should also be consistent with Service objectives. The content of all programs, including supplemental ones undertaken when primary themes are thoroughly covered, should be designed to transmit park values and encourage an appreciation of park resources, rather than exist as entertainment or education in their own right. Stated in another form, the park's entire interpretive and visitors services program and each activity within it should be designed so that it pertains specifically to the park's particular acreage and resources.

6. Off-site services should be provided consistent with Service energy-conservation strategies and management objectives when those services do not jeopardize full attention to on-site programs.

7. Special programs or activities are provided as resources permit to visiting groups with special interests.

INTERPRETIVE PRESENTATIONS

Interpretive presentations—including activities carried out in costume to dramatize historical activities or lifestyles; activities designed to demonstrate or teach a craft or skill; and activities undertaken to portray an event or idea through the use of performing or creative arts—all have both a special role in

NPS interpretation and require special consideration in use. Clearly, such presentations have an unusual potential to catch public interest and direct it to critical park values. At the same time, presentations as a category of interpretive activities are frequently personal and cost intensive; they are more easily and inappropriately treated as educational or entertainment ends in themselves rather than as vehicles for sparking further public interest in park resources; they have a greater potential to be out of step with principal park themes without that fact being readily apparent to us or to visitors; and they can more easily place an intangible barrier between interpreter—seen as a performer undertaking a performance—and visitors than some other forms of personal service. Hence, the use of interpretive presentations must meet the following standards in addition to those outlined above:

1. The need for interpretive presentations to interpret a central element of the park's primary themes has been established in the park's basic planning documents (including the interpretive planning components and Annual Statement of Interpretive and Visitor Services) as based on the park's legislated purpose. In parks established to commemorate major historical figures, specific events, or political/military actions and ideas, interpretive presentations that illustrate period lifestyles will usually not be appropriate. Pending approval of the necessary planning documents, the superintendent must determine that interpretive presentations are the most appropriate means to interpret the park's principal values to the public.

2. Program decisions on interpretive presentations or the design of any single presentation should be governed by the amount of "backstage" time required daily to give presentations. Backstage time refers not only to initial research, but to such things as feeding animals, preparing and maintaining equipment, preparing costumes, and rehearsals. If that kind of preparation detracts significantly from the time that interpretive personnel could be available to the public, the program may not be warranted.

3. Interpretive and visitors services personnel (employees, people under contract, and VIPs) involved in presentations are recruited and trained specifically to insure both safety and accuracy in presenting, portraying, or teaching the skills, attitudes, and/or values of the time period, locality, or activity being presented. Before personnel are hired for such presentations, their appropriateness for the individual tasks or role is thoughtfully assessed. If a person to be portrayed in a presentation was a member of an Indian tribe, ethnic group, or regional or local subculture, the knowledge and concerns of living persons who are members of that group will be given sensitive consideration. In some

cases it will be most appropriate to recruit a person who is a member of that group for the role.

4. Copies of documentary references which substantiate the accuracy of all presentation materials and practices are available to all staff members. Continuing well documented research is encouraged. Records of the experiences of the presenters during these activities are maintained.

5. Presentations designed to teach or upgrade an outdoor recreational or leisure time activity:

- Involve skills or activities relevant to the resources or themes of the park.
- Include safety and emergency preparedness information germane to the activity.
- Contain information to help minimize possible adverse impacts on the park's resources that can result from the skill or activity.

6. Presentations involving food or beverage preparation meet all applicable public health service standards, if the products are to be consumed by visitors or the park staff.

7. Presentations are given in such a way that visitors clearly understand the relationship between the presentation and park resources and the rationale for the use of that interpretive method in helping them to understand primary park values.

8. In a historical animated presentation, no major historic figure will be dramatically portrayed. Portrayals of past people must be of and must clearly be identified as "typical" people based on composite information about the lives of a variety of people.

9. All presentations dealing with history and prehistory must meet criteria for honesty as well as accuracy. Specifically:

- Presentations are not described or advertised as portraying "the past" but as limited illustrations of some scattered elements of previous activity, skills, or crafts.
- Facts, examples, and anecdotes are not selected or used out of context to make a particular point or to communicate personal or contemporary social or political beliefs.
- The reactions of historic people to past ideas and events are described in the context of past ideas and perceptions. We do not assume or suggest that historic people reacted to or felt about certain situations the way we would unless there is strong evidence to support that pattern.
- Costumes, equipment, speech patterns, etc., are specifically described to the public as being the most accurate reproductions we are able to obtain, rather than as "just like they had."

• The individual experiences, events, or ideas being portrayed are chosen and expressed in such a way as to portray the full contributions or "personalities" of the ethnic groups, cultures, or people whose history is being commemorated.

HISTORIC WEAPONS FIRING DEMONSTRATIONS

1. Only reproduction weapons will be used in NPS historic black powder weapon firing interpretive demonstrations. (Exceptions to this requirement may be justified in special situations. However, any exceptions must have been reached through the procedures outlined in Use of Original Historic Objects in this chapter.)
2. Firing demonstrations will use blank loads only.
3. Demonstrations involving firing at opposing lines are prohibited.
4. Every area administered by the National Park Service that conducts any type of historical black powder weapon firing demonstration, either using NPS personnel or outside groups or VIPs, must have on its permanent staff a supervisory employee who:

a. has successfully completed the Servicewide Historic Black Powder Weapon Certification course, sponsored jointly by the Division of Safety, WASO, and the Division of Interpretation and Visitor Services, WASO, and

b. is holding a valid certificate, issued by the WASO Divisions of Safety and Interpretation and Visitor Services, certifying him or her as trained and qualified to assume direct responsibility for, and to supervise, historic weapons firing interpretive demonstrations and the storage and handling of black powder used in those demonstrations.

Any NPS area that does not have a certified permanent supervisory employee, as described above, on site shall not allow any type of historic weapons firing demonstration to take place within its boundaries.
5. The only types of historical weapons that are authorized to be fired in a particular NPS area are those that the area's certified historic weapons firing supervisor has been officially trained and certified for, as listed on his or her certificate. Weapon types not listed on the certificate may not be fired in the park. This applies to outside individuals and groups and VIPs, as well as NPS personnel. There will be no exceptions.
6. All historic black powder weapons demonstrations in areas administered by the NPS will be in strict compliance with the official NPS Standards for Historic Black Powder Weapon Firing in Areas Administered by

the NPS and will follow exactly the approved NPS manuals for the particular weapon being demonstrated.

7. All NPS personnel involved in demonstrating the firing of historic black powder weapons in areas administered by the NPS must be trained and/or personally checked out and declared competent by the area's certified historic weapons firing supervisor before they will be allowed to participate in or conduct any firing demonstrations in that particular NPS area.

8. (This section was deleted from the original.)

9. The park will provide all outside individuals and groups with a copy of the sections of the Standards for Historic Black Powder Weapons Firing, and the appropriate approved NPS historic weapon manual, applicable to the intended firing demonstration at least a week prior to their participation in the park's program. It is the responsibility of the outside individual or group to certify in writing that they have read and will adhere to the standards they receive from the park. The written agreement must be received by the park at least 48 hours before the firing demonstration is scheduled to take place. Any violation of the standards by the individuals or group shall result in the immediate cancellation of the demonstration and the removal of the individual or group from further weapons firing demonstrations in the park.

10. The park's certified supervisor must personally supervise all firing demonstrations conducted by outside individuals and groups within the park's boundaries. The certified supervisor must be prepared and authorized by the park Superintendent to act immediately on any violation of the NPS Standards for Historic Black Powder Weapons Firing, including cancellation of the program and removing individuals or groups from further firing demonstrations in the park, as appropriate.

NON-PERSONAL SERVICES

1. The public use facilities, especially information and orientation centers, are kept open during times which serve the maximum numbers of visitors and provide maximum effective use of each facility.

2. NPS publications are kept accurate, up-to-date, and available in sufficient quantities to meet visitor needs.

3. All publications and sound recordings, including those sold by cooperating associations and concessioners, relate clearly to the basic interpretive themes of the park and related subjects and are accurate and free of avoidable religious, cultural, and ethnic biases. The publication mix includes literature for

young readers and foreign language materials as needed to meet the needs of park visitors.

4. Self guiding facilities that incorporate publications are checked regularly to insure availability to the public of the interpretive literature.

5. An appropriate, routine maintenance schedule is followed to keep the park exhibits clean and in good repair. Each permanent exhibit is inspected annually to determine whether its content remains accurate and appropriate, and whether its physical condition is satisfactory. Corrective action, if necessary, is coordinated with the regional office and Harpers Ferry Center.

6. Routine maintenance instructions for all audiovisual equipment issued by Harpers Ferry Center are followed, and written maintenance and repair procedures are readily accessible. All AV programs and equipment are reviewed periodically to insure that technical quality is acceptable, visuals are clean and fresh, and content is current.

7. Major changes proposed for existing media programs and facilities, or initiation of significant new exhibits or AV programs, are made through the Harpers Ferry Center or with their consultative assistance with coordination by the regional office.

USES OF ORIGINAL HISTORICAL OBJECTS

Original historical objects are an integral part of the park resources that the American people have entrusted to our care. Hence, our use of them must reflect the Service's responsibility to sustain the physical integrity of all such resources and to communicate to the public that particular responsibility. As park resources objects and object collections do have an interpretive value. Their carefully controlled use to produce imaginative insights that benefit interpretation is encouraged so long as the original objects are not subjected to unacceptable possibilities of wear, breakage, theft, or deterioration as a result of their use.

In cases where use of an original historical object would expose it to unacceptable wear, deterioration, or the real possibility of breakage or theft, it must be replaced by an accurate reproduction. In certain instances, the Regional Interpreter, the Regional Curator, and the Regional Historian may jointly exempt individual objects from the requirement if the park superintendent has submitted a justification and impact statement. The statement must demonstrate the purpose of the program in which the object used is critical to public understanding of the park's resources and values, and that use of a reproduction of an original or use of a reproduction is infeasible. Final approval of any exemption granted by a regional office will be made by the Assistant Director, Cultural Resources Management, WASO. The justification and impact statement from the park will contain the following sections:

- Description of the program and proposed use of the object.
- Description of the object to be used (and a copy of its catalog card).
- Explanation of how the activity in which the object will be used is critical to the public understanding of the park's primary values and resources.
- Explanation of how the activity is critical to the park management needs.
- Discussion of alternate activities or media which could be used to achieve the same or similar public understanding of the park's value.
- Explanation of why reproductions of the exact historic object or reproductions of similar historic objects are not available or cannot be feasibly used in this program.
- Measures proposed to mitigate the loss or physical damage that might be done to the object and to explain to the public why the Service is using historic objects.

No exemptions should be granted for use of objects in presentations or other activities that may lead to loss or deterioration of historical objects that are directly connected with or are prime survivors of the park's historical periods, events, or personalities. Even the exposure of some resources of that type to conditions outside those of a museum climate are damaging and should not be considered. These resources are, in a sense, the equivalent of wilderness resources whose value is great enough that availability to visitors should be limited.

Reproductions used in place of historical objects must be marked as such. They are controlled and accounted for either by normal property management regulations, with permanent records maintained in park files, or as curatorial guidelines require.

CURATORIAL ACTIVITIES

1. A scope of collections statement has been prepared by the interpretive staff and approved by the Regional Director. The statement clearly defines the needs and limits of its museum collection and is suitable as a guide for an active program of acquisition or disposal.

2. The museum collection is utilized in a beneficial but non-consumptive manner. The use of park museum specimens for scholarly research, interpre-

tive exhibits, or historical reference material are examples of such desirable uses.

3. The park interpretive program provides the visitor with an understanding and appreciation of the values of historical objects.

4. Every object in the park museum collection is properly numbered and catalogued in accordance with existing National Park Service museum records and procedures, and the records are housed in a physically safe and fire resistant location. (Proper record keeping includes accessioning, cataloguing, and marking as described in the Museum Manual.)

5. Each object is authoritatively identified and, whenever appropriate, authenticated in the museum records system. Letters pertaining to the uses made of an object, the persons owning an object, and the circumstances surrounding its acquisition are included in the permanent records.

6. All objects in the collection having a current value of $100.00 or more are inventoried annually. The inventory includes other objects, regardless of monetary value, which have special significance or desirability by collectors.

7. Each specimen is examined periodically by a trained employee and the suitability of its condition is determined. Specimens which are unstable or deteriorating are treated by an employee or professional conservator in the NPS Conservation Laboratories.

8. Every object in the park museum collection is either exhibited or stored under environmental conditions which will (resist) deterioration. This requires control of light, dust, temperature, and relative humidity. The museum collection has a security system appropriate to the value and significance of the specimens.

9. Films, tapes, books, research data, and other materials relating to park resources are properly housed, maintained, and recorded. Data are made available for use by park personnel and interested public.

PROGRAM EVALUATION

1. All interpretive activities conducted by permanent, seasonal, or VIP interpreters are audited by supervisory interpretive personnel at least twice during the visitor season. For new employees, the first audit occurs during the first two weeks of employment. The audit includes discussion with the employee and counseling as necessary. Concessioner and cooperative association interpretive activities are regularly monitored by experienced interpreters, and written reports and recommendations are filed with the superintendent.

2. Opinions on existing programs and activities and ideas for new efforts are continually solicited from seasonals and VIPs by the Chief Interpreter, acted upon expeditiously according to their merit, and summarized and discussed with the seasonals and VIPs at the end of the season.

3. A schedule for the annual review of the park's total interpretive and visitor services program (Statement for Interpretation and Visitor Services) is established by the park superintendent, preferably during the annual review of the park's Statement for Management. All interpretive activities are critically evaluated for relevance, effectiveness, and adherence to approved plans, objectives, and Servicewide guidelines for interpretation and visitor services. Those activities that do not meet these standards, although they may be popular or traditional, are revised, replaced, or eliminated.

4. Periodic quantitative measurements are made by the interpretive staff of visitor use of interpretive facilities to determine proportion of visitor populations contacted, average length of exposure to the park, etc.

5. The overall park interpretive program is reviewed at least annually by interpretive personnel in the regional office. Adherence to the Servicewide guidelines for interpretation is reviewed and a critique is conducted with the park staff.

PROGRAM ACCOUNTABILITY

1. A data recording system is maintained in the park that enables the chief interpreter to calculate accurately both the cost and productivity of each type of activity in the overall program.

2. At the end of each visitor season, program cost and productivity analysis is made evaluating the existing program against possible alternative methods of accomplishing the same objectives.

Appendix B

Antietam National Battlefield Rules and Regulations for the Volunteer Living History Groups

PART 1.

Performance

In effect, the group serves as an official representative of the National Park Service. All members will conduct themselves under the same ethical standards as government employees. They will serve the public in a helpful and courteous manner at all times. Differences in opinion with NPS policy, personnel, or interpretation of park themes should not be expressed publicly. Group members should refrain from making editorial comments. Group leaders are responsible for the behavior of their members.

New groups are on probation for their first year and should plan to participate in two (2) events.

In order to participate in programs at Antietam, all volunteers are required to complete the necessary park training once every three years.

The park VIP coordinator will be notified as soon as possible of any cancellation or schedule changes due to weather or other reason.

Groups should come prepared to give at least three formal presentations per day. If the park desires additional presentations, that shall be arranged between the group and volunteer coordinator prior to the weekend event.

Group presentations will be critiqued by the VIP coordinator. Groups will receive an annual performance evaluation.

The VIP coordinator will schedule a time for group leaders to fill out the necessary paperwork for reimbursement, etc.

Volunteers receive a 15% discount at the park bookstore. During special event weekends, group members participating in a living history program may only make purchases prior to 10:00 A.M. They are welcome to visit the bookstore and receive the discount any time they are not in uniform or costume, or actively engaged in a program.

Volunteers will restrict themselves to the campgrounds appointed by the park staff after dark, and will in no way disturb the quiet hours of the park neighbors. Firewood will be made available by the park. Washing of utensils, shaving and bathing will be conducted in the Visitor Center restrooms only between the hours of 7:00 P.M. and 8:00 A.M. Overnight camping is permitted with one campfire ring, and burning fires must be attended at all times. Lift the sod in squares, then dig a hole in the shape of a "V" for the fire. When ready to leave, put the fire entirely out, fill in the hole, and replace the sod squares. Leave no burned grass area so the appearance of the park area is unchanged. If a fire ring already exists at a camp site, use that one so only one area is impacted by a fire.

Volunteers must abide by the park rules, laws, and the Federal Code of Regulations. Possession or use of metal detectors in the park is prohibited. This violation will result in the removal of volunteers from the park Volunteer-in-the-Park (VIP) program. This includes the Piper Farm.

Alcoholic beverages and controlled substances (drugs) are prohibited within the park. This applies to employees and volunteers as well as the public.

PART 2.

Authenticity

All group members will be expected to meet park and impression standards for authenticity with regard to uniform, equipment and general appearance. New members who are not adequately equipped or trained are a liability to program authenticity and will not be allowed to participate in park programs except for training purposes. Groups will be inspected for authenticity and weapons safety.

There will be no individuals in period clothing associated with the groups who do not serve a function directly related to the specific theme of the program. In the interest of safety and authenticity, volunteers firing weapons must be at least seventeen (17) years old. Musicians with groups will be inspected for authenticity by the VIP coordinator, and must be at least fourteen (14) years old.

The VIP coordinator will establish specific themes for Living History events.

Since we are striving for authenticity, please avoid Twentieth Century affectations. For example, consumption of modern food or drinks will not be done in public view.

PART 3.

Safety

Weapons will be clean and ready for inspection upon arrival at the park. All members of the infantry shall come ready to fire (but with weapons unloaded).

Visitors are allowed to handle only inert cartridges and/or loose bullets carried for interpretive purposes. Cartridges will be made according to NPS-6 standards.

Volunteers will be permitted to carry edged weapons and unloaded firearms within the park only as required by designated duties. Off duty volunteers (not serving in an interpretive function for the benefit of the public) will not be under arms. When entering the Visitor Center, volunteers will check their arms at the Information Desk.

Arms and equipment should not be left unattended or unsecured beyond view in areas visited by the public. If muskets are stacked, a guard will be detailed to remain physically present at each stack of arms. The park cannot take responsibility for loss or damage to volunteer-owned materials used in park programs.

Visitors are not to handle edged weapons or firearms with fixed bayonets under any circumstances. Edged weapons may be drawn or fixed only under controlled circumstances when visitors are maintained at a fixed distance. Visitors may handle unloaded firearms provided the volunteer retains physical control of the weapon, especially the direction of the muzzle. Firearms are not to be pointed or aimed in the direction of anyone, volunteer, visitor or park personnel.

Horses will be under restraint and guarded, and visitor crowds controlled at a safe distance during drills, demonstrations and talks. Children are not permitted to pet animals.

Accidents (motor vehicle or personal injuries) please contact Park Ranger at the Visitor Center immediately. Do not attempt first aid unless you are qualified with an up-to-date certificate in First-Aid Training. Group members should report any accidents, injuries or incidents (witnessed illegal activities, etc.) and hazardous conditions as soon as possible.

Care of personal property of a volunteer while in the park will be the sole responsibility of the owner volunteer. The Park Service will not assume responsibility of any loss or damage to volunteer property.

PART 4.

Administrative

Visitor Contact Report forms are available at the Visitor Center and are required to be completed by each volunteer leader or individual volunteer on a daily basis and given to the VIP coordinator. Our VIP budget is based on volunteer hours, programs given and visitor contacts. Statistical reports are given at weekly staff meetings and are included in the regional bi-annual report. Please don't feel that they are a waste of time.

Volunteers may be reimbursed for certain expenses. If funding has been programmed, we are budgeted to provide a $2.00 meal per day, per person (for four hours or longer) and mileage (maximum 20 miles one way) at $0.20 per mile. Claim forms are available from the VIP coordinator.

The park VIP coordinator maintains a personal record file on all volunteers. This will contain their application, agreement, record of meals and mileage, and letters of appreciation or commendation. If letters are received at the volunteer's home address, the park would appreciate a copy for the park files. When the letters are sent to the park, the individual will receive the original copy.

Volunteer service is an opportunity to explore the National Park Service and is creditable experience for job opportunities within the National Park Service. It is also tax deductible.

We agree to abide by these guidelines and understand that failure to comply may result in suspension or termination from the volunteer program.

Appendix C

Antietam National Battlefield Park
Military Living History Uniform Guidelines

Military living history at Antietam National Battlefield is to be representative of soldier life during the Maryland Campaign of September, 1862.

When the proper research is done and a convincing impression is achieved, living history can be one of the most effective forms of historical interpretation. These guidelines have been adopted as a standard for anyone interested in doing living history at Antietam. These are not arbitrary rules. They are based on the latest research by authorities in the field.

Any variations or exceptions to these rules must be thoroughly documented and presented to the park staff. Upon approval they may be implemented.

BASIC GUIDELINES

The quality of period clothing available has improved greatly over the past several years, and more than a few dealers offer top grade reproductions. Of course, with this better quality comes a higher price, and usually a lengthy waiting period for the finished goods.

The "acme" brand of mass produced uniforms, though somewhat cheaper and certainly more readily available, are often the wrong grade of fabric, improperly patterned and entirely machine sewn.

So, when buying, remember that fabric, cut, and construction are all important to achieve a proper period look.

The minimum general standards are as follows:

SHOES: Must be of an appropriate mid-19th century style, leather (or possibly canvas) and have natural material laces. Boots must be of a mid-19th century style and construction. No modern styles of either.

TROUSERS: Must be cut and worn to mid-19th century standards: high-waisted, with cuffs slightly more narrow than the rest of the leg.

SHIRTS: Longer than modem styles. Mid thigh is about right.

UNDERGARMENTS: Although not a necessity, you are depriving yourself of one of the few comfortable items of wear if you don't have them.

VESTS: Should be of mid-19th century cut, either civilian or military style. Remember, most soldiers did not have vests, and in some Union units it was against regulations to have a civilian vest.

BANDANNAS: No bandannas or railroad scarves.

OTHER ACCESSORIES

INSIGNIA: Insignia should be displayed at a minimum. If well documented, unit designation or branch of service may be worn discreetly. When units brigade together for special events, insignia will only be appropriate if the scenario allows. No corps badges! No harps!

GLASSES: Unless it is absolutely necessary for you to function, we discourage the use of glasses. If glasses must be worn, they must be of mid-19th century style. No modern metal or plastic frames. No exceptions!

UNION SPECIFICATIONS

COATS AND JACKETS: The sack coat, frock coat, nine button state jacket, or a variation of a roundabout may be worn according to research and documentation of the unit represented.

A mixture is possible. Research shows that NCOs may have been issued frock coats as opposed to the rank and file's sack coat in some units.

All visible button holes should be hand sewn.

TROUSERS: Should be issued blue kersey wool. Any visible buttonholes should be hand sewn.

SHIRTS: Issue white cotton osnaburg, possibly gray. Button holes should be hand sewn.

FORAGE CAPS: A must. You must document evidence of kepis or slouch hats. Forage caps should not be overloaded with brass.

CONFEDERATE SPECIFICATIONS

CLOTH AND COLOR: Most Confederate uniforms were issued gray in color. Because of wear, weather, wood smoke, dust, perspiration, and other factors, this color sometimes faded and altered to variations commonly referred to as "butternut."

All uniform items must be gray or butternut as defined here. They must be made of proper jean cloth (a wool and cotton blend) and cut according to originals.

Civilian items must be of jean cloth or of period corduroy.

Butternut should be largely uniform within a unit. Brown jean cloth may be used for some civilian style trousers or vests.

JACKETS: Will be of shell type. Frock coats, worn mostly by officers and NCOs, can also be worn. All should be of proper pattern.

Piping, trim, belt loops and epaulets must be documented for your unit. All chevrons will be sewn directly on the sleeve. No backings.

Buttons will be script or block letter, wood, Union eagle, or if documented, state. NO CSA BUTTONS. All visible button holes will be hand sewn.

TROUSERS: Jean cloth, period corduroy. Some kersey may be worn in a unit, but not by more than one or two members. All visible button holes will be hand sewn.

SHIRTS: White cotton osnaburg dull homespun colors, possibly even dull red. Visible button holes should be hand sewn.

HATS: Slouch hats largely. Possibly even one or two forage/wheel caps per unit. NO BRASS OR CORDS ON SLOUCH HATS. Kepis must be documented. NO COWBOY, HILLBILLY OR MODERN SLOUCH HATS PERMITTED.

BELT BUCKLES: Frame. State, if documented.

Appendix D

Antietam National Battlefield
Rifle-Musket Misfire Plan

MISFIRE PREVENTION

Prior to the first demonstration, wipe excess oil from the bore using a dry patch on a .58 Cal. cleaning rod jag. Hammer should be at half-cock to allow air and excess oil to be forced out through cone. Then snap at least 2 caps (on range with no visitors present), to burn off remaining oil and to be sure that the vent is clear. (Fire second cap at ground and watch grass for a disturbance.)

MISFIRE PROCEDURE

All rifle-musket demonstrations will be performed by at least 2 persons: an interpreter and a demonstrator. If there is only one demonstrator and a misfire occurs during the 9-count loading drill (usually the first shot), the interpreter will explain the problem and the demonstrator will follow the commands of the interpreter through the misfire drill. If the misfire occurs while demonstrating continuous fire or if it is a group demonstration, the misfire drill will be performed automatically without individual commands.

    1st Misfire: (Hold weapon at AIM, count 10 seconds), PRIME (Recover arms), READY, AIM, FIRE.

2nd Misfire: (Hold weapon at AIM, count 10 seconds), PRIME (Recover arms, use vent pick), READY, AIM, FIRE.

3rd Misfire: (Hold weapon at AIM, count 10 seconds), SHOULDER ARMS, ORDER ARMS, GROUND ARMS.

DO NOT attempt to fire after the command CEASE FIRE, SHOULDER ARMS, or LOAD has been given. Come to the position of PRIME and wait until the command to fire is given again. If a problem other than ignition failure occurs while loading (ie: rammer stuck in bore, broken mainspring, etc.), and powder has been loaded, GROUND ARMS, and report the problem to the person in charge. After a weapon is grounded, the problem will be interpreted and the program concluded. Spectators will be asked to remain clear of the demonstration area.

WEAPON CLEARING PROCEDURE

1. The Park Demonstration Supervisor will retrieve the misfire kit and will assist the demonstrator in clearing the weapon. (Misfire kit shall consist of the following: water container, funnel, cleaning rod/ball puller, wiper, cone wrench, vent pick.)
2. Demonstrator will RAISE ARMS and, keeping the muzzle pointed in a safe direction at all times, will proceed with Park Demonstration Supervisor to a safe area away from the public.
3. The cone will be removed from the bolster, the vent cleaned with the vent pick, and the cone returned to the bolster. (Use fingers to seat cone, tighten with wrench.)
4. Prime and attempt to refire. If weapon fires, go to #9. If it still misfires, hold at AIM, count 10 seconds.
5. Place the butt of the weapon on the ground, keeping muzzle in a safe direction. Using the funnel, pour some water down the barrel. Do not fill entire barrel.
6. Pull the paper wad using the cleaning rod/ball puller or rammer/wiper combination—whichever works best.
7. Loosen the wet powder with the rammer/wiper, point muzzle down to drain barrel.
8. Add fresh water and repeat #7 until water comes out clear.
9. Spring rammer and snap a cap to be sure bore is clear.
10. The Park Demonstration Supervisor will determine the probable cause of the misfire upon inspection of the weapon. Appropriate action will be taken before the weapon is fired again.

Appendix E

American Civil War Commemorative Committee
and
Napoleonic Tactics, Incorporated
Gettysburg Reenactment Regulations, 1988

These rules are intended to demonstrate the amount of authenticity and accuracy that is required in doing a national event. New reenactors should read these rules as guidelines to what is expected of their portrayal. Many people may argue the validity or individual points of these regulations, but the whole of them should indicate what is expected at a major event.

ACWCC-NTI

GETTYSBURG REENACTMENT REGULATIONS

These are the rules that were passed around for the 125th Anniversary Reenactment of the Battle of Gettysburg. They were agreed to by the American Civil War Commemorative Committee (ACWCC) and Napoleonic Tactics, Inc. (NTI) who hosted the event.

1) All units should strive for an 1863 appearance. Units and individuals will be brigaded together by like appearing uniforms on a Company level. No ragged clothing in an unrepaired state will be allowed. All uniforms and accoutrements must be of period materials, styles and construction.

2) Recommended headgear for Federals are forage cap, used Hardee hat and

kepis, with correct hat devices and corps badges (optional). For Confederates, use forage caps, civilian hats or kepis. Other documentable variances will be allowed. A unit's headgear should be consistent.

3) For Federals, the recommended uniform is the four button fatigue coat and light blue trousers. For Confederates, the recommended uniform is a gray shell or frock, and any military or civilian style trousers. Butternut is permissible. Other styles and colors documentable to the Battle of Gettysburg are acceptable, but will not be brigaded with like appearing units.

4) Shoes and boots must be of period style and construction: Jefferson bootees and brogans, and period cut boots. No combat, cowboy or work boots, oxford style shoes or recognizable desert boots. For safety, no bare feet or burlap wrapping. Footwear is one item which has been allowed to slide in the past but will be closely monitored at Gettysburg.

5) Weapons for Infantry: 3-banded rifled or smoothbore muskets recommended, or proper 2-banded rifles and breechloaders if documentable to unit portrayal. No Remington zouaves, cut down muskets, carbines, Hawkins, shotguns, plains rifles, sporting guns or flintlocks allowed. For Cavalry: Carbine, revolver, and sabre. For Artillery: Full-scale, original or reproduction tube, 6- or 12-pounder carriage with a wheel diameter of 57", and of the following types: 6-pounder smoothbore/rifle (3.67"), 12-pounder Napoleon (4.62"), 10- and 20-pound Parrott, Ordnance Rifle, 12-pounder Howitzer and Whitworth. Other types will be considered on an individual basis, but nothing less than full scale need apply.

6) Horse tack for Federal should be 1858 McClellan only. For Confederates, can be McClellan, Grimsley, Campbell, Jenipher, Plantation, or English. All cavalrymen MUST BE MOUNTED. No horses may be ridden in the infantry camps. (It is recommended that all cavalrymen come with as good a Federal impression as possible. Confederates saw action only on the third day, and we would like as many as possible to be able to portray Buford's men on the first day in what would be the largest recreation of cavalrymen fighting dismounted ever.)

7) All officers must have the proper uniform and accoutrements. Overall and second level commanders (top four on each side) MUST BE MOUNTED. Battalion commanders may be, as well as all staff officers.

8) Colors must be full size and proper construction. National and regimental, and state for Federals. Army of Northern Virginia Battle Flag, 1st National or State for Confederate. Flags to be carried during the reenactments will be designated by the committee and respective overall commanders.

9) Camps will be open on Saturday, June 18th. No other than official personnel will be allowed on the property before that time. (Note exception in "Filming" section.) The authentic camps will be as at Manassas: Union and Confederate military camps, Union and Confederate family camps, and a civilian camp. On-site modern camping will be confined to the participant parking area, with no modern hookups. Improperly parked vehicles will be towed at owner's expense and risk. Anachronisms are forbidden from view of the authentic camps and on the field so such items as coolers should be kept in tents or in a period container. Please transfer modern foods and beverages to period containers. Proper period dress must be observed at all times in the encampment. No shirtless sunbathing and NO PETS ALLOWED. Firepits are allowed in designated areas only. Lights out at 1 A.M. each night.

10) Camps will not be accessible to vehicles to unload or set up. A shuttle service will be provided. This is to preserve the period integrity of the camps.

11) No live ammunition or fireworks are allowed. Gunpowder will be carried as pre-rolled cartridges only. No penny-wrappers, staples, gluetape, aluminum foil (except for artillery rounds) or waxed cartridges will be allowed. No discharging of firearms in the camp areas. Bayonets may be carried, but fixed only by order of the general commanding. A decision on ramrods will be made later. No hand-to-hand fighting except that specifically designated by the scenarios and rehearsed. Artillery crews will consist of at least six cannoneers, exclusive of officers.

12) No participant may carry a camera or audio-visual equipment on the field. Persons violating this rule risk confiscation of their equipment and expulsion from the event without refund or recourse.

13) Be sure to include each participant's rank on the pre-registration form. No participant shall have a rank higher than Captain without written authorization of the Committee. In general, there should not be more than one officer per 15 soldiers.

14) The minimum age for participation on the field is 13. Only those 16 years old or older may carry a weapon or service an artillery piece. Those 13 to 15 years old MUST be functional musicians (no flag bearers or couriers) and must be accompanied by a responsible adult. If you are registering anyone under 18, you should request a parental release form for minors, which must be submitted for participation. It is the responsibility of the minor or attendant adult to provide proof of age.

15) The registration fee is $3.00 per participant for pre-registrations postmarked by February 14, 1988. After February 14, the pre-registration fee

increases to $5.00. A participant is described as anyone who 'desires access to the property at times not open to the general public. All participants will receive an encoded photo ID, which should be carried at all times and must be presented at each inspection and for various services. Replacement of a lost pass will be $5.00. Pre-registration closes on May 31, 1988. Participant substitution by unit commanders will be allowed at the event. On-site registration will open at 10:00 A.M. on Saturday, June 18th, and remain open until 10 A.M., June 24th, and will also be open from 6:00 A.M. till 10:00 A.M. on both Saturday the 25th and Sunday the 26th. Everyone must sign a liability and photo release.

16) All participants are responsible for providing a few hours of provost and/or fatigue detail. The Commanders and civilian coordinator will publish a schedule prior to the event establishing your times for duty.

17) No illegal substances will be tolerated and violations will be referred to the appropriate authorities. Possession or consumption of alcoholic beverages is prohibited. Persons acting in an unsafe or uncooperative manner, or under the influence of alcohol or drugs, will be removed from the event.

18) Every unit and commander is responsible for the conduct of those listed on the registration form that they know, understand and abide by these rules and regulations. Any rules violations may be grounds for an individual or a unit to be suspended from the event, without refund or recourse, at the discretion of the Committee. Any officer who knowingly allows participation by any non-registered, disqualified or otherwise ineligible person subjects himself and his unit to immediate expulsion from this event and may preclude participation at any future event sponsored by the Committee.

SUTLER REGULATIONS

1) In the continuing effort to increase the authenticity as presented to the public, the semantics which deal with the sutlers is being changed. Please read the following rules carefully and pick your proper classification.

2) Authentic Sutlers will be defined only as people doing a portrayal of a period sutler, either as an exhibit or selling ONLY items sold by period sutlers at period prices. There is no additional fee for this type of portrayal. These will be set up in the authentic military camps as per original regulations.

3) Authentic Merchants (previously called Authentic Sutlers) are defined as persons working out of a semi-fixed facility (tents or wagons), predominantly selling items for use by reenactors portraying the 1860's persona. Items which

do not fall into this category include, but are not limited to: post 1865 topic books and artwork, non-period firearms, "souvenirs," and anything of obvious modern materials or construction. Nylon or other modern tentage or table coverings, aluminum poles, nylon ropes, modern tables without coverings, exposed modern sleeping gear, modern chairs and MODERN ARTIFICIAL LIGHTING are not allowed in the authentic area. Vehicles will only be allowed for unloading at specific times (to be announced) and reloading. The fee for authentic merchants (in addition to the participant fee) is the donation of merchandise (approximate retail value of $25.00) for an auction to benefit the Gettysburg Battlefield Preservation Fund.

4) Modern Merchants (previously called Modern Sutlers) are defined as vendors whose wares or sales facility do not meet the standards of an authentic merchant. The fee for modern merchants (in addition to the participant fee) is $25.00 to help support the expense of a separate camp area.

5) Concessionaires are businesses selling food and drink, are not covered by these rules and should contact us separately for those regulations. Authentic and modern merchants are not allowed to sell food and drinks.

6) All locations for sutlers and merchants will be assigned on a first come, first served basis. Only pre-registered sutlers and merchants are allowed to sell non-food merchandise on the property.

CIVILIAN AUTHENTICITY

There are no absolute rules for governing authenticity of dependents. General guidelines would be that you use your own judgement for WBTS period dress. However, in order to encourage authenticity among civilians, a new registration category has been established: AUTHENTIC CIVILIANS. This category differentiates participatory civilians from on-lookers and dependents. Participation in this category is purely by choice, but all civilians chosen for public activities or filming must be Authentic Civilians. Authentic civilians must have the following requirements:

HAVE A PERSONA: More than simply putting on different clothes, put on an identity! You should know the age, occupation of the head of the household, and economic status of the persona you portray.

APPEAR AS THOUGH THEY COULD HAVE EXISTED AT THE TIME: Avoid the appearance of having items which did not exist or were not available at that time. Fabric and trim should have the look and feel of items which were available.

Obvious synthetics such as nylon net and double knits are prohibited.

Fasteners must be those that existed at that time: hooks and eyes, buttons and (less frequently) lacings. Anything plastic, snaps, zippers and Velcro are prohibited.

Anachronisms such as wrist watches, modern eyeglasses, shoes with "tread" on the soles, plastic parasols and colored fingernail polish, as examples, are prohibited.

APPEAR AS THEY WOULD HAVE WANTED TO APPEAR AT THE TIME: Dress in a manner appropriate for your persona for July, 1863 in southern Pennsylvania. Recognize that the existence of an item does not ensure that it was available or used by everyone here and now.

Although armscyes, the seams which connect the sleeve and garment, were vertical in the 18th century and into the 19th century, during the Civil War period all garments had armscyes which appeared as diagonal or horizontal lines when the garment was worn.

Although eyeliner pre-dates Cleopatra, respectable women of the period would not wear it, or noticeable eyeshadow or mascara. Confine whatever rouge is worn to the front of the cheeks. Again, colored fingernail polish is not correct.

Ladies' day dresses of the period generally fasten at the center or side front. The dresses of teens and children may fasten at the center back. All blouses, children, teen or adult, fasten at the center front.

Ladies wear their hair confined to a hairstyle which hides the ends of individual hairs. Most ladies wear their hair parted in the center front. Bangs should be pulled back so they are less noticeable than in modern hairstyles. Children may wear their hair short and unconfined. Children under the age of eight should not wear snoods. Boys' hair should be parted on the side.

Adult women must cover their shoulders and chest to the nape of the neck, or a shallow "V" neckline, when outdoors during the day. Low, wide necklines during the day are acceptable only for teenagers and young girls, who may also wear short sleeves.

Dress hems for young girls should be below the knee, but closer to the knee than the ankle. For teens the hems should be ankle length, and longer as she approaches adulthood. Day dresses for adults should be ankle length or longer. The exception is a camp or work dress as would be "worn in the field," which might be slightly shorter.

The diameter of day dress hoop skirts should not exceed 50 to 70% of the lady's height. Hoops are optional, especially with a work or camp dress. Children under six should not wear hoops.

Men should wear cotton or wool shirts with front fasteners and long sleeves. Pants should ride high at the waist and fit loosely.

APPEAR AS THEY WOULD HAVE BEEN ABLE TO AFFORD TO APPEAR: Dress in a manner appropriate to the economic status of your persona. Just as people today do not dress like fashion models in *Vogue,* the average person in the nineteenth century did not have the money or inclination to dress exactly as the fashion plates of the period indicate.

All fabric, trims and styles should be consistent with what your persona could afford—even if that means wearing clothing several years out of fashion (pre-Civil War). These may or may not have been modified with trim in an effort to update them. Specifically, be extremely judicious in the use of lace, which was very expensive at that time.

Clothing and accessories should be made with an eye toward practicality. Detachable collars and cuffs were liberally used to cut down on laundering garments. For children, the presence of "growth tucks" in skirts or pants gives evidence [that] it is expected to last.

Let us emphasize that these guidelines are not meant to discourage your participation, but to encourage a level of authenticity equal to that expected of soldiers at this event. Not meeting these requirements WILL NOT keep you out of the encampments or the Ball or other participant-only social activities.

ADDENDUM

There will be a series of educational seminars offered free of charge during the event dealing with a variety of topics to help improve everyone's impression. The Civil War Lifestyles Institute, as we are calling it, will be held on June 23rd to June 25th, and may include as many as ten individual sessions. We are currently searching for speakers on a variety of non-military topics. The Institute should be of interest to anyone who does serious living history; it should be noted that everyone of the period was a civilian, even soldiers, and there are many facets of life which would have been common knowledge regardless of your occupation or lifestyle. There will be greater details on this later on.

Appendix F

U.S. Infantry Tactics
for the Instruction, Exercise, and
Manoeuvres of the
United States Infantry,
including Infantry of the Line,
Light Infantry, and Riflemen
May 1, 1861
As Revised by the
National Park Service
1979

MANUAL OF ARMS

INTRODUCTION

Before commencement of the actual loading and firing procedures, it is important that the recruit learn the proper manner in which to carry his weapon. Presented at the beginning are the required basic positions for carrying the weapon from which the loading takes place.

I. Manual of Arms

A. Principles of Shouldered Arms

121. The piece in the right hand—the barrel nearly vertical and resting in the hollow of the shoulder—the guard to the front, the arm hanging nearly at its full length near the body, the thumb and forefinger embracing the guard, the remaining fingers closed together, and grasping the swell of the stock just under the cock, which rests on the little finger.[1]

122. Recruits are frequently seen with natural defects in the construction of the shoulders, breast and hips. These the instructor will labor to correct in

the lessons without arms, and afterwards, by steady endeavors, so that the appearance of the pieces, in the same line, may be uniform, and without constraint to the men in their positions.

123. The instructor will have occasion to remark that recruits, on first bearing arms, are liable to derange their position by lowering the right shoulder and the right hand, or by sinking the hip and spreading out the elbows.

124. He will be careful to correct all these faults by continually rectifying the position; he will sometimes take away the piece to replace it the better; he will avoid fatiguing the recruits too much in the beginning, but labor by degrees to render this position so natural and easy they may remain in it a long time without fatigue.

125. Finally, the instructor will take great care that the piece, at a shoulder, be not carried too high or too low; if too high, the right elbow would spread out, the soldier would occupy too much space in his rank, and the piece made to waver; if too low, the files would be too much closed, the soldier would not have the necessary space to handle his piece with facility, the right arm would become too much fatigued, and would draw down the shoulder.

B. Support Arms and Return to Shoulder Arms

128. Each command will be executed in one time (or pause), but this time would be divided into motions, the better to make known the mechanism.

129. The rate, or swiftness of each motion, in the manual of arms, with the exceptions herein indicated, is fixed at the ninetieth of a minute; but, in order not to fatigue the attention, the instructor will, at first, look more particularly to the execution of the motions, without requiring a nice observance of the cadence, to which he will bring the recruits progressively, and after they shall have become a little familiarized with the handling of the piece.

130. As the motion relative to the cartridge, to the rammer, and to the fixing and unfixing of the bayonet cannot be executed at the rate prescribed, not even with a uniform swiftness, they shall not be subjected to that cadence. The instructor will, however, labor to cause these motions to be executed with promptness, and, above all, with regularity.

131. The last syllable of the command will decide the brisk execution of the first motion of each time (or pause). The commands two, three, and four will decide the brisk execution of the other motions. As soon as the recruits shall well comprehend the positions of the several motions of a time, they will be taught to execute the time without resting on its different motions; the

mechanism of the time will nevertheless be observed, as well as to give a perfect use of the piece as to avoid the sinking, or slurring over, either of the motions.

132. The manual of arms will be taught in the following progression. The instructor will command:

Support—Arms

One time and three motions

133. (First Motion) Bring the piece, with the right hand, perpendicularly to the front and between the eyes, the barrel to the rear; seize the piece with the left hand at the lower band, raise the hand as high as the chin, and seize the piece at the same time with the right hand four inches below the cock.

134. (Second Motion) Turn the piece with the right hand, the barrel to the front; carry the piece to the left shoulder, and pass the forearm extended on the breast between the right hand and the cock; support the cock against the left forearm, the left hand resting on the right breast.

135. (Third Motion) Drop the right hand by the side.

136. When the instructor may wish to give repose in this position, he will command:

Rest

137. At this command, the recruits will bring up smartly the right hand to the handle of the piece (small of the stock) and the right foot drops back slightly. They will not be required to preserve silence, or steadiness of position.

138. When the instructor may wish the recruits to pass from this position to that of silence or steadiness, he will command:

1. Attention 2. Squad

139. At the first word, the recruit will draw his attention to the instructor, and at the second word, the recruits will resume the position of the third motion of support arms.

Shoulder—Arms

One time and three motions

140. (First Motion) Grasp the piece with the right hand under and against the left forearm; seize it with the left hand at the lower band, the thumb and

fingers extended; the palm against the ramrod; detach the piece slightly from the shoulder, the left forearm against the stock.

141. (Second Motion) Carry the piece vertically to the right shoulder with both hands, the rammer to the front, change the position of the right hand so as to embrace the guard with the thumb and forefinger, slip the left hand to the height of the shoulder, the fingers extended and joined, the right arm nearly straight.

142. (Third Motion) Drop the left hand quickly by the side.

Order—Arms

One time and two motions

147. (First Motion) Seize the piece briskly with the left hand near the upper band, and detach it slightly from the shoulder with the right hand; loosen the grasp of the right hand, lower the piece with the left, re-seize the piece with the right hand above the lower band, the little finger in rear of the barrel, the butt about four inches from the ground, the right hand supported against the hip, drop the left hand by the side.

148. (Second Motion) Let the piece slip through the right hand by opening slightly the finger, and take the position about to be described.

Position of Order Arms

149. With the hand low, the barrel between the thumb and forefinger extended along the stock; the other fingers extended and joined; the muzzle about two inches from the right shoulder; the rammer in front; the toe (or beak) of the butt against, and in line with, the toe of the right foot, the perpendicular.

150. The instructor may wish to give repose in this position; he will command:

Rest

151. At this command, the recruits will not be required to preserve silence or steadiness.

152. When the instructor may wish the recruits to pass from this position to that of silence and steadiness, he will command:

1. Attention 2. Squad

153. At the first word the recruit will draw his attention to the instructor, and at the second word, the recruit will resume the position of Order Arms.

Shoulder—Arms

One time and two motions

154. (First Motion) Raise the piece vertically with the right hand to the height of the right breast, and opposite the shoulder, the elbow close to the body; seize the piece with the left hand below the right, and drop quickly the right hand and grasp the piece at the swell of the stock, the thumb and forefinger embracing the guard; press against the shoulder with the right arm nearly straight.

155. (Second Motion) Drop the left hand quickly by the side.

C. Right Shoulder Shift

Right Shoulder Shift—Arms

One time and two motions

210. (First Motion) Detach the piece perpendicularly from the shoulder with the right hand, and seize it with the left between the lower band and guide sight, raise the piece, the left hand at the height of the shoulder and four inches from it; place, at the same time, the right hand on the butt, the beak between the first two fingers, the other fingers under the butt plate.

211. (Second Motion) Quit the piece with the left hand, raise the piece on the right shoulder with the right hand, the lock plate upwards; let fall, at the same time, the left hand by the side.

Shoulder—Arms

One time and three motions

212. (First Motion) Raise the piece perpendicularly by extending the right forearm to its full length, the elbow at ninety degree angle, the rammer to the front; at the same time seize the piece with the left hand between the lower band and guide sight.

213. (Second Motion) Quit the butt with the right hand which will immediately embrace the guard, lower the piece to the position of shoulder arms, slide the left hand to the height of the shoulder, the fingers extended and closed.

214. (Third Motion) Drop the left hand by the side.

II. Loading and Firing Procedures

A. Load in Nine Times (done from shoulder arms)

1. LOAD

One time and one motion

156. Grasp the piece with the left hand as high as the right elbow, and bring it vertically opposite the middle of the body, shift the right hand to the upper band, place the butt between the feet, the barrel to the front, seize it with the left hand near the muzzle, the arm extended full length from the body; carry the right hand to the cartridge box; and unfasten it.

2. HANDLE—Cartridge

157. Raise the flap, and withdraw a cartridge. Seize the cartridge with the thumb and next two fingers, and place it between the teeth.

3. TEAR—Cartridge

158. Tear the paper to the powder, hold the cartridge upright between the thumb and first two fingers, near the top; in this position place it to the side of and near the muzzle—the back of the hand to the right.[2]

4. CHARGE—Cartridge

One time and one motion

159. Empty the powder charge into the bore. Then, using the first finger and thumb of the right hand, quickly place the empty cartridge paper into the bore. (Note!—Take care to place the cartridge paper in the bore as quickly as possible without needlessly exposing the hand before the muzzle. Do not use the first finger to poke the cartridge paper into the bore!) Seize the head of the rammer with the thumb and forefinger of the right hand, the other fingers closed.

5. DRAW—Rammer

One time and three motions

160. (First Motion) Half draw the rammer by extending the right arm; steady it in this position at the pipes, with the left thumb; grasp the rammer near the muzzle with the tips of the fingers and thumb of the right hand, the little finger uppermost, the nails to the left, the thumb extended along the rammer.

161. (Second Motion) Clear the rammer from the pipes by again extending the arm; the rammer in the prolongation of the pipes.

162. (Third Motion) Turn the rammer, the little end of the rammer passing near the left shoulder; touch the head of the rammer to the right side of the muzzle, keeping it clear of the muzzle. The back of the hand is to the front.

6. RAM—Cartridge

One time and one motion

163. Insert the rammer as far as the right hand allows and quit the rammer with the right hand. Seize the rammer at the small end with the thumb and forefinger of the right hand, the back of the hand to the front; press the cartridge home.

164. Draw the rammer out, and grasp it near the muzzle with the finger tips and thumb tip of the right hand, the little finger uppermost, the nails to the front; clear the rammer from the bore by extending the arm, the nails to the front, the rammer in the prolongation of the bore.

165. Turn the rammer, the head of the rammer passing near the left shoulder, and insert in the pipes until the right hand reaches the muzzle, the nails to the right.

7. RETURN—Rammer

One time and one motion

166. Force the rammer home by placing the little finger of the right hand on the head of the rammer, the thumb toward the body; pass the left hand down the barrel to the extent of the arm, without depressing the shoulder.

8. PRIME

One time and three motions

167. (First Motion) With the left hand, raise the piece till the hand is as high as the eye, grasp the small of the stock with the right hand; half face to the right; place, at the same time, the right foot behind and at right angles with the left, the hollow of the right foot against the left heel. Slip the left hand down to the lower band, the thumb along the stock, the left elbow against the body; bring the piece to the right side, the butt below the right forearm, the small of the stock against the body and two inches below the right breast, the barrel upwards, the muzzle on a level with the eye. (With live firing, the muzzle is pointed directly down the range with the weapon parallel to the ground.)

168. (Second Motion) Half cock with the thumb of the right hand, the fingers supported against the guard and the small of the stock; remove the old cap with one of the fingers of the right hand, and with the thumb and forefinger of the same hand, take a cap from the pouch, place it on the cone, and press it down with the thumb; seize the small of the stock with the right hand.

173. (Third Motion) Cock, and seize the piece at the small of the stock without deranging the position of the butt. (NPS Note: Normally, the ninth

count is Shoulder—Arms with Ready, Aim, and Fire having no designated numbers. Due to safety problems the shoulder arms command has been eliminated and the 9th count has been re-assigned to Ready.)

9. READY

One time and one motion

170. With the thumb of the right hand, bring the hammer to full cock making sure that the fingers of the right hand are outside the trigger guard.

AIM

174. Raise the piece with both hands, and support the butt against the right shoulder, the left elbow down, the right as high as the shoulder; incline the head upon the butt, so the right eye may perceive quickly the notch of the hause, the front sight, and the object aimed at; the left eye closed, the right thumb extended along the stock, the forefinger on the trigger.

FIRE

One time and one motion

177. Press the forefinger against the trigger, fire, without lowering or turning the head, and remain in this position.

178. Instructors will be careful to observe when the men fire, that they aim at some distinct object, and that the barrel be so directed that the line of fire and the line of sight be in the same vertical plane. They will often cause the firing to be executed on ground of different inclinations, in order to accustom the men to fire at objects either above or below them.

B. Recover Arms (if the weapon has not been discharged)

To cause the recruit to recover his weapon from the aim to the ready, the command is as follows:

RECOVER—Arms

One time and one motion

184. At the first part of the command, withdraw the finger from the trigger; at the command Arms, retake the position of the third motion of READY.

III. Inspection Arms

This procedure should be executed before and after a demonstration, at least in principle. (Executed from Order Arms.)

INSPECTION—Arms

One time and two motions

227. (First Motion) Seize the piece with the left hand below and near the upper hand, carry it with both hands opposite the middle of the body, the butt between the feet, the rammer to the rear, the barrel vertical, the muzzle about three inches from the body; carry the left hand reversed to the sabre-bayonet, draw it from the scabbard and fix it on the barrel; grasp the piece with the left hand below and near the upper band, seize the rammer with the thumb and forefinger of the right hand bent, the other fingers closed.

228. (Second Motion) Draw the rammer straight out, and introduce the threaded end to the barrel, and let it glide gently to the bottom of the bore; replace the piece with the left hand opposite the right shoulder, and retake the position of ordered arms.

229. The instructor will then inspect in succession the piece of each recruit, in passing along the front of the rank. Each, as the instructor reaches him, will raise smartly the piece with his right hand, seize it with the left between the lower band and guide sight, the lock to the front, the left hand about the height of the chin, the piece opposite the left eye; the instructor will take it with the right hand at the handle, and, after inspecting it, will return it to the recruit, who will receive it back with the right hand, and replace it in the position of ordered arms.

230. When the instructor shall have passed him, each recruit will retake the position prescribed at the command inspection arms, return the rammer, and resume the position of ordered arms.

231. If, instead of inspection of arms, the instructor should merely wish to cause bayonets to be fixed, he will command:

FIX—Bayonets

232. Take the position indicated in No. 227, fix the bayonets as has been explained, and immediately resume the position of ordered arms.

233. If it is to be the wish of the instructor, after firing, to ascertain whether the pieces have been discharged, he will command:

SPRING—Rammers

234. Put the rammer in the barrel as has been explained above, and immediately retake the position of ordered arms.[3]

235. The instructor, for the purpose stated, can take the rammer by the head, and spring it lightly in the barrel, or cause each recruit to make it ring in the barrel.

236. Each recruit, after the instructor passes him, will return the rammer, and resume the position of ordered arms.

** No firing demonstration will be conducted unless the demonstrator is wearing natural fiber clothing (cotton, wool, etc.). Synthetics are very dangerous if there is an accident in that synthetic fibers melt, whereas natural fibers smolder. As most National Park Service uniforms are all or in part synthetic fabrics, they must never be worn for firearms demonstrations.

Appendix G

Reenactors and Taxes

The tax laws change each year, but there are a few general rules that are fairly constant. Always check with the IRS or a tax advisor for correct, up-to-date information.

The IRS allows volunteers to deduct from taxes "un-reimbursed expenditures, made incident to rendition of services to a qualifying organization." Charitable, educational, and veterans groups often qualify, and some reenactment organizations may be considered charitable or educational organizations. Before deducting any expenses, make sure the organization qualifies.

Theoretically, if an organization has a written requirement for special equipment, uniforms, or other clothing to be used for charitable or educational purposes, any equipment or clothing purchased to fulfill that requirement should be tax-deductible. But I have yet to meet anyone who has managed to deduct the total reenactment uniform and equipment costs.

Here are a few guidelines so that you will be prepared at tax time:

Always ask for and keep receipts, especially those from the charitable institutions themselves. They are your proof of expenses and will justify your deductions. Among other things, a receipt from an NPS bookstore will show that you were there on that day. A receipt that shows a VIP discount proves that you were a volunteer at the park or historic site that day.

Get the organization's qualifying IRS number (sometimes called an EN) or state tax number.

Keep records of automobile costs, tolls, mileage, and any other expenses. You can deduct the mileage costs of attending educational events, or you can deduct actual costs instead of mileage. Keep records of both.

In order to take a deduction, you have to have spent the money. The money you are deducting must actually have been paid out, and not just be a pledge, and it must have been paid in the tax year for which you are filing. The qualifying organization must have been approved by the IRS before you spent the money and claimed the deduction. With some West Coast organizations coming to the East Coast for reenactments, and other groups going to Europe, some big bucks are being shelled out. Looking into tax deductions may be worthwhile.

You cannot deduct for your time in donating services or meals unless there is overnight travel for yourself or dependent care expenses.

You may find that the time spent keeping records and receipts and completing government paperwork isn't worth the deductions. If you do a short form or take the standard deduction, keeping track of expenses and payments may not be worth the savings. Nevertheless, it may pay to check into it.

For your regiment or historic site to be qualified as a charitable or educational organization, there are a number of forms to be filled out for both state and federal taxes. These can be a yearly paperwork headache. Any group that has a tax exempt number, however, has some advantages in attracting new members who may want to deduct some of their expenses.

Appendix H

Civil War
Reenactment Organizations and Sutlers

CIVIL WAR VETERANS AND GENEALOGICAL ORGANIZATIONS

These are nonprofit organizations with little money for overhead. A stamped, self-addressed envelope is always appreciated when you write for information or an application.

Many of the local chapters are fairly independent from the national organizations. Ask for the names and addresses of the local chapters and officers when writing to the national offices; otherwise, you may be signed up only in the national organization and not the local one.

Auxiliary to the Sons of Union Veterans of the Civil War, 1016 Gorman Street, Philadelphia, PA 19116–3719

Dames of the Loyal Legion of the United States of America, Daughters of Union Veterans of the Civil War, 1861–1865, 503 S. Walnut Street, Springfield, IL 62704–1932 <DUVCW@aol.com>

GAR Civil War Museum and Library, 4278 Griscom Street, Philadelphia, PA 19124–3954. (215–673–1688) <garmuslib@aol.com> or <suvcw.org/garmus.htm> Civil War and G.A.R. artifacts.

Hood's Texas Brigade Association, c/o the Harold B. Simpson Confederate Research Center, Hill College, PO Box 619, Hillsboro, TX 76645.

Military Order of the Loyal Legion of the United States (MOLLUS), National Headquarters, Civil War Library and Museum, 1805 Pine Street, Philadelphia, PA 19103.

Military Order of the Stars and Bars (MOSB), PO Box 59, Columbia, TN 38041. <www.scv.org>

Military Order of the Zouave, Militia and Volunteers of the United States (MOZMVUS), 6788 S. Congress Avenue, Lantana, FL 22462.

National Society of Andersonville (NSA), PO Box 48, Andersonville, GA 31711. Descendants of the Andersonville POW Camp.

National Victorian Women's Speaker's Forum, 622 3rd Avenue SW, Pipestone, MN 56164. (507–825–3182) <cwlady@rconnect.com> Programs and presentations.

North-South Skirmish Association (N-SSA), PO Box 361, Bloomfield Hills, MI 48303–0361. (248–258–9007) <www.n-ssa.org> Preserves Civil War heritage through live-fire competitions.

Point Lookout Prisoner of War Camp, 3587 Windmill Drive, Virginia Beach, VA 23456. <members.tripod.com/~PLPOW/plpow.htm> Descendants of Point Lookout, MD, POW Camp.

Sons of Confederate Veterans, PO Box 59, Columbia, TN 38401. (800–380–1896) <www.scv.org>

Sons of Sherman's March to the Sea (SSMS), c/o Stan Shirmacher, 1725 Farmer Avenue, Tempe, AZ 85281.

Sons of Union Veterans of the Civil War (SUVCW), David Hann, National Secretary, 440 Clark Drive, Hammonton, NJ 08037. (609–567–7527) <Colellet@erols.com> or <www.suvcw.org>

Women's Relief Corps, Auxiliary to the GAR, Lucille Streeter, 782 W. Girad Road, Sherwood, MI 49089, <streeterla@cbpu.com>

REENACTMENT SUTLERS AND MANUFACTURERS

Many of these sutlers have mail-order catalogs. Some will request a few dollars to help with printing costs, or at least a stamp or two for postage. This is not a complete list, nor are all the items sold authentic. Before you buy, check with other members of your unit for their suggestions and find out your unit's requirements. All good reenactment units have written guidelines for their uniforms and equipment. Get the essentials (boots, uniform, leather gear, and rifle) first.

In reenacting, there are two kinds of sutlers. First are the manufacturers, who make the goods. These people sell their goods directly to the reenactors, and to other sutlers, who retail the goods to reenactors as well. There is a need for both. The retail sutlers can carry lines from several manufacturers and can carry a wider, more extensive line of products. The manufacturers usually concentrate in only a few lines, such as clothing or leather gear, and can't supply all needs.

Many manufacturers can make individual uniforms from specific instructions. As with any handmade products, however, it takes time and effort to do it right. For off-the-shelf products, it's best to go to a sutler retailer, who will have items in stock. If you want a uniform or dress made especially to your specifications, go to one of the manufacturers.

In most cases, these people are reenactors themselves and have a marvelous nineteenth-century outlook to customers and life. They treat their customers with respect, and they demand the same respect in return. Most sutlers have a slower, more personal way of doing business than is customary today, and this is a valid part of the reenacting experience.

There are a few retailers who pander to the public specifically and sell "farb" items and souvenirs at high prices. Most sutlers take great pains to sell only authentic and correct materials, however, and you can ask them any number of questions that they can answer with authority. Very few make a living at this; at most, it is a sideline for very dedicated people. Many of their materials are manufactured by themselves, because there is no one else who can make them correctly. Often, a sutler's catalog is in itself a document to learn from.

The following are sutlers and suppliers of uniforms, clothing, and equipment. Most sutlers in this list are small businesses, prefering to work slowly and correctly. Be patient and ask questions. For the computer literate, a number of websites also have posted sutler lists. A search on your favorite web browser for the terms "sutler," "sutlers," or "sutlery" should bring up a few good web addresses. Many lists differ from each other, and no list is complete (including this one). Most sutlers want the publicity, but many others do not want to be part of a published list, since some do specialized work for specific units or organizations where they are members. Some sutlers manufacture items on request only; others do only contract work. Some engage in sutlery as a hobby and refuse to be overwhelmed by success, which would turn their avocations into real work.

Abraham's Lady, Donna Abraham, 1402 St. Matthew Drive, Verga, NJ 08093. (609-853-6882) <abraham@citent.com> New store location at: 47 Steinwehr Avenue, Gettysburg, PA 17325 (717–338–1798). Notions, trims, and accessories.

Tim Allen, 1429 Becket Road, Eldersburg, MD 21784. (410–549–5145) Men's hats.

Amazon Drygoods, Janet Brugess, 2218 E. 11th, Davenport, IA 52803. (800–798–7979 for orders) (319–322–4003 Fax) <www.amazondrygoods.com> Reenactment suppliers and manufacturers, books, patterns, and shoes.

Elizabeth Ann, PO Box 716, Middlefield, OH 44602. (440–632–9808) Sutler.

Antique Optics, Malcolm Addoms. (804–648–7616) <antqoptics@aol.com> Field glasses, telescopes, etc.

AoP Press, PO Box 1863, Santa Barbara, CA 93116. Military manuals.

Artifakes, Don Rademacher, 1608 W. Pearl Street, Stevens Point, WI 54481. (715–341–5893) Hardee hats, haversacks, knapsacks, shelter halves.

G. H. Bent Company, 7 Pleasant Street, Milton, MA 02186. (617–698–5945) (617–696–7730 Fax) <ghbent@aol.com> Hardtack.

Benckendorf Pipes, PO Box 30062, Des Moines, IA 50310–3330. (515–255–0838) Reproduction and collectible pipes.

Blanket Brigade, PO Box 534, Kunkletown, PA 18058. (610–381–4400) Blankets and clothing.

Blockade Runner, 103 Blackman Boulevard, Wartrace, TN 37183. (931–389–8426) (931–389–0486 Fax) <www.blockaderunner.com> General reenactment supplies.

Blue Heron Mercantile, James Jacobs, 4202 Hillside Drive, Lafayette, IN 47901. (765–474–8426) <Blueheron48@aol.com> Green coffee, parched corn, rope and twine, eighteenth-century items.

Border State Sutler and Museum, Billy D. Byrd, 112 West Kentucky Avenue, Franklin, KY 42134. (502–586–9343) <byrd@kih.net> Period clothing, leather gear, books, and weapons.

Border States Leatherworks, Douglas Kidd, 1158 Apple Blossom Lane, Springdale, AR 72762. (501–361–2642) <cavsaddler@aol.com> Cavalry and artillery goods.

Bowdoin Explosive Company, 287 John Tarr Road, Bowdoin, ME 04287. (207–737–2630) (207–737–5747 Fax) <www.bowdoinexplosives.com> Black powder.

Broadfoot Publishing Company, 1907 Buena Vista Circle, Wilmington, NC 28411. (910–686–4816) (800–537–5243 for orders) Book publisher.

Lynn E. Bull, 809 North Spence Avenue, Goldsboro, NC 27534. (919–778–7032) Historical clothing 1760–1865.

C & C Sutlery, 3353 Fuller Road, Emmett, ID 83617. (208–398–7279) General reenactor supplies.

M. J. Cahn Company Inc., 510 West 27th Street, New York, NY 10001–5506. (212–563–7292) <daniel@inch.com> Cloth for uniforms, clothing, headgear.

California Millinery Supply Company, Irene Arroyo, 721 South Spring Street, Los Angeles, CA 90014. (213–622–8746) (213–622–0438 Fax) <calmil@loop.com> Vintage supplies for hatmaking.

Caps and Kepis, 2665 Longfellow Drive, Wilmington, DE 19808. (302–994–6428) <capskepis1@aol.com> Forage caps and kepis.

The Carpetbagger, 7805 Main Street, Middletown, VA 22645. (540–869–7732) (800–840–1865 for orders) <sales@thecarpetbagger.com> Carpetbags, haversacks, and traveling bags.

Carrico's Leatherworks, 811 5000 Road, Edna, KS 67342. (316–922–7222) (316–922–3311 Fax) Saddles, slings.

Cartridges Unlimited, 4320 A Hartford Street, St. Louis, MO 63116. (314–664–4332) Black powder, caps, and cartridges.

Cathleen's, 1122 Grand Avenue, Frankfort, KY 40601. (502–223–7208) <Cathleens1@aol.com> Clothing for ladies and gentlemen.

Cavalry Shop, 9700 Royerton Drive, Richmond, VA 23228. (804–266–0898) Infantry, cavalry, and artillery gear.

Chattahoochee Black Powder Arms, 4153 Drew Road, Cumming, GA 30040. (888–889–3711) Firearms.

Mrs. Christen's Miscellanea, Glenna Jo Christen, 28078 Universal Drive, Warren, MI 48092. <gwjchris@rust.net> or <rust.net/~gwjchris/ GCATALOG.HTML> Antique, reproduction, and vintage items for ladies.

Cinderella Flower and Feather, Division of Margola Import Company, Neil Chalfin, 48 W. 37th Street or 62 W. 38th Street, New York, NY 10018. (212–840–0644) Flowers, feathers, and assorted trim.

Civil-La-Tea, 39 York Street, Gettysburg, PA 17325. (717–334–0992) Women's accoutrements, tea.

Civil War Lady Dry Goods Store, 622 3rd Avenue SW, Pipestone, MN 56164. (507–825–3182) <cwlady@rconnect.com> Women's historical clothing store.

Civil War Vintage Watches, Michael D. Clark, PO Box 641, Williamsburg, OH 45176. (513–724–3167) (513–732–3463 Fax) Antique and period pocket watches.

Clearwater Hat Company, HC 73, Box 646, Clearwater Road, Newnata, AR 72680. (870–746–4324) (870–746–4294 Fax) <www.clearwaterhats.com> Hats for men and ladies.

John A. Coffer and Company, 1236 Dombroski Road, Dundee, NY 14837–9443. Traveling photographer.

The Commissary, Randy Jackson, 825 11th Street, Charleston, IL 61920. (217–345–6386) Contracts to provide period provisions to Civil War units.

The Company Quartermaster, 258 Zimmerman Street, N. Tonawanda, NY 14120–4509 (716–693–3239) Firearms.

The Confederate Postmaster, PO Box 1864, Middletown, CT 06457–1864. (860–632–5004) Envelopes and stationery.

Confederate Socks, Michael Black, 6378 U. S. Highway 601, Salisbury, NC 28147. (704–637–3331) Authentic Confederate and period socks.

The Confederate Treasury, 1100 North Main Street, Tennessee Ridge, TN 37178. (931–721–3303) (800–632–2383 for orders) <www.Confederate Treasury.com> Reproduction CSA money.

Confederate Yankee, Dennis Semrau, PO Box 192, Guilford, CT 06437–0192. (203–453–9900) Men's and women's clothing, 1800–1940s.

Coon River Mercantile, 1152 Amos, Des Moines, IA 50315. (515–287–8315) (515–287–6607 Fax) General reenactment supplies.

County Cloth, Charles R. Childs, 13797-C Georgetown Street NE, Paris, OH 44669. (216–862–3307) Makes uniform kits, material, buttons, blankets.

Crane Mercantile and Manufacturing, 4829 Coleman Road, Villa Ridge, MO 63089. (314–451–2551) (314–451–2553 Fax) Civil War saddles and hardware.

Crescent City Sutler, 17810 N. Highway 57, Evansville, IN 47711, (812–938–4217) Uniforms, tents, boots, and books.

P. M. Cunningham, 1034 Park Ave., Madison, IN 47250. (812–273–4193) Tinware.

T. Czekanski Leatherworks, 925 Montegut Street, New Orleans, LA 70117–7201. (504–945–8797) <Tczekanski@aol.com> Leather gear such as belts, knapsacks and cartridge boxes.

D & N Mercantile, 82 Newcomb Drive, Ventura, CA 93003. (805–644–7858) <dnmerc@rain.org> General reenactment supplies.

C. J. Daley Historical Reproductions, 105 West Green Street, Middletown, MD 21769. (301–371–5792) <chrisdaley@erols.com> Federal clothing and haversacks.

Davis Distributing Company, PO Box 743, Findlay, OH 45839. (419–422–2227) (419–422–3937 Fax) GOEX Black Powder.

Dell's Leather Works, David E. Dellacato, 83 First Avenue, Kingston, NY 12401. (914–339–4916) <www.dellsleatherworks.com> Leather goods, slings, suspenders.

Dirty Billy's Hats, Bill Wickham, 7574 Middleburg Road, Detour, MD 21757. (410–775–1865) <dirtybillyshats.com> Retail shop: 430A Baltimore Street, Gettysburg, PA 17315. (717–334–3200). Hats and kepis.

Dixie Gun Works Inc., PO Box 130, Union City, TN 38261. (800–238–6785) <www.dixiegun.com> Weapons and supplies.

Dixie Leather Works, PO Box 8221, Paducah, KY 42002–8221. (502–442–1058) (800–888–5183 for orders) Leather goods, trunks, hats.

Drummer Boy, Christian Hill Road, RR 4, Box 7198, Milford, PA 18337. (717–296–7611) Uniforms, buttons, leather goods, insignia.

Mrs. Eddins Fine Sewing Emporium, Nancy Eddins, 186 Hayes Circle, Rex, GA 30273. (707–389–1470) <mrseddins@yahoo.com> Custom sewing for men and women.

Elephant Black Powder, 7650 US Highway 287, #100, Arlington, TX 76001. (800–588–8282) <www.elephantblackpowder.com>

Mary Ellen and Company, 100 North Main Street, North Liberty, IN 46554. (219–656–3000) (800–669–1860 for orders) Ladies clothing, accessories, patterns, and books.

Euroarms of America, PO Box 3277, 208 E. Piccadilly Street, Winchester, VA 22604. (540–662–1863) (540–662–4464 Fax) Replica rifles and pistols, and black powder.

Fair Oaks Sutler Inc., Dennis D. Boettcher, 9905 Kershaw Ct., Spotsylvania, VA 22553. (540–972–7744) <www.fairoakssutler.com> General reenactor supplies.

Fall Creek Corporation, PO Box 92, Whitestown, IN 46075. (765–482–1861) (765–482–1848 Fax) <http://fcsutler.com> PO box 530, Freedom CA 95019. (408–728–1888) (408–728–1853 Fax) Reenactment supplies and accoutrements.

Family Heir-Loom Weavers, David Kline, 775 Meadow View Drive, Red Lion PA 17356. (717–246–2431) Patrick Kline, 125 O'San Lane, Red Lion, PA 17356. (717–246–5797) <www.familyheirloomweavers.com> Weaves period fabrics and does commission weaving.

First Corps Books, Mike Wadsworth, 126 Silvermill Road, Columbia, SC 29210–4428. (803–798–5513) <FirstCorps@msn.com> Out of print books.

Foot Mountain Cobblery, Jim Yeiser, 420 South Washington Street, Baltimore, MD 21231. <www.civilwarshoes.com> Handmade boots and shoes.

Forge and Anvil, Charles Keller, PO Box 51, Newman, IL 61942. (217–352–0803) Blacksmith.

Fort Branch Supply, Ken Bucher, 146 Country Farm Road, PO Box 190, Windsor, NC 27840. (919–794–5400) <www.entgroup.com/fbs> Wooden canteens, trunks.

Frazer Brothers, 5641 Yale Boulevard, Suite 125, Dallas, TX 75206. (214–428–1865) (214–361–9137 Fax) Canteen halves and tinware.

Fugawee Corporation, 3127 Corrib Drive, Tallahassee, FL 32308. (800–749–0387) <www.fugawee.com> Boots, shoes and buttons.

Genteel Arts Academy, Carolann Schmitt, PO Box 3014, Gettysburg, PA 17325. (717–337–0283) <www.cvn.net/~cschmitt/> Men's and women's clothing seminars.

Gettysburg Sutler, Ron Palese, 1180 Hanover Road, Gettysburg, PA 17325. (717–337–9669) (717–337–3245 Fax) Men's and women's clothing.

Gohn Brothers, 105 South Main, PO Box 111, Middlebury, IN 46540–0111. (219–825–2400) (800–595–0031 Orders) Amish and plain clothing.

Goldberg Textiles, Patrick Brown, 2495 S. Alden Street, Salt Lake City, UT 84106. (801–467–2343) (801–944–8204 Fax) Clothing kits and tinware.

Goose Bay Workshops, 990 Greenwood Road, Crozet, VA 22932. (540–456–7111) (540–456–6990 Fax) Tin, copper and brass cookware and related items.

Grand Illusions, Sunny and Maurice Whitlock, 705 Interchange Boulevard, Newark, DE 19711. (302–366–0300) <www.grand-illusion.com> Retail store: 100 Baltimore Street, Gettysburg, PA 17325 (717–337–1220) Classic attire.

Grand Spectacle, 528 W. Water Street, Elmira, NY 14905. (607–732–7500) (607–732–6045 Fax) <www.thegrandspectacle.com> Period prescription glasses.

Jefferson Grant Woodworks, PO Box 291, Newark, DE 19715. (302–368–1650) Period furnishings, toys, accessories.

Guns and Stuff, 6379 Griffith Highway, Whitwell, TN 37397. (423–942–3844) Firearms and supplies.

Hand Sewin' Shirts, Jodee Himebaugh, 26723 N. Isabella Parkway #103, Canyon Country, CA 91351–4892. (805–251–7143) <USDragoon@aol.com> Tailoring.

Hanover Brass Company, PO Box 550, Norge, VA 23127. (757–564–0606) <www.hanoverbrass.com> Handcast brass buckles, etc.

Harriet's TCS, PO Box 1363, Winchester, VA 22604. (540–667–2541) Retail Store: Millwood Crossing, Winchester, VA 22601. (540–662–5157) Handmade clothing.

Hatcrafter's Inc., Victor H. Heantze, 20 N. Springfield Road, Clifton Heights, PA 19018. (610–623–2620) (610–284–2620 Fax) <www.Hatcrafters.com> Period hats and materials.

Haversack Depot, 1236 River Acres Drive, PO Box 311262, New Braunfels, TX 78131. (830–620–5192)

Heirloom Emporium, 24 Leffingwell Drive, Orwell, OH 44076. (440–437–8563) Ladies' and childrens' clothing.

Heritage Reproductions, Kelly Krause, 1811 Jeanette Avenue, Evansville, IN 47714. (812–473–5233) Authentic cage crinolines and other accessories.

Historic Clothiers, Nick Sekela, 16 Boonton Ave., Butler, NJ 07405. (973–283–0800) <www.HistCloth.com> Federal enlisted man's uniforms, headgear, and footwear.

Honest Tom's Sutlery, 6920 Yuma Way, Bakersfield, CA 93308–6469. (805–589–8452) <honesttomssutler@aol.com> General reenactment supplies.

House of Times Past, 102 E. Pickens Street, Abbeville, SC 29620. (864–459–0325) <hotp@thepast.com> General reenactment supplies.

I. C. Mercantile, 122 East Jewel Street, Republic, MO 65738. (417–732–8495) Army and civilian boots.

Ironman Forge, Bruce Noordzy, 572 Hollow Horn Road, Ottsville, PA 18942. (610–847–2748) <Ironforg@epix.net> Traditional blacksmithing.

James Country Mercantile, 111 N. Main Street, Liberty, MO 64068. (816–781–9473) (816–781–1470 Fax) <JAMESCNTRY@aol.com> General reenactor supplies.

C & D Jarnagin, PO Box 1860, Corinth, MS 38834–1860. (601–287–4977) (601–287–6033 Fax) <www.jarnaginco.com> General reenactment supplies.

Jessup Mercantile Company, F. Addison, Route 1, Box 20–B, Westfield, NC 27053. (336–351–3604) Clothing, shoes, accessories.

The Jeweler's Daughter, Susan Saum-Wicklein, 2–4 W. Washington Street, Hagerstown, MD 21740. (301–733–6741) <www.jewelersdaughter.com> Victorian reproduction jewelry.

Johnnie O's, PO Box 25083, Providence, RI 02905. (401–781–0725) Period watches and chains.

K & P Weaver, PO Box 1131, Orange, CT 06477–7131. (203–795–9024) <KPWEAVER@aol.com> Clothier for men.

Kentwood Sutlery and Manufacturing, PO Box 88201, Kentwood, MI 49518. (616–531–7645) Wooden items, watches.

Kathy Kleiman, 10264 Eagle Nest Court, FairFax, VA 22032. <dortheadix@aol.com> (703–323–1219) Knitted socks and other items to order.

L & H Hats, Jim McMicking, 179 Melville Street, Dundas, ON L9H 2A9 Canada. (905–627–7492) Men's and women's made-to-order hats.

Lady Deborah's Historical Fashions, Debbie Hudson, 15 Hickory Court, Webb, AL 36376. (334–793–7920) Seventeenth to nineteenth century clothing.

Robert Land, 593 Willow Road, Guelph, ONT N1H 7J8 Canada. (519–836–0747) (519–836–2689 Fax) Footwear.

Legendary Arms Inc., PO Box 479, Three Bridges, NJ 08887–0479. (800–528–2767) Edged weapons.

Lepierre Sutler, Fred M. Healy, 3727 Verona Caney Road, Lewisburg, TN 37091. (615–364–7424) Leather and accoutrements

Levi Ledbetter, Sutler, Frank Lanning, 7032 Mineral Springs Road, Oakboro, NC 28129. (704–485–4746)

Liberated Goods, Dave Henshall, 15251 Eclipse Drive, Manassas, VA 20112–4028. (703–897–1861) Retail outlet at: Featherstone Square Antique Mall, 14567 Jefferson Davis Highway, Woodbridge, VA 22191 (703–491–9099) <liberatedgoods@erols.com> Used reproduction uniforms, clothing, and equipment.

Lodgewood Mfg., William Osborne, PO Box 611, Whitewater, WI 53190. (414–473–5444) <lodged@idcnet.com> Firearms and parts.

Lucinda's Sewing Room, 14961 Rea Magnet Road, Laurinburg, NC 28352. (910–280–1970) Accessories and underpinnings for ladies.

Mac's Sutlery, Bill MacIntosh, No. 1235 Battery Avenue, Baltimore, MD (410–962–8503) Mercantile goods of all sorts: "I don't do catalogs."

Mad Hatter Millinery, Carol Mitchell, 4530 Bailey Road, Dimondale, MI 48821 (517–646–6103) Jennifer Mitchell, 3248 Creston, Lansing, MI 48917. (517–374–9631) <cmmitch@juno.com> Headgear and hairpieces.

Maki's Boxes and Mercantile, 1521 Franklin Avenue, Lexington, MO 64067. (660–259–2200) Shipping boxes, tin cans, labels.

S. G. Marinos Company, PO Box 3192, Gettysburg, PA 17325–3192. (717–334–6568) General reenactment supplies.

Heidi Marsh Patterns, 3494 North Valley Road, Greenville, CA 95947. Ladies' and men's patterns for military and civilian clothing.

Martha's Authentic Designs, Martha Aytes, PO Box 1714, Fletcher, NC 28732. (828–684–5557) (828–684–5572 Fax) <maytes1860@aol.com> Women's clothing.

Mattimore Harness, 509 South Second Street, Laramie, WY 82070. (307–745–8460) Brogans and civilian shoes, shoe repair, belts, slings.

Mrs. Martin's Mercantile and Millinery, 4566 Oakhurst Drive, Sylvania, OH 43560–1736. (419–474–2093) Ladies clothing, seminars and instruction.

McKechnie-Lid Design and Research, 1146 N. Centra Avenue, #110, Glendale, CA 91202–2506. (818–500–8725) (818–243–8328 Fax) <Mckechlid@aol.com> Ladies' and men's civilian clothing.

Mechanical Baking Company, PO Box 513, Pekin, IL 61554. (309–353–2414) <jlarkin@mtco.com> Bakers of army-style hardtack biscuits.

Media Magic, 3120 Pine Tree Road, Lansing, MI 48911. (517–393–3100) Videotapes of army drill.

Mercury Supply Company Sutler, 101 Lee Street, Livingston, TX 77351. (409–327–3707) (409–327–3791 Fax) <mercurys@livingston.net>. General reenactment supplies.

Butch Meyers, 6507 Horsepen Road, Richmond, VA 23226. (804–288–9380) Leather gear.

Mill Creek Mercantile and Millinery, Carol Lee Peter, PO Box 428815, Cincinnati, OH 45242–8815. (513–891–6709) Custom-made ladies' clothing.

Miller's Millinery, Lynette R. Miller, PO Box 8077, Lancaster, PA 17604–8077. (717–285–3373) (717–285–3629 Fax) <http://bonnets.com> Period head wear patterns and custom items.

Missouri Boot and Shoe Company, Robert Serio, 951 Burr Crossing Road, Neosho, MO 64850. (417–451–6100) Boots and shoes.

Morningside Bookshop, 260 Oak Street, Dayton, OH 45410. (800–648–9710) <www.morningsidebooks.com> Bookshop and republisher of out-of-print Civil War books.

Navy Arms Company, 689 Bergen Boulevard, Ridgefield, NJ 07657. (201–945–2500) (201–945–6859 Fax) <www.navyarms.com> Firearms.

Needle and Thread, 2215 Fairfield Road, Gettysburg, PA 17325. (717–334–4011) Period fabrics and patterns.

New Richmond Depot, Chris White, 2308 M Street, Richmond, VA 23223–7238 (804–644–0601) <cwhite@aol.com> Confederate jackets and pants.

Old Dominion Forge, Howard Pohn, 709 Cattail Road., Winchester, VA 22603. (540–722–2139) Handforging and designs.

Old Sutler John, John W. Ferry, PO Box 174, Westview Station, Binghamton, NY 13905. (607–775–4434) General reenactment supplies.

Ole Church Emporium, 1187 Burrville Road, Sunbright, TN 37872. (423–628–5528) General reenactor supplies, firearms.

Wendy K. Osman, 5424 Elliott Avenue S., Minneapolis, MN 55417. (612–823–4009) Buttons, officers' insignia, tinware.

Owens Accouterments, James Owens, 2114 Belvedere Boulevard, #2, Silver Spring, MD 20902. (301–681–7462) Federal haversacks, slings, scabbards, cap box.

Panther Primitives, PO Box 32, Normantown, WV 25267. (304–462–7718) (304–462–7755 Fax) <Pantherlodges.com> Manufacturer of canvas tents and multi-period camping goods.

Past Patterns, PO Box 2446, Richmond, IN 47374–2446. (765–962–3333) (765–962–3773 Fax) <www.pastpatterns.com> Patterns for men's and ladies' clothes.

Paulson Brothers Ordnance Corporation, PO Box 121, Clear Lake, WI 54005. (715–263–3300) Artillery parts.

Peninsula Firearms and Sutlery, Terry Cummings, 7116 78th Street N., Pinellas Park, FL 33781. (727–547–6471) (727–547–6174 Fax) General reenactment supplies.

Period Impressions, 1320 Dale Drive, Lexington, KY 40517. Patterns for clothing.

Petticoat Junction, 307 Lakeside Avenue, Angola, NY 14006. (716–549–4998) <Livhis@aol.com> Women's civilian clothing.

Quartermaster Shop, Jeff O'Donnell, 5565 Griswold Road, Kimball, MI 48074–1906. (810–367–6702) (810–367–6514 Fax) General reenactment supplies.

R & K Sutlery, 1015 1200th Street, Lincoln, IL 62656. (217–732–8844) <www.sutlery.com> Uniforms and civilian wear.

Ragged Soldier Sutlery, PO Box 10311, Burke, VA 22009–0311. (703–978–3925) <mmescher@mail.erols.com> Children's toys and books.

Re-enactment Eyewear, Don Griffin, 1738 E. Third Street, #346, Williamsport, PA 17701. (570–322–9849) Period prescription eyeglasses.

Regimental Quartermaster, PO Box 553, Hatboro, PA 19040. (215–672–6891) <http://members.aol.com/regtqm> Retail Store: 45–47 Steinwehr Avenue, Gettysburg, PA 17325. (717–338–1864) General reenactor supplies.

Richmondville, PO Box 407, Aurora, OR 97002. (503–678–1675) Tinware.

Ron's Photography, Ronald A. Burgess, 770 State Route 97 E., Bellville, OH 44813. (419–886–4835)

Running Iron Outfitters, PO Box 205, Sonoita, AZ 85637. (520–455–5858) Boots, brogans, and shoes.

S & S Firearms, 74–11G Myrtle Avenue, Glendale, NY 11385. (718–497–1100) <www.ssfirearms.com> Original and reproduction rifle parts, insignia.

Sands Sutler of Gettysburg, Tim Sheads, PO Box 218, 135 Kime Avenue, Bendersville, PA 17306–0218. (717–677–7580) <sheads@mail.cvn.net> General reenactment supplies.

Santa Fe Sales, 1 Ranch Club Road, Suite 3–402, Silver City, NM 88061. Historical accessories, books, and manuals.

Chris Schreiber, 143 Ravenhurst Avenue, Staten Island, NY 10310. (718–442–5997) Leather gear.

Servant and Company, 230 Steinwehr Avenue, Gettysburg, PA 17325. (800–GETTYS–1) <www.servantandco.com> General reenactment supplies.

Shamrock Hill, Ed O'Dwyer, 12725 Bethany Road, Alpharetta, GA 30004–1080. (770–569–1802) (770–569–1801 Fax) <http://Bookguy.com> Books for the reenactor, muskets, videos.

Sidekick Sutler, PO Box 53733, Indianapolis, IN 46523. (317–293–0587) Canteens, plates, cups, bowls.

Luther Sowers, 5050 Statesville Boulevard, Salisbury, NC 28147. (704–633–4170) Federal bayonet scabbards.

Spectacle Accoutrements, Gregg Crockett, 2918 N. Rolling Road, Baltimore, MD 21244. (410–281–6069) Period prescription glasses.

Stoney Brook Company, Chris Sullivan, 50 Porreca Drive, Millville, NJ 08332. (609–825–7307) <sullivan@algorithms.com> Federal trousers, shirts.

Sullivan Press, PO Box 1711, West Chester, PA 19380–0057. (610–286–7905) <sullpress@aol.com> Paper goods, a few books.

The Sutler of Mount Misery, G. Gedney Godwin, 2139 Welsh Valley Road, Valley Forge, PA 19481. (610–783–0670) (610–783–6083 Fax) <gggodwin.com> Seventeenth- and eighteenth-century items.

Swamp Fox Sutlery, Craig Pierce, RR 1, Box 3090, DeKalb, MO 64440. (816–685–3215) <missouriswampfox.com> Hats and uniforms.

Benjamin Tart, PO Box 28, Spring Hope, NC 27882. (252–478–7668) Sumac-dyed jeans, buttons.

Tentsmiths, Peter Marques, Box 1748, Conway, NH 03818. (603–447–2344) <tentsmiths.com> Tents from Vikings to present.

Thistle Hill Weavers, Rabbit Goody, 101 Chestnut Ridge Road, Cherry Valley, NY 13320. (518–284–2729) <www.quilthistory.com/rabbit.htm> Reproduction period cloth and textiles.

Mike Thompson, 3519 Loganview Drive, Dundalk, MD 21222. (410–288–5284) Knapsacks, haversacks.

Jas. Townsend and Sons Inc., 133 North First Street, PO Box 415, Pierceton, IN 46562. (800–338–1665) <www.jastown.com> Mostly Revolutionary War, but some Civil War.

T, P & H Trading Company, 121 Carriage Drive, Birdsboro, PA 19508. (610–582–0327) "Double bow" hats.

Trans Mississippi Depot, PO Box 5273, Santa Barbara, CA 93150. (805–969–2328) (805–969–4749 Ext.51 Fax) Roller buckle belts and personal items.

Uniforms of Antiquity, Mike and Bette Bradley, 122 Sweetgum Lane, Mena, AR 71953. (870–389–6308) <pbradley@cswnet.com> Made to order uniforms and clothing.

Upper Mississippi Valley Mercantile Company, 1607 Washington Street, Davenport, IA 52804. (319–322–0896) (319–383–5549 Fax) <musket@mcleodusa.net> Weapons, uniforms, insignia, accessories.

Uriah Cap and Clothier, PO Box 93, 220 Old Route 30, McKnightstown, PA 17343. (717–337–3929) Union forage caps types I and II.

USA History Store, PO Box 109, Middleboro, MA 02346. (508–947–8866) <usahistorystore.com> Brass candlesticks, flags, bunting, pottery.

Victoria Louise, PO Box 266, Jefferson, MD 21755. (301–473–4140) Patterns, lace, fine sewing, and millinery.

Village Tinsmithing Works, Bill and Judy Hoover, PO Box 539, Hamptonville, NC 27020. (336–468–1190 Fax 1191) A variety of tin items.

Spence Waldron, PO Box 51, Cherry Valley, NY 13320. (607–264–3678) Federal uniforms.

Ward Family Knitgoods, Patti Ward, 1731 Beauregard Drive, Lilbum, GA 30047. (770–978–6423) <Wardfamily7@mindspring.com>

John M. Wedeward, 1900 Pleasant View Drive, Stoughton, WI 53589. (608–873–8503) Sack coats.

Winchester Sutler, 270C Shadow Brook Lane, Winchester, VA 22603–8509. (540–888–3595) General reenactment supplies.

Wisconsin Veterans Museum, 30 West Mifflin Street, Madison, WI 53703. <http://badger.state.wi.us/agen> or <cies/dva/museum/giftshop.html> Authentic blankets.

Women's Nation, 325 Avenel Street, Avenel, NJ 07001–1534. (732–726–1716) Ladies' jewelry.

Zangroniz Photography, Julio Zangroniz, 4011 Muncaster Mill Road, Rockville, MD 20853. <marzan@idsonline.com> Photography, calendars.

John A. Zaharias, Sutler (The Button Baron), PO Box 31152, St. Louis, MO 63131. (314–966–2829) <JAZSUTLER@worldnet.att.net> General reenactor supplies, buttons.

John G. Zimmerman, PO Box 1351, 1195 Washington Street, Harpers Ferry, WV 25425. (304–535–2558) <www.edsmart.com/jz> Firearms.

Appendix I

Reenacting Periodicals

There are many magazines that teach the history of the mid-nineteenth century—almost too many to mention. The most popular among Civil War reenactors are *Civil War Times Illustrated, Military Images, Blue and Gray, American Heritage,* and *Gettysburg.*

All of the magazines listed here have articles on history, living history, and reenacting; calendars of forthcoming events; and advertising by suppliers of reenactment materials. Names and address of suppliers and sutlers are listed in the newspapers *(Camp Chase Gazette, Civil War Lady,* and *Civil War News).* You can often borrow a copy from another member of the regiment. This book also includes an appendix (H) listing sutlers and suppliers.

Before any equipment purchase, a new recruit should always consult with another regimental member concerning the authenticity of the item. A reenactor who uses or wears unauthentic materials is known as a "farb" or "polyester soldier" and is often not allowed to participate in reenactment events.

Although there are many other magazines available on the WBTS period and military history, the following seem to be of the most interest to reenactors:

Camp Chase Gazette, Citizen's Companion, PO Box 707, Marietta, OH 45750. (800–449–1865) Magazines for reenactors. $24.00 per year

The Civil War Courier, 2503 Delaware Avenue, Buffalo, NY 14216. (800–418–1861)

Civil War Lady: Women in Reenacting, 622 3rd Avenue SW, Pipestone, MN 56164. (507–825–3182) <cwlady@rconnect.com> $21.00 per year

Civil War News, 234 Monarch Hill Road, Tunbridge, VT 05077. (800–777–1862) <www.civilwarnews.com> $27.00 per year (11 issues)

Harper's Weekly, 128 The Great Road, PO Box 365, Bedford, MA 01730–9858. (87–OLDNEWS) <www.harpersweekly.com> A subscription to the reprinted original weekly newspaper

Harriet's Then and Now, 1 North Nabby Road, Danbury, CT 06811. (203–730–2122) $30.00 per year (6 issues)

Living History, PO Box 77, Fairfax, VA 22030. <Livinghistoryonline.com>

Military Images, Route 1, Box 99-A, Henryville, PA 18322. <www. civilwar-photos.com> $24.00 per year (6 issues)

Our Young Folks, 1865, New England and Virginia Co., PO Box 8511, Salem, MA 01971–8511. Reprint of the original magazine for children. $35.50 per year

Peterson's Magazine, 1864, New England and Virginia Co., PO Box 8511, Salem, MA 01971–8511. Reprint of the original magazine. $57.00 per year

Smoke and Fire News, PO Box 166, Grand Rapids, OH 43522. (800–766–5334) $18.00 per year (monthly), $2.00 for sample issue

The Watchdog, PO Box 1675, Warren, MI 48090–1675.<watchdog@rust. net> $15.00 per year

Notes

1: REENACTMENT, LIVING HISTORY, AND TEACHING HISTORY

1. For the growth of pageantry and the movements at the turn of the century, see David Glassberg, *American Historical Pageantry: The Uses of Tradition in the Early Twentieth Century* (Chapel Hill, NC: University of North Carolina Press, 1980).
2. For a history of the GAR, see Stuart McConnell, *Glorious Contentment: The Grand Army of the Republic, 1865–1900* (Chapel Hill, NC: University of North Carolina Press, 1991).
3. Michael Kammen, *Mystic Chords of Memory: The Transformation of Tradition in American Culture* (New York: Knopf, 1991), 456.
4. John Bodnar, *Remaking America: Public Memory, Commemoration, and Patriotism in the Twentieth Century* (Princeton, NJ: Princeton University Press, 1992), ISBN: 0691047839. 213–26.
5. John Skow, et al., "Bang, Bang! You're History, Buddy," *Time* (August 11, 1986): 58.
6. There are many theories for the origin of the word "farb." In a letter in the February–March 1995 *Civil War News*, Ross M. Kimmel states that it was used at the Manassas reenactment in 1961. He affected the term "pharbie." According to another theory, the term "farb" came from the joking use of "Far be . . ." During the Bicentennial, when many of the ideals of authentic reenacting were

established, one unit had a historian who was so exact that he would comment, "Far be it from me to criticize, but you seem to have twelve stitches per inch in your shirt cuff, when most Revolutionary War soldiers only had ten." Another suggestion is that it is from Farberware, a manufacturer of bright aluminum or stainless steel pots and pans. Farbe is a German word meaning "color," so it may have some reference to bright or inappropriate colors, and the German word for "manufactured" is farbische. Juanita Leisch calls it "Fast And Researchless Buying," and other sources insist it came from the Bicentennial and Revolutionary War groups and means "Fairly Authentic Royal British."

The last word on the origin of the word "farb" comes from Burton K. Kummerow, executive director of the National Museum of Civil War Medicine in Frederick, Maryland (private correspondence, September 26, 1995). Mr. Kummerow states that in 1960 he was involved with a reenactment group called "The Black Hats, C.S.A." One of the members had a particularly lively choice of expressions, sprinkled with fake German, that he regularly shared. This member coined the word "farb" one Sunday in reference to another member of the group. The rest of the Black Hats loved it and used it wherever they went. George Gorman and his 2nd North Carolina picked up the term at the First Manassas Reenactment in 1961 and enjoyed using it constantly with condescension and sarcasm directed toward other units. When the reenactment group split off finally and completely from the North-South Skirmish Association in 1962, the word was part of the baggage that left with the reenactors. It has been in use ever since.

7. Warren Leon and Margaret Piatt, "Living History Museums," in *History Museums in the United States: A Critical Assessment,* ed. Warren Leon and Roy Rosenzweig (Urbana, IL: University of Illinois Press, 1989), 91–92.

8. Freeman Tilden, *Interpreting Our Heritage* (1957; revised, Chapel Hill, NC: University of North Carolina Press, 1978), 7–8.

9. *Ibid.,* 9-10.

10. William J. Lewis, *Interpreting for Park Visitors* (Philadelphia: Eastern Acorn Press, 1981), 81–88.

11. *Ibid.*

12. *Ibid.*

13. Daphne White, "Patriot Games: If the Williamsburg Show Ever Gets an Oscar, It Should Be for Lighting," *Washington Post,* September 13, 1995, B9.

14. Lewis, *Interpreting for Park Visitors,* 27–28.

15. Patricia F. Black, *The Live-In at Old Economy* (Ambridge, PA: Harmonie Associates, 1972), 17–18.

16. Lewis, *Interpreting for Park Visitors,* 81–88.

17. Leon and Piatt, "Living History Museums," 85. For another example of how this is done for more modern history, see Craig Stoltz, "Lawyers on Stage: Reenactment of Famous Trials at the Smithsonian Institution's Folklife Festival," *Association Management* (November 1986), 34–36.

18. William T. Alderson and Shirley Payne Lowe, *Interpretation of Historical Sites,* rev. ed. (Nashville: American Association for State and Local History, 1987), 107. Reprinted with permission from the publishers.

19. Lewis, *Interpreting for Park Visitors,* 81–88.
20. *Ibid.,* 38.

2: REENACTMENT FOR INFANTRYMEN

1. Chris Roberts, Editorial, *The Rebel Boast: The Newsletter of the 26th Regiment, North Carolina State Troops,* December 1991.
2. Ross Kimmel, "Looking Your Best: Authentic Gear and Clothing" (1993 Volunteer Training Seminar for Antietam and Monocacy National Battlefields, Hagertown, Maryland, March 20, 1993).
3. Class A is also sometimes used to refer to the dress uniforms, or at least the most presentable, that are worn on parade or at parties and balls. Class B then means the fatigue uniforms or older, more worn uniforms.
4. Fannie L. Lowe, "Flag of the North Carolina Grays," in *Brief Sketches of the North Carolina State Troops in the War Between the States,* ed. James C. Birdsong (Raleigh, NC: Josephus Daniels, State Printer, 1894), 154–55.
5. *Revised U.S. Army Regulations of 1861,* 463.
6. *Ibid.,* 74.
7. *Ibid.,* 23.
8. Christina Walkley and Vanda Foster, *Crinolines and Crimping Irons* (London: Owen Press, 1978), 40.
9. There is some controversy over wearing the cartridge box under the belt. Hardee's drill indicates that the belt was worn under the cartridge box sling, since the box had to be held by the left hand when bending over to ground arms, or found and opened by the right hand as one step in the loading sequence.
10. One of the reviewers of this manuscript said that this was a questionable conclusion, since some Union infantrymen, particularly Zouaves, did wear the cartridge box looped on their belts. But by far, most photographs show them worn on the leather sling. If you want to wear the box on your belt, check with your unit historian for accuracy and permission.
11. Anne L. MacDonald, *No Idle Hands: The Social History of American Knitting* (New York: Ballantine Books, 1988), 124.
12. *Ibid.,* 109.
13. James 1. Robertson, Jr., *The Civil War* (Washington, DC: U.S. Civil War Centennial Commission, 1963), 49–50.
14. *Revised U.S. Army Regulations of 1861,* 467.
15. Cigarettes were supposed to have been invented by French troops during the Crimean War, and there are numerous other examples of cigarettes or cigarette-like items from remote history. The Oxford English Dictionary documents at least six uses of the word "cigarette" and diminutives before 1852, and the oldest cigarette package dates from Finland in 1860 *(Guiness Book of World Records).* In any case, cigarettes were not typical of Civil War soldiers or officers.
16. *Revised U.S. Army Regulations of 1861,* 42.

17. William J. Hardee, *Hardee's Rifle and Light Infantry Tactics* (1860; reprint, Cornith, MS: C & D Jarnigan Co., 1981), 181.

3: CAMP LIFE

1. Bell I. Wiley, *The Life of Billy Yank* (Baton Rouge, LA: Louisiana State University Press, 1978), 55. The *U.S. Army Regulations* state that one tent should accommodate seventeen soldiers, plus a stove.

4: CIVILIAN REENACTING

1. Both Union and Confederate army regulations allowed four women to each company as washerwomen.
2. Juanita Leisch, "Commentary," *Glass House Gazette (1987),* 3. This has been rewritten for her book, *Who Wore What?*
3. Cecil Willett Cunnington, *Feminine Attitudes in the Nineteenth Century* (New York: Haskell House, Publishers, 1973), 195–97.
4. Walkley and Foster, *Crinolines and Crimping Irons,* 9, 30–31.
5. *Ibid.*
6. *Ibid.,* 128–29.
7. James Laver, *Children's Fashions of the Nineteenth Century* (London: B. T. Batsford, Ltd., 1951), 3–4.
8. Walkley and Foster, *Crinolines and Crimping Irons,* 127–8.

5: REENACTING ETIQUETTE

No notes.

6: HEALTH AND COMFORT

1. Jeffrey Mosser, "Civil War 'Potpourri' II," *Camp Chase Gazette,* XVIII (8) (July1991), 31. Reprinted with permission.
2. *Ibid.,* 30.

7: HOSTING A CIVIL WAR REENACTMENT

1. National Park Service, *Interpretation and Visitor Services Guideline* (Washington, DC: National Park Service, 1980), chapter 2, pages 1–2.

APPENDIX F: U.S. INFANTRY TACTICS

1. The paragraph numbers refer to the paragraph numbers in Hardee's Tactics. Since this is an abbreviated text, the numbers are not necessarily in order or sequential.
2. A variation of this is done at some parks, in which the cartridge is held between the top two fingers but the thumb is kept lightly over the top of the opened cartridge until it's time to pour in the powder. This position with the thumb on top will prevent a flying spark from igniting the powder in the hand. When the cartridge is held next to the muzzle, it should be a bit below the opening.
3. Other parks often use a different method. After placing the rammer down the barrel, especially if the rifle may still be charged, the rifle is placed in the position described in the first position load, except that the right hand is placed over the wrist of the left. If there is still a charge in the rifle and it should go off, the rifle will be pointing away from the body.

Glossary

accoutrements: Usually, the items attached, strapped, or belted to the soldier, including the haversack, canteen, blanket roll, and belt. Additionally, it means anything else attached or carried. Diminutives are the nickname "cooter," usually attached to a younger child who hangs about his older brother; "cootie," the lice and other bugs that "hitch a ride" for the duration; and "couter up," the command to put on the gear and get ready to "fall in."

anachronism: An item that doesn't fit into the time period portrayed. This could mean wearing Mexican War (1840s) or Indian War (1870s) uniform articles during a WBTS (1860s) reenactment. If an item must be out of period, it is more authentic to go backward than forward in time.

approximator: Someone whose clothing, equipment, and activity only outwardly approximates the look of the period, such as wearing a ball gown with a zipper down the back or making up infantry drill commands. The approximator knows this is not correct and settles for it, rationalizing convenience rather than adhering to authenticity.

authentics: People who take great care in their uniform and accoutrements. They are "authentic" reenactors, as opposed to "farbs" or "fanatics." Reenactor Bob Sullivan summed it up nicely: "Authentics—what we do; farbs—those who cut more corners than we do; fanatics—those who cut less corners than we do."

Awkward Squad: A term used when drilling new recruits, who are still awkward. Seasoned soldiers will join the awkward squad as "ballast" so that new recruits can follow the actions of the other soldiers while they learn.

BFH: A term used on the march to warn soldiers behind that there is a "Big f—king hole" ahead. Other warnings include "Step" or "Curb" when there is an obstruction ahead. The warning is passed down the ranks on the march in a low tone.

BOB: "Better Off Bowling." This generally refers to someone who is so out of tune with reenacting that they don't have clue about authenticity.

bridge: A person who acts as a "bridge" between visitors and first-person reenactors, answering questions in today's terms and providing information. See also *dodo*.

camp dress: A practical form of Civil War–period dress without the hem (trail) dragging on the ground or dress hoops; useful for walking around obstructions such as fire pits and road apples when visiting or working in the reenactment site. It is similar to a day dress but is appropriate at all times, whereas other types of women's clothing are dependent on the situation: a day dress for work around the house, a Sunday "go-to-meeting" dress for church, an evening dress for supper, a ball gown for formal dances, and so on. One sign of a lady was her ability to know when to wear what for whom. Some people don't like the term because it doesn't come from the period but describes a dress used during reenactments.

camp followers: Men and women who traveled with the troops. These included sutlers, gamblers, some preachers, and some relatives. Although generally a disparaging term, especially for women, not all camp followers were of ill repute.

camps: A reenactment site is divided into different camps. Besides the Confederate and Union camps, there are often camps for sutlers, or merchants, and civilians. There also may be a modern camping area for those who want to use a camper or modern conveniences. The rest of the camps are authentic and use only period tents and sleeping arrangements. Don't mistake the authentic civilian camp for the modern camping area.

chiefing: The Cherokee in North Carolina use this term to refer to the practice of tourist center staffers wearing the brighter, less authentic Plains Indian "sundance" outfits, with chemical-dyed turkey feathers, instead of traditional Cherokee attire, since this is what the visitors expect because of television misrepresentations and ignorance. The visitors get exactly what they expect and learn nothing new. The living-history people are simply embarrassed because of "farb" outfits.

contraband: A Civil War-period army term for escaped slaves, often applied to both black troops and civilians.

costumed interpreter: A National Park Service term for a third-person interpreter. Reenactors do not especially care for this term because we do not like to refer to our uniforms or civilian clothing as a "costume." See also *living history.*

cowboy: A "farb" or nonauthentic reenactor. Also, one who does not follow rules concerning safety and acts silly or dangerously, or is a glory hound.

daughters: Generally, members of the Daughters of Union Veterans of the Civil War, the United Daughters of the Confederacy, or some other similar organization.

death march: An overly active and physically exhausting reenactment.

death marcher: A disparaging term for an officer who gets the troops lost.

docent: A volunteer at a historic site who gives tours and answers questions. Also, reenactors who lecture to the public and explain what is happening during drills and tacticals. Similar to the "dodo."

dodo: A person who does not take part in the reenactment but acts as an interpreter. Although it sounds silly, this is not a disparaging term and can refer to an interpreter, a sentry who remains in camp while his regiment goes off on drill, or a third-person interpreter and guide in a group of first-person interpreters.

early war or late war: An early-war event is a reenactment of an event that took place during the first or second year of the war, 1861 or 1862. A late-war event is a reenactment of an event from the period 1863 to 1865. For Confederate reenactors, it usually means a change in uniforms.

elephant: To "see the elephant" is to have seen action. A new recruit who has not taken part in a tactical has not "seen the elephant."

fan: A piece of ordnance used by women to capture men. Normally used for cooling, a fan was also an important part of the flirting conventions of the era.

farb: Nonperiod, non-authentic equipment, or the person who uses it, also known as "cowboy" or "polyester soldier." Variations on the term include farbette, farble, farb-fest, farb-a-thon, farb-wannabe. There are many theories on the origin of the word, such as adaptions of "Far be it for me to criticize, but . . ." or "Fast and Researchless Buying" or "Fairly Authentic Royal British" or an acronym for barf. The last word on its origin comes from Burton K. Kummerow (private correspondence, September 26, 1995). Mr. Kummerow states that in 1960 he was involved with a reenactment group called The Black Hats, CSA. One of the members had a particularly lively choice of expressions, sprinkled with fake German, that he regularly shared with the rest of the group. This member coined the word "farb" one Sunday in reference to another member of the group. The rest of the Black Hats loved it and used it wherever they went. George Gorman and his 2nd North Carolina then picked up the term at the Centennial Manassas Reenactment in 1961 and enjoyed using it with condescension and sarcasm directed toward other units. When the reenactment group split off from the North-South Skirmish Association in 1962, the word became part of the language that left with the reenactors. It has been in use ever since.

file closer: A noncommissioned officer placed at either end of a line who makes sure that the men keep in place when marching. This man may be sent to a particular spot, and the rest of the line will then "close," or line up next to him. When moving forward, he will be in advance of the line to show where the ends of the line should wind up. The file closer often carries a small flag, called a "guidon," and any man in line can see his place by looking first to the flags in the center of the line, and then to the outside guidon. He then can "guide on" the colors.

first person: A first-person impression is done in living history when the actor assumes the role of a person and acts only in the character of that person. He or she will not come out of character, so spectators feel that they are actually meeting someone from the period portrayed. The term comes from the use of the first person singular: "I marched from Cashtown to Gettysburg, a distance of twelve miles, in three hours last July for the big battle."

five-yard rule. A rule for authenticity, in which an object must be indistinguishable from an original object at a distance of five yards (in decreasing authenticity, some people use ten yards, or fifteen yards, or two miles, and so on).

frag or fragging: A modern term for the deliberate assassination (shooting in the back) of unpopular and dangerous officers or noncoms. Also known as "skagging."

fresh fish: New recruits. Their equipment shines, and they stink.

front-rank material: The front rank is the most seen and watched by spectators. Traditionally, a company will try to have the most accurately uniformed and most experienced men in the front rank, and those who best know the drill. New recruits are often placed in the rear rank, because they are not yet "front-rank material." For safety reasons, however, new recruits are sometimes placed in the front rank, since they may not place their musket barrels correctly over the shoulders of the front-rank men. Often, just before the order to fire, the more experienced front-rank man will discreetly trade places with a new recruit. For authenticity, the height of the soldiers should determine their placement in rank.

galvanize: To change sides. Many times at a reenactment, there will be too many on one side and not enough on the other. Some of the men on one side will volunteer to change sides to make them more equal, and thus become "galvanized" Union or Confederate. Also, many regiments field men on both sides. Oneregiment I belong to does the 26th Regiment, North Carolina Infantry as its main reenactment unit, but also dons Yankee blue as needed as the 19th Regiment, Maine

Infantry. When I first started reenacting in the South, events were small and my unit was the only one around, North or South. We were required to get both Confederate and Union uniforms. The last ones to show up at an event were "punished" by becoming galvanized Yankees.

gods: The inspectors who pass through the ranks of men before the reenactment and check for authenticity and to make sure there are no anachronisms. They have the authority to ask someone inappropriately dressed to fall out, and so are the "gods" or overseers of the event.

guide right (guide left): On the march, a command to move over to one side or the other. Most often used when car traffic is coming down the road. "Guide right" means to move the column over to the right, "guide left," to the left.

ham: A reenactor who overacts for spectators.

hardcores: The ultra-authentics, who would take authenticity to extremes, trying to attain as close to 100 percent accuracy as possible. Many prefer the term "progressive."

hardtack: This was a staple of WBTS food, and was a hard baked biscuit. "Tack" is an old English work for leather, and "hardtack" explains itself. It is guaranteed not to do two things: It will never go bad and it will never taste good.

haversack talk: A "haversack talk," "uniform talk," or "flag talk" is an informal lecture given by members of a unit concerning the types of equipment and clothing used during the Civil War. (Some joker in the unit will always pipe up, "Gee, how do you get a haversack to talk?") It is usually given by a member in front of a tent to passersby, although sometimes several members can join in for a more formal "fashion show." Keep such talks short, and slip in a plug for the conservation and preservation of historic sites.

hayfoot: A new recruit. Many recruits were from small farms and didn't know their left from their right. NCOs would tie bits of hay to the left foot and straw to the right foot, and give the cadence for marching as "Hay foot, straw foot." Since troops march off starting with the left foot—the "hay foot"—a soldier who couldn't even get that right was called a "strawfoot," which meant "dumb recruit," but "strawfoot" most often seems to be applied to an experienced reenactor who makes an obvious mistake. Shortly after the WBTS, these terms were expanded to newcomers out West, and such terms as "sugarfoot" and "tenderfoot" also came into the American vocabulary.

horseshoe: A U-shaped metal plate nailed to the leather heel of the boot. This slows wear on the heel and provides some traction on mud and grass. It's also a tool to test infantry coffee. If a rusty horseshoe thrown in the old coffeepot doesn't float and come up shiny, then the morning coffee isn't ready yet.

hot dog: A reenactor who becomes too active during an event and does something foolish and dangerous, such as engaging in impromptu hand-to-hand fighting.

independent: A person who does not belong to an established regiment. Independents go to whatever event they want to, and fall in with other units as the fancy takes them. Often, these independents portray skilled or technical specialists, such as a blacksmith, doctor, nurse, or signaler. There weren't regiments of such specialists, so it is reasonable for them to be independent. Also, this is a disparaging term used on a battlefield for a person or unit that doesn't obey orders, as in "independent command."

intrusion: One of the pet peeves of civilian reenactors at events: the intrusion of "farby" or modern camping into their authentic area. When event organizers don't know what to do with unauthentic folks, they sometimes send them to the civilian camps. This is a big no-no!

iron underwear: A unit that won't take hits or suffer casualties is said to wear "iron underwear." Also called "ironclads."

Kentucky windage: Originally, in black-powder shooting, to aim slightly away from or above a target to allow for crosscurrents of wind and distance. Now used by reenactors to describe a gross exaggeration.

lean in and look out: A general rule for turning a long line of men in a maneuver called a "wheel," where the men turn like a wheel spoke on an axle. The men lean slightly inward on their comrades and look outward in order to keep the line straight and to prevent a "bow."

living history: Authentic portrayal of a real or fictitious person from another time. The living historian interprets and demonstrates the way of life in that period. Also, National Park Service term for a first-person portrayal. See also *costumed interpreter*.

mannequin: A reenactor who is dressed correctly but does not behave with social or historical accuracy, for example, discussing current sports events during the reenactment.

MOLLUS: An acronym for the Military Order of the Loyal Legion of the United States, a historical and genealogical society made up of descendants of commissioned officers of the United States during the Civil War.

MOSB: An acronym for the Military Order of the Stars and Bars, a historical organization made up of descendants of commissioned officers of the Confederate States.

mule collar: The rolled blanket or quilt that WBTS soldiers wore diagonally across their shoulder to carry their goods. Although many people insist that they be worn only from right shoulder to left hip, Civil War photographs show that it was worn from left shoulder to right hip almost half the time. Many Union troops used the mule collar instead of the heavy backpacks, particularly toward the end of the war, so check with your unit for authenticity. Also called a "horse collar" by the more fastidious.

museum quality: Said of a reproduction item that is so well done that it is suitable for display in a museum. Such a reproduction is often made as an exact copy of an existing example or from an original template.

NPS: National Park Service.

N-SSA: North-South Skirmish Association. Members are into black-powder target shooting, dressed in WBTS costumes.

orphan: A member of a regiment at an event where other members of the regiment don't come. The lone soldier usually falls in with another regiment for that event. He is called an "orphan" and is considered different from an "independent."

penny wrapper: A cheap tube of heavy paper used to roll coins for banks. Unfortunately, these are sometimes incorrectly used by reenactors to make cartridges, in part because they are so convenient. The paper is heavy, however, and when wadded in the barrel of a musket, it becomes potentially lethal and may leak gunpowder into the cartridge box. Such cartridges are dangerous and will not pass inspection.

powder burner: An event that has a great deal of shooting. Also, a dangerous person who shoots wildly.

progressive: New term for hard-core reenactors, it implies someone who is going further into research and a correct impression.

provenance: An item's history. Often a reenactor will show an item and be asked about its provenance. Is it an heirloom or gift, or was it purchased? Is there proof it was used in the WBTS, such as a photograph or other documentation? Archivists and art historians use this term to establish the authenticity of a document, and the term migrated over to reenacting. Also called "pedigree."

provost: Military police, called variously the provost guard, provost marshal, or PMO (Provost Marshal's Office).

reenactment: A scripted enactment of a historical event, such as the Battle of Franklin or the Gettysburg Address.

reproduction: A piece of equipment or clothing newly manufactured in a traditional manner or by authentic standards. It is preferable to using an antique item. Often shortened to "repro."

resurrection: The time at the end of the event when the troops who have taken hits stand up and fall back in line.

road apples: A euphemism for horse droppings.

Scarlett O'Hara: A woman who overacts or overdresses as a "grande dame." Also called a "Magnolia." In either case, a much more polite term than "ham." Variations include "Scarlett Fever."

scenario: A scripted action. A scenario can be big or little and might include a reenactment of a mythical event, such as a skirmish on the Rapidan River in 1864 or mail call in a Confederate camp in 1863. It can be as elaborate or as "loose" as historical accuracy and imagination can supply.

shebang: An interesting lean-to contraption of foraged spare lumber, oilcloth, and canvas, used in lieu of a tent. Very comfortable in warm, dry weather.

site specific: National Park Service term used for any historical interpretation that refers to a specific site, park, or historical area. Confederate uniforms worn at First Manassas in 1861 would not be appropriate for historical interpretation at Appomattox, and thus would not be site specific. The NPS and other organizations want as much as possible to have all historical interpretations be site specific.

snood: A cloth mesh covering for ladies' hair.

sons: Generally, members of the Sons of Confederate Veterans (SCV), descendants of officers and men of the Confederate States, and the Sons of Union Veterans of the Civil War (SUVCW), male descendants of Union veterans.

stitch counter: Originally based on superauthentics from the Revolutionary War camp, who were famous for fatuous statements such as "Far be it from me to criticize, but on this kind of shirt, there were only eleven stitches per inch on the cuff, and I see you have thirteen stitches—you may want to go back and check your sources. . . ." Wes Clark says it is based on an article in the Camp Chase Gazette that never existed: a satire called "The Efficacy of Seam Threads Used in Federal Western Theater Trowsers, April, 1862 to May, 1864." In either case, it describes a kind of reenactor we all know perfectly.

sutler: A merchant who sold goods to the troops. The term applies to both "authentic sutlers," who know and sell authentic reproductions to reenactors, and "gimcrack merchants," who sell cheap souvenirs to the crowds. Also, to "go sutlering" is to go shopping.

tactical: A form of reenactment where the opposing units maneuver and apply authentic military tactics according to WBTS studies. Sometimes they are closed events, in which the public is not invited to observe. Some tacticals take all weekend, and what is taken in on Friday evening is what the soldier eats, sleeps, and fights with over the entire weekend until Sunday afternoon.

tactical lane: A refereed event in which a patrol, company, or regiment proceeds down a "lane" where they will be challenged by another unit. Of most importance are the element of surprise, the refereeing of casualties, and the post-scenario analysis.

TBG: "Tubby Bearded Guy." Disparaging term used by female soldier reenactors to refer to their male counterparts, who criticize them for being unauthentic.

time bandit: A historical researcher, usually a professional historian, who does reenacting as a means of applying scientific principles (testing a hypothesis) to prove or disprove a historical theory. Rarely seen at WBTS reenactments.

time warp: An occasional feeling that the reenactor has actually gone back in time. Giving an emotional jolt, a time warp happens when the environment is so authentic that the historical presentation appears natural, and modern times seem but an intrusion.

Virginia private: A disparaging term for a person of self-appointed higher rank. For example, if a regiment that consists of four members is made up of a general, a colonel, a major, and a captain, they might be referred to as "Virginia privates." I don't like this term, as it singles out one state, but it is used by North Carolina, Kentucky, and Maryland troops, as well as a number of western regiments. There is a perception, perhaps wrong, that many Virginia units are brass heavy. One source thought it was a reference to the inordinate number of Virginians in the General Officer Corps.

virtual regiment (VR): The people from around the world who take part in electronic discussions on the Internet and other electronic bulletin boards and media. The recent growth in popularity of this form of communication is astounding. At some computer literate but historically unauthentic camps, the @ sign from the Internet addresses sometimes appears on a small swallowtail flag.

vivandière: A vivandière (or cantiniere) is a woman or girl who helps keep the spirits of the men raised by helping out in camp. Girls are often accepted as mascots or regimental pets (as was Shirley Temple in the movie *The Little Colonel*). Women usually helped out with chores and were company for the troops. They often wore a feminine variation of the regiment's uniform. A few accounts mentioned the vivandières bringing water to the troops, even while under enemy fire. A reenactment unit should not encourage women to participate in this capacity unless it is documented for that regiment, however.

zebra convention: A disparaging term for any event where there are more noncommissioned officers (referring to their noncom stripes) than was typical of the period.

Bibliography

1: REENACTMENT, LIVING HISTORY, AND TEACHING HISTORY

Anderson, Jay. *Living History Sourcebook*. Nashville: American Association for State and Local History, 1985, ISBN: 0910050759. An excellent introduction to living history in the United States. All time periods are covered, and there is a nice selection of books, suppliers, and annual events.

———. *Time Machines*. Nashville: American Association for State and Local History, 1983. An excellent introduction to the history of authentic reenactment from a historian's perspective. Anderson gives a history of reenactment, the movement toward living history at museums and affairs, and some excellent tips on first-person impressions and reenactment.

Daily, Brian. *The Basics: How to Get Started in Civil War Reenacting*. Austin, IN: privately printed. Illustrated by Ward Williams. A brochure that covers the basics of Civil War reenacting. Originally for new recruits in a reenactment regiment, it covers the history of the 49th Indiana, with information on what is needed to get started as a member of the regiment. Available through interlibrary loan.

Dennison, Will. *Springing to the Call! How to Get Started in Civil War Reenacting*. Marietta. OH: Camp Chase Publishing Company, 1990. 36 pages. An excellent book, with much needed information and advice on how to get started. Recommended as a first purchase.

Hardee, William. *Hardee's Rifle and Light Infantry Tactics, Including the School of the Soldier and the School for the Company.* New York: School of the Soldier J. 0. Kane Publishers, 1860. Reprint. Corinth, MS: C & D Jarnigan Co. This is *the book* of regulations for the infantry soldier reenactor. It has the drills for marching and the tactics used by the individual soldier as well as the company, and was followed by both the Federal and Confederate armies. (A few different regiments followed other tactical books, but on the whole, the standard for both armies for light infantry was Hardee's.) Every member should get a copy and read it thoroughly.

In addition to Hardee's Tactics, there were a number of other tactics and drill books that were used during the WBTS. Tactical tracts by Silas Casey, Winfield Scott, William Gilham, and several other authors were all used during the war, and these have recently been reprinted for reenactors. Learn which manual is used by the regiment you want to join, and follow their instructions. Hardee's is by far the most commonly used drill manual in Civil War reenacting, however.

Living History and Interpretation
The following items are concerned with the interpretation and presentation of history, although not necessarily with Civil War reenactment.

Alderson, William T., and Shirely Payne Lowe. *Interpretation of Historical Sites* (rev. ed.). Nashville: American Association for State and Local History Press, 1987. ISBN: 0910050732. This paperback is affordable and informative and is one of the better books on interpretation. Highly recommended.

Alexander, Edward P. *The Interpretation Program of Colonial Williamsburg.* Williamsburg, VA: The Colonial Williamsburg Foundation, 1971. Regrettably, trying to get information from Colonial Williamsburg is like pulling teeth. Letters seem to fall into a black hole and are seldom answered except with an appeal for membership and funds.

American Association for State and Local History. *Interpreting Healy House.* Nashville: American Association for State and Local History Press, n.d. Audio-tape, slides, and booklet.

American Living History Resource Directory: Annual Resource Directory Spanning 1500s through the 1800s. Volume 1, Portland, OR: Living History Publishers, 1998. Good collection of miscellaneous living history suppliers. Planned additions for December 1999 are volume 2, "Early American Museums," and volume 3, "Internet Web Sites."

Anderson, Jay. *The Living History Sourcebook.* Nashville: American Association for State and Local History Press, 1985. ISBN: 0910050759. This is an excellent, although dated, source of information. It covers so much that it is almost overwhelming, but I still highly recommend it.

———. *Time Machines: The World of Living History.* Nashville: American Association for State and Local History Press, 1984. ISBN: 0910050716. An excellent book on living history of different types. It has top-notch chapters on different periods of living history, although only a small section of the book is specific to the Civil War period.

Anderson, Lorinda Amy. "Historical Interpretation and Park Management: Voyageurs National Park, Minnesota." Master's thesis, University of Minnesota, 1976. 201 pages.

Anderson, Ralph H. *Information Please: Training Bulletin for Field Employees of the National Park Service.* Washington, DC: Department of the Interior, 1955. The National Park Service is enormously irritating in having good items discontinued or infrequently published. This one is hard to get hold of.

Association of Interpretive Naturalists. *AIN 80 Program: Interpreting Cultural and Natural Interpretation, October 6–10, 1980.* Derwood, MD: The Association of Interpretive Naturalists, 1980. 283 pages. Many of the methods, ideas, and works on interpretation by natural-history experts are also appropriate to historical interpretation.

Ballantyne, Roy. "Interpreters' Conceptions of Australian Aboriginal Culture and Heritage: Implications for Interpretive Practice." *The Journal of Environmental Education* 26, no. 4 (1995): 11–17. An excellent work from "Down Under" that discusses the perils of interpreting the culture of a different race and heritage.

Barnes, Frank. "Viewpoint: Living History, Clio or Cliopatria." *History News* XXIX (September 1974): 202–3. Clio was the muse of history in ancient Greece, and this article concerns the application of real history instead of making up "history" that never was.

Barnes, Lois J., "Living History in the Junior High School Classroom." *History Teacher* 11, no. 4 (August 1978): 509–513. A course in U.S. and Kentucky state history where the students assume the personalities of historical figures, and speak as that character about life in his or her era.

"Bates County Civil War Reenactment III: 1992." Butler, Mo.: n.p., 1992. Official souvenir program guide of presentation "Where the Civil War Began."

Black, Patricia F. *The Live-In at Old Economy: An Experiment in a Role Playing Educational Program in the Museum.* Ambridge, PA: Harmonie Associates, 1972. This small book recounts earlier attempts at living history and environmental role playing, in which students were brought in to live for a day at Old Economy. Excellent teaching resource.

———. "Today's Youth, Tomorrow's Heritage: Teenage Docents at Old Economy." *Historic Preservation* XXIV (April–June 1972): 18–21. ISSN: 0018–2419. Of more interest to museum directors than anyone else, this article shows how teenagers were used to work with the public and teach the mission of the village.

Blatti, Jo, ed. *Past Meets Present: Essays about Historical Interpretation and Public Audiences.* Washington, DC: Smithsonian Institution Press, 1987. Some information about interpretation, but little on living history.

Bodnar, John. *Remaking America: Public Memory, Commemoration, and Patriotism in the Twentieth Century.* Princeton, NJ: Princeton University Press, 1992. ISBN:0691047839. Has an interesting section on the 1961 reenactment of

Manassas.

Bond, Brian. "Some Attractions and Pitfalls of Military History." *Military Revue* 45, no. 2 (1965): 87–96. Mostly concerned with twentieth-century military reenactments.

Booth, Jeanette Hauk, Gerald H. Krockover, and Paula B. Woods. *Creative Museum Methods and Educational Techniques.* Springfield, IL: Thomas Co., 1982. ISBN:0398046948. An excellent book with an interesting chapter on educational techniques.

Brockman, Christian Frank. *Evolution of National Park Service Interpretation.* Privately published, 1976. 107 pages. A history and chronology of the NPS. Mostly about natural resources and interpretation.

Burke, James. *The Day the Universe Changed.* A book and a ten-part PBS video series produced in 1985 on the history of technology; it uses reenactors to illustrate events and is an excellent example of living history as a teaching tool.

Campbell, H. Dean. *A Second Impression, 1673–1973.* Trivoli, IL: Campbell Press, 1974. A 1970s reenactment of the exploration of the Mississippi River.

Carlton, Mary Anne. "Interpreter's Handbook: History, Regulation, Walks, Interpretation of Lodgepole Sequoia National Park." Master's thesis, San Jose State University, 1980. 275 pages.

Carson, Barbara G., and Cary Carson. *Interpreting the Historical Scene: Landscapes, Structures and Artifacts.* Correspondence course produced by the American Association of State and Local History for the National Park Service, 1983.

Carter, R. W. *Interpretation: An Approach to the Conservation of the Natural and Cultural Heritage of Australia.* Queensland National Parks and Wildlife Service, n.d.

Clotti, Jack. *The American Civil War.* Falls Church, VA.: Landmark Media, 1998. Explains to young viewers what life was like for the Civil War soldier.

Confederate Receipt Book: A Compilation of Over 100 Receipts, Adapted to the Times. Richmond, 1863. Reprint. Mattituck, NY. Amereon Press, 1983. ISBN:0848800079.

Courtney, Kent. *Returning to the Civil War: Grand Reenactments of an Anguished Time.* Photographs by Al Thelin. Salt Lake City, UT: Gibbs Smith, 1996. A photographic album of reenactments and a good coffee-table book.

Custer's Last Stand: A Re-enactment. Hardin, MT.: Hardin Chamber of Commerce and Agriculture, 1991. Videotape of the reenactment with 200 Indian riders and 100 cavalrymen, scripted by Joe Medicine Crow.

Daily, Brian. *The Basics: How to Get Started in Civil War Reenacting.* Illustrated by Ward Williams. Austin, IN: Privately printed by the author, 1984. This is one of the better recruiting books I have seen, with concise information on reenacting and how to join up.

DeLong, Martha. "Bringing History to Life: Locations that the National Capital Parks Service have redone and provided with live reenactments of the events that made them important in history." *Parks and Recreation* 8, no. 6, (June 1973): 44–46.

DeVries, Willem A. "Meaning and Interpretation in History." *History and Theory* 22, no. 3 (1983): 253–63. The use of reenactment and other methods of interpretation.

Ermann, Natalie. "A Gettysburg Address: NY Group Revives Local Artillery Unit." *New Orleans Magazine* 32, no. 7, (April 1998): 37–38. Account of how a New York unit represented the Washington Artillery from New Orleans.

Grzych, Richard. *Civil War Breaks out at Buckley Homestead.* Cedar Lake, IN.: R. Grzych, 1994. Videotape scenes from a reenactment at Buckley Homestead County Park.

Hagan, Dave and Joan Hagan. *Civil War Reenactment.* Arglen, PA.: Schiffer Publishing, 1996. Color photos of a reenactment.

Hake, Metta. *Advanced Training Handbook for Tour Guides.* Sacramento, CA: California Department of Parks and Recreation, 1971. Haven't been able to get a copy.

Handler, Richard and Eric Gable. *New History in an Old Museum: Greeting the Past at Colonial Williamsburg.* Durham, NC: Duke University Press, 1997. Observations on the expression of historical truth at Williamsburg.

Hanna, John W., and Valeen Adams Silvy. *Visitor Observations for Interpretive Programming.* College Station, TX: Texas A&M University, Department of Recreation and Parks, 1978.

Harris, Joseph E. *Afro-American History Interpretation at Selected National Parks.* Washington, DC: Howard University, 1978. Prepared by the History Department Research Team, Howard University, September 1978. 238 pages.

Hilker, Gordon. *The Audience and You: Practical Dramatics for the Park Interpreter.* Washington, DC: National Park Service, 1974. A good how-to book on dramatics, needed for the "actor" in the reenactor.

Hinchberger, Christian. *Visit From a Civil War Soldier.* First-person video of a private from the 78th Pennsylvania.

Hirzy, Ellen C. *Open Conversations: Strategies in Professional Development in Museums.* Chicago: Chicago Department of Education, Field Museum of Natural History, 1988.

Horne-Jaruk, Honour. "Even Ground—Reenactors and Disabilities." *Recreating History* 2, no. 4, iss. 7, (Aug.–Sept. 1996): pages 12–15, 21. An interesting and much-needed article about reenactors and spectators with disabilities.

Hughes, Susan Lyons. *First Impressions: Getting Started in Civilian Reenacting.* Marietta, OH: Camp Chase Press, 1994.

Inglis, K. S. "Remembering Australia." *Historian* 19 (1988): 3–8. An account of a reenactment of the founding of the British settlement in Sydney.

Isemonger, Paul Lewis. *Wellington's War: A Living History.* Far Thrupp, Gloucestershire, England: Sutton Publications, 1998. Reenactment information about the Napoleonic Wars.

Junkelmann, Dr. Marcus. A Bavarian military historian and archaeologist, Junkelman has written a number of publications, unfortunately, almost all in German. This includes *Die Legionen des Augustus, der Romaische Soldat im Archaologischen Experiment, Romische Kampf und Turnierrustungen,* and *Legio XXI Rapax.* He has re-created an Augustan-era legion that in 1985 marched from Verona, Italy, to Augsburg, Germany, over the course of 23 days, using only Roman-period equipment and supplies in an experiment in "practical archaeology."

Kay, William Kennon. *Keep It Alive! Tips on Living History Demonstrations.* Washington, DC: National Park Service, 1970. Small brochure on living history, mainly for site managers.

Kietz, Bill. "The Reenactor's Art." *Civil War Times, Illustrated* (March 1987): 22–36. ISSN: 0009–8094. Good review of reenacting.

Knudsen, Peter A. and Vicki I. Speir. *Saltbrush & Sagebrush: The Jubilee Overlanders.* Kent Town, South Australia: Peacock Publishers, 1986. A reenactment of horse-and-wagon treks across South Australia and Texas.

Krockover, Gerald H., and Jeanette Booth Hauck. *Training for Docents: How to Talk to Visitors.* Nashville: American Association for State and Local History, 1980. Technical Leaflet #125. A short brochure on how to talk to and, more important, how to listen to visitors.

Leon, Warren, and Roy Rosenzweig. *History Museums in the United States: A Critical Assessment.* Urbana, IL: University of Illinois Press, 1989. ISBN: 0252014006. Chapter 3, "Living History Museums," by Warren Leon and Margaret Piatt, is exceptionally well written.

Lewis, William J. *The Fine Art of Interpretive Critiquing.* Washington, DC: National Park Service, Division of Interpretation, 1975.

———. *Interpreting for Park Visitors.* Philadelphia: Eastern Acorn Press, 1981. ISBN:0890620792. Although mainly aimed at natural-history interpretation, this is still a good introduction to park interpretation at the national parks.

Lowe, Shirley P. *Historic Site Interpretation: The Human Approach.* Nashville: American Association for State and Local History, 1965. Technical Leaflet #32.

Mackintosh, Barry. *Interpretation in the National Park Service: A Historical Perspective.* Washington, DC: National Park Service, History Division, 1986. This is an interesting work—a history of interpretation. Marred, however, by incomplete citations and lack of bibliography.

Malcolm-Davies, Jane. "Keeping It Alive: The Use of Live Interpreters in Historical Museums; A Conference Sponsored by Cadbury's, Birmingham, England. *Museums Journal* 90 (1990): 25–29.

Martin, Rex. *Historical Explanation: Re-enactment and Practical Inference.* Ithaca, NY: Cornell University Press, 1977. ISBN: 0801410843. Looks at how to extrapolate information from a time period.

Meadows, G. Parker. *Enlist! A Video guide for Civil War Reenactors.* Richmond, VA.: Meadows Video Productions, 1994. Introduction to the hobby with advice on uniforms, firearms, accessories, and some money-saving tips.

Meltzer, Suzanne. *Witness to History: Using Hands-On Activities—A Guidebook for High School History Teachers.* Washington, DC: ERIC Report ED 387416, Eric Clearinghouse, 1995. An interesting guide to using hands-on projects to teach American history from Colonial days to turn of the century. A good source of ideas for living-history projects and school activities.

Miller, Kimberly A. "Gender Comparisons within Reenactment Costume: Theoretical Interpretations." *Family and Consumer Sciences Research Journal* 27, no. 1, (Sept. 1998): 35–61. Explores why people dress in costumes: Women dress in costume primarily to assume another persona, while men dress in costume because of their love of history.

National Park Service. *Campfire Programs: Training Bulletins for the Field Employees of the National Park Service*. Washington, DC: National Park Service, 1955. Geared to park personnel, this is mainly a brochure on how to use public relations to get people to use the parks.

————. *History: National Park Service Interpretive Series*. Washington, DC: U.S. Government Printing Office, 1942.

————. *Interpretation and Visitor Services Guideline, NPS-6 (National Park Standard-6)*. Release Number 2. Washington, DC: National Park Service, March 1980. A ponderous document.

————. *Interpretive Training Package*. Washington, DC: National Park Service, n.d. Audiotaped examples of interpretive talks and tours, with accompanying manual.

————. *In Touch: Interpreter's Information Exchange. Produced in and for the NPS (National Park Service) People Concerned with Interpretive and Visitor Services*. Washington, DC: NPS Division of Interpretive and Visitor Services, WASO,1974. Irregular journal from 1974 to 1986.

————. *Living History in the National Park System*. Washington, DC: National Park Service, 1976. 20 pages. Mostly a listing of national parks that have living-history programs.

————. *Talks: Training Bulletin for Field Employees of the National Park Service*. Washington, DC: National Park Service, 1953.

————. *Training Methods Manual: A Training Guide for Supervisors and Other Instructors to Enable Them to Increase the Effectiveness of All National Park Service Training Activities*. Washington, DC: National Park Service, 1967.

National Park Service, Division of Interpretation. *The Fine Art of Interpretive Critiquing*. Washington, DC: National Park Service, Division of Interpretation, 1970.

————. Arlington, VA: National Recreational and Park Association, 1978. Videotaped examples of supervisors critiquing and evaluating interpretive programs, with an accompanying information booklet.

————. *Resources for Interpreters*. Washington, DC: National Park Service, Division of Interpretation, 1982. Revised, 1986.

Nice Boom! The American Civil War Artillery Reenactor's Handbook. Rochester, N.Y.: S. McAdoo, 1996. Handbook for field artillery reenactors.

Nichols, Susan K. *Working Papers: Historians, Artifacts and Learners*. Washington, DC: Smithsonian Institution, Museum Reference Center Publications Office, 1982.

Nichols, Susan K., Mary Alexander, and Ken Yellis, eds. *Museum Education Anthology, 1973–1983: Perspectives on Informal Learning*. Washington, DC: Museum Education Roundtable, 1984. Living history is slightly reviewed.

The Old Sturbridge Village, a Center for Living History. Sturbridge, MA: Old Sturbridge Village, 1953. A one-page pamphlet on living-history interpretation.

The Park, the Visitor and the Interpreter: A Personal Training Program for Interpreters. Washington, DC: National Park Service, n.d. A communication skills training curriculum package for individual study, consisting of a syllabus workbook and accompanying videotape.

Pressly, Thomas. *Americans Interpret Their Civil War*. New York: Free Press, 1962. A centennial book on the Civil War.

Princeton 76: A Revolutionary Battle: Plan for Interpretation. Trenton: State of New Jersey, Department of Conservation and Economic Development, 1968. 70 pages.

Reenactment of the Battle of Newport Barracks, February 2, 1864: Echoes of Dixie. Raleigh, NC: North Carolina Division, Sons of Confederate Veterans, 1996.

The Reenactors. Narrated by Gerald McRaney. Lansing, MI: Media Magic, 1995. Videotape of two reenactors, Kyth Bass and Dave Roberts, explaining their reasons for and experiences in reenacting.

Reenactor's Guide to Clothing and Fabrics in the Civil War. Fall Creek Sutlery (317–482–1861). Fifty-page booklet with bibliography. Good introduction to fabrics.

Reibel, Daniel B., and Patricia B. Reibel. *A Handbook for Interpreters. Washington Crossing Historic Park, Washington Crossing, Pennsylvania.* Harrisburg, PA: Pennsylvania Historical and Museum Commission, 1981.

———. *A Manual for Guides, Docents, Hostesses, and Volunteers of Old Economy.* Ambridge, PA: Harmonie Associates, 1974.

Replica Resource List. Pendleton, IL: ALHFAM Replica Resource Committee, Fall 1997. This is a new item that I haven't seen. It includes 350 suppliers of replica items for living history, with 100 topical headings.

Roos, Marita. "An Approach to the Interpretation of Women's History for an Urban Cultural Park in Seneca Falls, New York." Master's thesis, University of Georgia, 1989. 85 pages.

Saari, H. "Reenactment: A Study on R. G. Collingwood's Philosophy of History." Dissertation, Swedish University of Abo, 1985.

Seevil Wawah: Faces of Smiles. Columbia, MD: Classic Images, 1990. Videotape of classic bloopers from the 125th anniversary commemoration of the war.

7th Annual Civil War Weekend, Sept. 27–28, 1997. Wade House & Wesley Jung Carriage Museum and Historic Site, Greenbush, Wisconsin: Kautzer-Zenk Video Productions. Videotape of the reenactment of the battle of Brawner's Farm.

Severa, Joan. *Authentic Costuming for Historic Site Guides.* Nashville: American Association of State and Local History Press, 1979. Leaflet #113. Although this is a short leaflet, it is valuable as a first resource for authentic costuming.

Sharpe, Grant W. *Interpreting the Environment.* New York: Wiley, 1982. ISBN: 0471778966. From a geological point of view, but some of the information on interpretation is relevant.

Smith, David. *Civil War Reenactor's Blackpowder Guide.* Gettysburg, PA: Rusty Musket Enterprise, n.d.

Smith, Jim. *The Battle of Droop Mountain.* French Creek, WV: Filming America, n.d. A reenactor turned videographer produced a videotape of a reenactment.

Smith, Randy. *The Black Powder Plainsman: A Beginner's Guide to Muzzleloading and Reenactment on the Great Plains.* Bountiful, UT: Horizon Publishers, 1992. A good introduction to "Rendezvous" and western reenacting.

Stagner, Howard Ralph. *Conducted Trips: Training Bulletin for Field Employees of the National Park Service.* Washington, DC: National Park Service, 1951.

Stanton, Cathy. "Being the Elephant: The American Civil War Reenacted." Master's thesis, Vermont College of Norwich University, 1997. An interesting study of reenactors as a social organization.

Stover, Kate F. "Is It Real History Yet? An Update on Living History Museums." *Journal of American Culture* 12 (Summer 1989): 13–17.

Tennent, William Lawrence. "The John Jarvie Ranch: A Case Study in Historic Site Development and Interpretation." Master's thesis, Utah State University, 1980. 180 pages.

The Tennessee Campaign of 1864 and the Fight for Nashville. Kansas City, MO: Video Post, 1996. Videotape of a reenactment of the battle of Nashville.

Tilden, Freeman. *Interpreting Our Heritage: Principles and Practices for Visitor Services in Parks, Museums and Historic Places.* Chapel Hill, NC: University of North Carolina Press, 1957. Revised, 1978. The grandfather of all books on interpretation, and still one of the best. Highly recommended.

———. *The National Parks: What They Mean to You and Me.* New York: Knopf, 1951. Mostly about natural-history parks; of limited value to living history, but has good discussions of interpretation and interpretive education.

Trilling, Jeffery D. "Civil War Portraiture: Civil War Reenacting Used as a Method to Gain Insights into the Workings of a 19th Century Field Photographer." Master's thesis, Columbia College, Chicago, 1984.

Walls, Donnie, et al. *Civil War in Pulaski County [Virginia], 1864.* Newbern, VA: Wilderness Road Regional Museum, 1992. Reenactment of Cloyd's Mountain.

Wellikoff, Alan. *The Historical Supply Catalog: A Nineteenth Century Source Book.* Charlotte, VT: Camden House, 1993. Reprint of the *American Historical Supply Catalogue,* 1984.

Wexler, Henrietta. "The Way Things Really Were: Living History Museum Researchers Delve Deeper." *Museum News* 66 (January–February 1988): 62–63.

Whitney, Jeanne, and Jane Strauss, eds. *Colonial Williamsburg Interpreter: A Handbook.* Williamsburg, VA: Colonial Williamsburg Foundation, Department of Interpretive Education, n.d. Special issue of the bimonthly *Colonial Williamsburg Interpreter.*

Yu, Jessica. *Men of Reenaction.* New York: Carousel Films & Video, 1995. Documentary video explores the reasons why people reenact.

Zen, E-an, and Alta S. Walker. *Rocks and War: Geology and the Civil War Campaign of Second Manassas.* Shippensburg, PA: White Mane.

Historical Farms

Bearss, Edwin C. *The Burroughs Plantation as a Living Historical Farm (Booker T. Washington National Monument).* Washington, DC: National Park Service, Division of History, Office of Archeology and Historic Preservation, 1969. The farm's history, as well as a discussion of crops and methods used in the nineteenth century.

———. *Lincoln Boyhood as a Living Historical Farm.* Washington, DC: National Park Service, Division of History, 1967. An interesting slant on living-history farms, calling for livestock and period crops to be cared for today as they originally were. If possible, period hybrids instead of modern ones should be used. The book includes a listing of documented livestock and crop types.

Clawson, Marion. "Living Historical Farms: A Proposal for Action." *Agricultural History* 39, no. 2 (1965): 110–11. ISSN: 0002–1482.

Farm Museum Directory: A Guide to America's Farm Past. Lancaster, PA: Stemgas
    Publishing, n.d. This is a guide to living-history farm museums from all time
    periods in the U.S. and Canada.
Kelsey, Darwin P. *Farming in the New Nation: Interpreting American Agriculture,
    1790–1840.* Washington, DC: Agricultural History Society, 1972.
———. "Harvests of History." *Historic Preservation* 28, no. 3 (1976): 20–24.
    ISSN:0018–2419.
———. "Historic Farms as Models of the Past." *ALHFAM Annual* 1 (1975): 33–39.
———. *The Living Historical Farms Handbook.* Washington, DC: Smithsonian Insti-
    tution Press, 1972.
———. "Outdoor Museums and Historical Agriculture." *Agricultural History* 46
    (1976): 105–27. ISSN: 0002–1482.
Schlebecker, John T. *Living Historical Farms: A Walk into the Past.* Smithsonian Pub-
    lication Number 4747. Washington, DC: Smithsonian Institution, 1968.
———. *The Past in Action: Living Historical Farms.* Washington, DC: Living Histori-
    cal Farms Project, Smithsonian Institution, 1967.
———. "Social Functions of Living Historical Farms in the United States." *Museum*
    (Paris) 36, no. 3 (1984): 146–149.
Williams, Sharon. "Historical Interpretation of Leonis Adobe and Plummer House
    Museum and Living Farm Exhibit: An Analysis of Two Restoration and Preser-
    vation Projects in Process." Master's thesis, University of California at Los
    Angeles (Department of Urban Planning), 1986. 30 pages.
Woods, Thomas A. "Living Historical Farming: A Critical Method for Historical
    Research and Teaching about Rural Life." *Journal of American Culture* 12 (Sum-
    mer 1989): 43–47.

2: REENACTMENT FOR INFANTRYMEN

Regimental Histories and Personal Narratives

There are many sources providing information about the many regiments and
organizations in the Civil War. The following sources will direct you to other
sources with information about your unit's history.

The Banner. Official publication of the Union Veterans.
Bilby, Joseph G. *Forgotten Warriors: New Jersey's African American Soldiers in the
    Civil War.* Hightstown, NJ: Longstreet House, 1993. Accounts of the soldiers
    from primary sources.
Brinton, John Hill. *Personal Memoirs of John H. Brinton, Civil War Surgeon,
    1861–1865.* New York: Neale Publishing, 1914. Reprinted 1996. Accounts of
    medical care during the war by a Union physician.
Confederate Veteran. Official publication of the United Confederate Veterans,
    1895–1932.
Coulter, Ellis Merton. *Travels in the Confederate States: A Bibliography.* Norman,
    OK, 1948. Reprint. Wendell, NC: Broadfoot's Bookmark, 1981.

Dawson, Francis Warrington. *Reminiscences of Confederate Service, 1861–1865*. Baton Rouge, LA: Louisiana State University Press, 1993. Personal experiences in the Army of Northern Virginia.

Dornbush, C. E. *Military Bibliography of the Civil War*. New York: New York Public Library, 1967–1972. Three volumes with new editions published by Morningside Press. One of the best places to find out what has been written about the regiments from each state.

Miller, Edward A. *The Black Civil War Soldiers of Illinois: The Story of the 29th US Colored Infantry*. Columbia: University of South Carolina Press, 1998. History of the unit from formation to the postwar fate of many of the soldiers.

Military Order of the Loyal Legion of the United States (MOLLUS). This organization was made up of commissioned officers of the Union army. A personal narrative series was produced by many of the state commanderies, usually designated as MOLLUS followed by the state name, e.g., MOLLUS-Maine.

Nathanson, David. *Sunshine and Shadows: A Catalog of Civil War Unit Histories and Personal Narratives in National Park Service Libraries*. Harpers Ferry, WV: National Park Service, 1982.

Nevins, Allan, James I. Robertson, and Bell I. Wiley. *Civil War Books: A Critical Bibliography*. Baton Rouge, LA: Louisiana State University Press, 1969. Two volumes.

Official Records of the War of the Rebellion. Washington, DC: U.S. Government Printing Office. Reprinted several times. Multiple volumes and series. It is now out on a CD-Rom for computers. This is the official correspondence of the Union and Confederate armies, with most of their records. Excellent resource, and indexed to people as well as regiments.

Personal narratives. Rhode Island Soldiers and Sailors Historical Society.

Phillips, Stanley S. *Excavated Artifacts from Battlefields and Campsites of the Civil War 1861–1865*. Lanham, MD: Walsworth Press, 1974, with a 1980 supplement.

Report of the Select Committee Relative to the Soldiers' National Cemetery . . . March 31, 1864. Report of Samuel Weaver. Excellent resource that inventories the pocket contents of the soldiers buried at Gettysburg.

Scribner, Benjamin Franklin. *How Soldiers Were Made; Or the War As I Saw It Under Buell, Rosecrans, Thomas, Grant and Sherman*. New Albany, IN. and Chicago, IL.: Donahue & Henneberry, 1887. Personal account by the colonel of the 38th Indiana Veteran Volunteers, later a brigadier in the XIV Army Corps, Army of the Cumberland.

Southern Historical Society. *Southern Historical Society Papers*. 52 vols. Richmond, VA, 1876–1959.

Stillwell, Leander. *The Story of a Common Soldier of Army Life in the Civil War, 1861–1865*. Kansas City, MO: Franklin Hudson Publishing, 1920. Reprinted by Time–Life Books, 1983. Personal account of life in an Illinois Regiment.

Taylor, Richard. *Destruction and Reconstruction: Personal Experiences of the Late War*. New York: Appleton Press, 1879. Reprinted 1955, 1995. Personal account of life in the Confederate army.

Todd, Frederick, et al. *American Military Equipage, 1851–1872*. Multivolume. Hartford, CT: Company of Military Historians. Most excellent book of equipment with truly awesome line drawings.

Wiley, Bell Irvin. *The Life of Billy Yank: The Common Soldier of the Union*. Baton Rouge, LA: Louisiana State University Press, 1952. (Reprinted several times.) This book and the next one are the best guides for understanding the life of the common soldier and should be among your first purchases.

————. *The Life of Johnny Reb: The Common Soldier of the Confederacy*. Baton Rouge, LA: Louisiana State University Press, 1952. (Reprinted several times.)

Wills, Charles Wright. *Army Life of an Illinois Soldier, Including a Day-to-Day Record of Sherman's March to the Sea: The Letters and Diary of Charles W. Wills*. Compiled by Mary E. Kellog. Washington, DC: Globe Publishing, 1906. Reprinted by Illinois University Press, 1996. Excellent account of life in the mid-western regiments.

Worsham, John H. *One of Jackson's Foot Cavalry: His Experience and What He Saw During the War, 1861–1865; Including a History of "F" Company, Richmond, Virginia, 21st Regiment Virginia Infantry, Second Brigade, Jackson's Division, Second Corps, Army of Northern Virginia*. New York: Neale Publishing, 1912. Reprinted by Time-Life Books, 1982. Good personal narrative of life in the Army of Northern Virginia.

Civil War-Era Photographs

Much information can be gathered by studying Civil War-period photographs with a good magnifying glass. Keep in mind, however, that photographs taken in studios were sometimes done with props (extra pistols, swords, flags, sashes) and with the soldiers in their best uniforms. Studio pictures may not be typical of uniforms and accoutrements actually worn in the field or off the parade ground. The following are some excellent sources of Civil War-era photographs and information on uniforms and equipment.

American Historical Images on File. *The Civil War*. Carter Smith, executive ed. New York: Facts on File, 1989. Annotated images, good for reproducing with high school and college reports.

Barnard, George N. *Photographic Views of Sherman's Campaign*. New York: Dover Press, 1977. ISBN: 0486234452. Nice reproductions of photos, mostly landscape shots.

Civil War: A Centennial Exhibition of Eyewitness Drawings. Washington, DC: National Gallery of Art, Smithsonian Institution, 1961. Black-and-white drawings held by the National Gallery.

Civil War Photographs, 1861–1865: A Catalog of Copy Negatives Made from Originals Selected from the Mathew B. Brady Collection in the Prints and Photographs Division of the Library of Congress. Washington, DC: Library of Congress, 1961, 1977. Reprint. List of negatives held in the collection. Useful only if you are looking for something specific, such as a photo of a general.

Divided We Fought: A Pictorial History of the War, 1861–1865. New York: Macmillan Company, 1952. Excellent introduction to Civil War photography with many photos of troops.

Echoes of Glory. Three volumes: *Arms and Equipment of the Confederacy, Arms and Equipment of the Union,* and *Illustrated Atlas of the Civil War.* Alexandria, VA: Time-Life Books, 1991. This excellent series has a number of photographs of original equipment. Unfortunately, unique items in this series are used by some to argue in favor of uncommon uniforms.

The First Battles: A Sourcebook of the Civil War. Carter Smith, ed. American albums from the collections of the Library of Congress. Brookfield, CT: Milbrook Press, 1992. ISBN: 056294262X. Lithographs, maps, and photos from the Library of Congress's many collections, for the period from 1861 to 1862. Other books in the series are *Prelude to War; 1863: The Crucial Year; The Road to Appomattox; Behind the Lines; One Nation Again.*

Frassanito, William A. *Antietam: The Photographic Legacy of America's Bloodiest Day.* New York: Scribner's Sons, 1978. Excellent review of the photographs taken on the battlefield.

———. *Gettysburg: A Journey in Time.* New York: Scribner's Sons, 1975. Excellent and unusual book. Rephotographed portions of Gettysburg, with annotated text describing each scene.

———. *Grant and Lee: The Virginia Campaigns, 1864–1865.* New York: Scribner's Sons, 1982. ISBN: 0684178737. His usual excellent analysis of the period photographs.

Gardner, Alexander. *Gardner's Photographic Sketch Book of the Civil War.* New York: Dover, 1959. Good collection of photos.

Garofalo, Robert, and Mark Elrod. *Pictorial History of Civil War Era Musical Instruments and Military Bands.* Charleston, WV: Pictorial Histories Publishing Co., 1985. ISBN: 0933126603. Includes a record and good bibliography.

Horan, James David. *Mathew Brady: Historian with a Camera.* New York: Crown Publishers, 1955. Although primarily a biography, this book does reproduce a number of Brady photos.

Horsemen Blue and Gray: A Pictorial History. New York: Oxford University Press, 1960. Excellent set of photos, unfortunately marred by too many cavalrymen.

Hunt, Christopher John, and G. A. Embleton. *The American Civil War.* New Malden, MA: Almark Publishing Co., 1974. ISBN: 0855241675.

Mast, Greg. *State Troops and Volunteers: A Photographic Record of North Carolina's Civil War Soldiers.* Volume 1 (1861–1862). Raleigh, NC: North Carolina Department of Cultural Resources, Division of Archives and History, 1995. ISBN:0865262640. Excellent resource of original information concerning North Carolina troops and some civilian clothing and equipment.

Military Collector and Historian: The Journal of the Company of Military Historians. Company of Military Historians, North Main Street, Westbrook, CT 06498. A two-part special Confederate issue was printed in the fall and winter 1989 issues.

Military Images magazine. East Stroudsburg, PA: Harry Roach. ISSN: 1040–4961 or 0193–9866.

Miller, Francis T. *The Photographic History of the Civil War in Ten Volumes.* New York: Thomas Yoseloff, 1957. Although the photos are reproduced a bit dark, this is an excellent source for period photography.

National Historical Society. *Image of War. Pictorial Reporting of the American Civil War*. New York: National Historical Society Press, 1984.

Neely, Mark E. *The Confederate Image: Prints of the Lost Cause*. Chapel Hill, NC: University of North Carolina Press, 1987. ISBN: 0807841978. Reproductions of prints, many quite romanticized, from the South.

Nelson, Christopher. *Mapping the Civil War: Featuring Rare Maps from the Library of Congress*. Japan: Starwood Publishing, n.d. A fine reproduction of maps held in the Library of Congress.

Price, William H. *The Civil War Centennial Handbook*. A Civil War Research Associates Series. Arlington, VA: Prince Lithograph Co., 1963. Reprint of a number of the usual photos.

Severa, Joan L. *Dressed for the Photographer: Ordinary Americans and Fashion, 1840–1900*. Kent: Kent State University Press, 1995. Excellent reproductions of various period photographs and discussions of the clothes and styles.

Stern, Philip van Doren. *They Were Here: The Civil War in Action as Seen by Its Combat Artists*. New York: Crown Publishers, 1959. Good selection of drawings by combat artists. Nice studies of troops around camps.

Uniforms of the Civil War: Federal Enlisted Uniforms of the Civil War Period. Washington, DC: Smithsonian Institution and Roberts Video Publishing, 1990. Videotape, 83 minutes.

Voices of the Civil War. Alexandria, VA: Time-Life Books, Inc., 1994. Good collection of photos, drawings, and portraits. Gettysburg ISBN: 0783547005. Second Manassas ISBN: 0783547013.

Ward, Geoffrey C. *The Civil War: An Illustrated History*. New York: Alfred A. Knopf, 1990. Based on the series produced with Ken Burns, this is a modern reproduction of many period photos.

Wiley, Bell I. *Embattled Confederates: An Illustrated History of Southerners at War*. New York: Harper and Row, 1964. Photos of people and equipment, some drawings.

———. *They Who Fought Here*. New York: Macmillan Co., 1959. Good text and photos, many of soldier life.

Army Drill and Regulations

The following are some drill and tactical studies from the WBTS. Most contemporary works from the Civil War on infantry drill and tactics are now hard to find except in special history bookstores or large university libraries.

Cary, Richard Milton. *Skirmisher's Drill and Bayonet Exercises (as Now Used in the French Army) with Suggestions for the Soldier in Actual Conflict*. Richmond: West and Johnson, 1861. Has 56 pages of bayonet drill.

Casey, Silas. *Infantry Tactics; for the Instruction, Exercise and Manoeuvres of the Soldier, a Company, Line of Skirmishers, Battalion, Brigade or Corps d'Armee*. New York: Van Nostrand, 1862. 3 vols. (Reprinted several times.)

Chandler's Tactics: Manual for Drill for Wisconsin Volunteers. I have not seen a copy, but this was supposedly published in 1997 and has specific materials for Iron Brigade troops.

Confederate States of America War Department. *Regulations for the Army of the Confederate States: Corrected and Enlarged with a Revised Index.* Richmond, VA: J. W. Randolph, 1863. (Another copy was printed by West and Johnson of Richmond, again in 1863, but with 432 pages. The Randolph version is considered the more correct.) The how-to book for CS Army reenactment. The Randolph edition was republished by the National Historical Society, Harrisburg, PA, in 1980.

————. *Southern Military Manual. Containing All the Confederate Military Laws, Articles of War, Army Regulations, Field Artillery, Mahan's Treatise on the Effects of Musketry and Artillery, and the Means of Directing the Fire as to Obtain the Best Results, Hardee's Manual of Arms, Fully Illustrated, Military Ordinances of Louisiana and Napoleon I., Health Hints for Volunteers, etc.* Jackson, MS: J. L. Power, 1861. 125 pages.

————. *A System for Conducting Musketry Instruction, Prepared and Printed by Order of General Bragg, for the Army of Tennessee.* Richmond, VA: *Enquirer's* Office, 1863.

Cooke's Cavalry Tactics: Instructions, formations and movements of the Cavalry of the Army and Volunteers of the United States. Reprint of the 1861 edition.

Dal Bello, Dominic J. *Instructions for Guards and Pickets.* Manual on guard duty for reenactors.

————. *Parade, Inspection and Basic Evolutions of the Infantry Battalion: Being a Manual for Company Officers and Noncommissioned Officers of Civil War Living History Units on the Movements of a Battalion of Infantry.* 2d ed. Santa Barbara, CA: Army of the Pacific Press, 1995. (P.O. Box 1863, Santa Barbara, CA 93116.)

Duffield, William Ward. *School of the Brigade and Evolution of the Line.* Philadelphia: J. B. Lippincott & Co., 1862.

Dufour, Guillaume Henri. *Strategy and Tactics.* Translated from the French by William P. Craighill. New York: Van Nostrand Press, 1864. Translation of *Cours de Tactique* (Course of Tactics).

Ellsworth, Elmer Ephraim. *Manual of Arms for Light Infantry Adapted to the Rifled Musket, with, or without, the Priming Attachment, Arranged for the U.S. Zouave Cadets, Governor's Guard of Illinois.* Chicago: n.p. 1859. 110 pages.

French, W. H. *Field Artillery Tactics.* Reprint of the 1864 edition for the Union army.

Gilham, Maj. William. *Manual of Instruction for the Volunteers and Militia of the United States, with Numerous Illustrations.* Philadelphia: Charles DeSilver, 1861. Reprint. Inman, SC: B&B Historical Research, 1985. Also reprinted by Company A, 4th Virginia Infantry. This manual, popularly known as Gilham's, is used by heavy infantry and is a storehouse of information on band music, courts-martial, and drill.

Great Britain War Office. *Field Exercises and Evolutions of Infantry, as Revised by Her Majesty's Command, 1862.* London: Her Majesty's Stationery Office, 1862. Drill, tactics, and bugle music for the Brits; also used by some regiments in the United States.

Greenleaf, Charles Ravenscroft. *A Manual for the Medical Officers of the United States Army.* Philadelphia: Lippincott, 1864. Recently reprinted.

Griffith, Paddy. *Battle Tactics of the Civil War.* New Haven, CT: Yale University Press, 1989. ISBN: 0300042477. Revised edition of *Rally Once Again* from 1987.

Halleck, Henry Wager. *Elements of Military Art and Science: Or, A Course of Instruction in Strategy, Fortification, Tactics of Battles Etc., Embracing the Duties of Staff, Infantry, Cavalry, Artillery and Engineers; Adapted to the Use of Volunteers and Militia.* 3d ed. New York: D. Appleton & Company, 1863.

Hardee, William Joseph L. *Infantry and Rifle Tactics.* Mobile, AL: S. H. Goetzel, 1861. "This is the only complete, correct and revised edition, and this edition only contains the improvements and changes I have recently made adapting the manual to the use of arms in the hands of the troops of the Confederate States. Col. William J. Hardee, Colonel, CSA."

———. *Rifle and Infantry Tactics, Revised and Improved, by Brig. Gen. W. J. Hardee, C.S. Army, and Infantry Tactics; or Rules of Exercises and Manoeuvres of Infantry, by Major-General Scott, Evolutions of the Line. Published by order of the Governor for the use of North Carolina Troops.* Raleigh, NC: John Spelman, 1862. (Recently reprinted.)

———. *Rifle and Light Infantry Tactics for the Exercise and Manoeuvres of Troops When Acting as Light Infantry or Riflemen. Prepared under the direction of the War Department, by Brevet Lieutenant Colonel W. J. Hardee.* Philadelphia: J. B. Lippincott & Co., 1861. 2 vols.

———. *Rifle and Light Infantry Tactics for the Exercise and Manoeuvres of Troops When Acting as Light Infantry or Riflemen.* Philadelphia: Lippincott, Grambo & Co., 1855. 2 vols.

Heitman, Don. *Hardee's Simplified and Guard Mount.* Santa Barbara, CA: Army of the Pacific Press, n.d. (P.O. Box 1863, Santa Barbara, CA 93116.) An interpretation of General Hardee's drill manual for reenactors.

Jervis-White-Jervis, Henry. *Manual of Field Operations—Adapted for the Use of Officers of the Army.* London: J. Murray Company, 1852. 428 pages.

Le Louterel, Francois Philippe. *The Field Manual for Battalion Drill: Containing the Exercises and Manoeuvres in the School of the Battalion, Arranged in a Tabular Form, for the Use of Officers of the U.S. Infantry, Translated and Adapted to the U.S. Infantry Tactics, from the Latest French Authorities, by Capt. Henry Coppee.* Philadelphia: J. P. Lippincott & Co., 1862.

Lewis, George Cooper. *The Soldier's Companion: Containing an Abridgement of Hardee's Infantry Tactics; with the Heavy Infantry and Rifle Manuals, Skirmish Drill and Bayonet Exercise, Field Fortification, Picket and Outpost Duty, with Various Regulations, Forms, &c, That Will Be Found Useful to the Soldier in Camp and on the March; with an Appendix Containing Fancy Movements for Volunteer Companies, Uniform and Dress of the Army, &c.* Raleigh, NC: John Spelman, Printer, Office State Journal, 1863.

Lippitt, Francis James. *A Treatise on the Tactical Use of the Three Arms: Infantry, Artillery and Cavalry.* New York: D. Van Nostrand Press, 1865.

Manual of Arms (Percussion) for Heavy Infantry, with the Loadings and Firings. Charleston, SC: Steam Power Presses of Evans and Cogswell, 1861.

McConnell, David. *British Smooth-bore Artillery: A Technical Study to Support Identification, Acquisition, Restoration, Reproduction, and Interpretation of Artillery at National Historical Parks in Canada.* Ottawa: National Historic Parks and Sites, 1988. 595 pages. Issued also in French as *L'Artillerie Lisse Britannique.*

McMullen, Kiernan E. *Marches and Shelter for Horse Drawn Artillery with Notes for Artillery Scouts.* Scholar of Fortune Publications, 1993. Artillery drill, tactics, and military camps.

McWhiney, Grady. *Attack and Die: Civil War Military Tactics and the Southern Heritage.* University, AL: University of Alabama Press, 1982. ISBN: 0817300732.

Moore, S. P. *Regulations of the C.S.A. Medical Departments.* Reprint of the 1862 edition.

Morris, [Brig. Gen.] William Hopkins. *Infantry Tactics: Comprising the School of the Soldier; Instruction for Skirmishers; School of the Battalion; Evolutions of the Brigade and Directions for Manoeuvering the Division and the Corps d'Armee (Including Music and Bugle Calls).* New York: D. Van Nostrand, 1865. 2 vols.

Moseley, Thomas Vernon. *Evolution of the American Civil War Infantry Tactics.* Chapel Hill, NC: University of North Carolina Press, 1967.

Revised Regulations of the Army of the United States, 1861. Philadelphia: J. G. L. Brown, printed by authority of the War Department. Republished by the National Historical Society, Harrisburg, PA, 1980. These are the regulations in force for the first year of the WBTS.

Richardson, John H. *Infantry Tactics; or Rules for the Exercise and Manoeuvres of the Confederate States Infantry in the Evolutions of the Line. Compiled, Arranged and Adapted to Hardee's Drill.* Shreveport, LA: Caddo Gazette, 1864. Also, Richmond, VA: West & Johnson, 1862.

Scharr, Reinhold. *Die Technik im Dienst der Operativen Tutigkeit einer kavallerieddivision.* (Technology in the service of the operational activity of a cavalry division.) Berlin: A. Bath, 1904. An application with reference to the North American War of Secession in Virginia and a map as well as 35 figures in the text.

School of the Soldier. Videotape of drill taken from Hardee's and Casey's manuals. Program I: Facings, Manual of Arms, Bayonet. Program II: Loading, Firing, Marching. Lansing, MI: Media Magic. Not seen.

Scott, Winfield. *Infantry Tactics.* New York: Harper and Brothers, 1854, 1861. 3 vols. (Reprinted in part or whole several times.)

United States War Department. *Abstract of Infantry Tactics: Including Exercises and Manoeuvres of Light Infantrymen and Riflemen; for Use by the Militia of the United States.* Philadelphia: Moss and Brothers, 1853.

———. *Infantry Tactics: Or Rules for the Exercises and Manoeuvres of the Infantry of the United States Army.* Washington, DC: Davis and Force, 1852. 2 vols.

———. *Revised United States Army Regulations: 1861; With an Appendix Containing the Changes and Laws Affecting Army Regulations and Articles of War to June, 1863.* Yuma, AZ: Fort Yuma Press, 1980. 594 pages. Reprint of the 1863 edition published by the U.S. Government Printing Office. These are the set of rules and regulations governing all aspects of army life—from allotments sent home to courts-martial to dress-uniform requirements. Also useful as a reference for Confederates, who had many of the same regulations.

————. *U.S. Infantry Tactics, for the Instruction, Exercise and Manoeuvres of the Soldier, Company, Line of Skirmishers, and Battalion for the Use of Colored Troops of the United States Infantry.* Washington, DC: U.S. Government Printing Office, 1863. 400 pages of text on drills, music, and tactics.

————. *U.S. Infantry Tactics, for the Instruction, Exercise and Manoeuvres of the United States Infantry, Including Infantry of the Line, Light Infantry and Riflemen. Prepared under the Direction of the War Department, and Authorized and Adopted by the Secretary of War, May 1, 1861.* Philadelphia: J. B. Lippincott & Co., 1861.

von Buckholtz, L. *Tactics for Officers of Infantry, Cavalry and Artillery: On the Science of War.* Richmond: J. W. Randolph, 1861.

Wheeler, Joseph. *A Revised System of Cavalry Tactics, for the Use of Cavalry and Mounted Infantry, Confederate States of America.* Mobile, AL: S. H. Goetzel & Co., 1863.

Williams, Lemuel D. *The American Illustrated Military Text-Book: Manual of Arms, Facings, Steps, Positions, etc., Employed in Heavy and Light Infantry and Rifles, According to Scott and Hardee Tactics, and the Army Regulations, 1857; Every Motion Being Fully Illustrated, Adapted to Self-Instruction and for Volunteer Uniform Corps: Also, Embracing the Principles of Alignments, Front and Rear, Column, About, Flank, Counter, Oblique Movements, Wheelings, Turns, etc., etc., for Squad Exercises.* Baltimore: J. Murphy, Printers, 1861. 175 pages.

Woodward, Joseph Janvier. *Hospital Steward's Manual: For the Instruction of Hospital Stewards, Ward-Masters, and Attendants, With their Several Duties. Prepared in Strict Accordance With Existing Regulations and the Customs of Service in the Armies of the United States of America, and Rendered Authoritative by the Order of the Surgeon General.* Philadelphia: Lippincott, 1862. Recently reprinted.

3: CAMP LIFE

Descriptions of camp life are found in the military manuals of the period, and in numerous diaries and personal recollections of the soldiers themselves.

Any reenactment camp will depend on the ground, the layout of the opposing forces, and the allocation of space to artillery parks, horses and the sutlers, authentic civilians, and modern camping. These camps are all complicated by the positions of parking lots, toilets, spectator access, and other modern encumbrances.

The basic street layout for a military camp is described in detail in the Army Regulations of both sides. However, camps showing "campaign" camping are very different from "garrison" camps. As a new recruit, you will basically be told where to pitch your tent, and how to do it. (That is one of the nice things about being a private—other people are always telling you how you are wrong and how to do things "properly.") Let more experienced reenactors show you how to pitch your camp, or let the historic site representatives lay out what they want.

Union Soldier Life

The following resources concern the camp life and experiences of Union troops. In looking for material giving accurate portrayals, original writing by veterans, especially material written near the time of the war, is the best. Reminiscences after the war, and sometimes significantly after the war, may be suspect. Details become vague after only a few years, and writers may leave out incidents or rewrite history for various purposes.

Also, many memoirs were written by senior officers. Reenactors strive to portray the lives of privates and NCOs, so you should look for the accounts of men on the line, not higher commands.

Books written by researchers should be suspect if they do not include footnotes. If there are no footnotes, there is no way of leading to the primary resources needed by authentic reenactors. Books written for the public, for children, and by nonhistorians have few if any footnotes. Avoid these. Look for books that have good footnotes and original photographs and that are referred to by other historians.

Ayers, James T. *Diary of James T. Ayers, Civil War Recruiter.* Springfield, IL: State of Illinois, 1947. This Union soldier recruited blacks in Alabama.

Bardeen, Charles William. *A Little Fifer's War Diary: With 17 maps, 60 Portraits, and 246 Other Illustrations.* Syracuse, NY: C.W. Bardeen, 1910. Both good and bad experiences in camp as seen by a young man.

Bear, Henry Clay. *The Civil War Letters of Henry C. Bear: A Soldier of the 116th Illinois Volunteer Infantry.* Harrogate, TN: Lincoln Memorial University Press, 1961.

Billings, John D. *Hardtack and Coffee, or the Unwritten Story of Army Life.* Boston: Smith Co., 1888. (Reprinted several times.) Excellent book with many fine illustrations.

Bockmiller, Stephen R. *The United States Marine Corps Aboard the USS* Constellation, *1855–1868.* Baltimore: Ship's Company, 1999. An excellent introduction to U.S. Marine Corps history.

Bopp, Lawrence J. Sailor Life Aboard the USS Constellation, *1855–1868.* Baltimore: Ship's Company, 1999. An excellent introduction to U.S. Naval living history.

Carter, Robert Goldwthaite, ed. *Four Brothers in Blue, or Sunshine and Shadows of the War of the Rebellion: A Story of the Great Civil War from Bull Run to Appomattox.* Austin, TX: University of Texas Press, 1913, 1978. ISBN: 0292724268. Letters home to Maine and Massachusetts from the Army of the Potomac.

Gavin, William G., ed. *Infantryman Pettit: The Civil War Letters of Corporal Frederick Pettit.* New York: Avon Books, 1990. ISBN: 038071437X. Pettit was a member of the 100th PVI.

"Guns of the Civil War." Malibu, CA: Monterey Movie Company, 1993. Part 1: "A Greater Moral Force"; Part 2: "Measure for Measure"; Part 3: "Against the Thunderstorm." An interesting three-part documentary video (three hours long), it is an examination of the long arms used during the war, with a lot of good information and some interesting shots of the rifles. Especially good for learning about the various arms used and goes beyond the usual infantryman's experience.

Hess, Earl J. *The Union Soldier in Battle: Enduring the Ordeal of Combat.* Lawrence: University Press of Kansas, 1997. Impressive descriptions of combat experiences and the psychology of Union soldiers.

Johnson, Paul D. *Civil War Cartridge Boxes of the Union Infantryman.* Examines the four basic types of issued cartridge boxes.

Jones, Jenkins Lloyd. *An Artilleryman's Diary.* Madison, WI: Wisconsin Historical Commission, 1914. A narrative of service in Battery 6, Wisconsin State Artillery.

Kautz, A. *Company Clerk: Showing How and When to Make Out All the Returns, Reports, Rolls and Other Papers, and What to Do With Them.* Reprint of the 1863 Union army manual.

Kays, Steven. *The 19th Indiana: Gone but Not Forgotten.* n.p., 1994. Videotape history of this regiment of the Iron Brigade, narrated by Lonnie Perkins.

Keller, Kenneth. *Sutler Paper Money.* Sutlers often printed tokens and script, which they gave back in change or sold at a discount or advanced as loans, and that were only good at their own sutlery.

Kingsbury, Allen Alonzo. *The Hero of Medfield: Containing an Account of the Journals and Letters of Allen Alonzo Kingsbury, Member of Co. H, Chelsea Volunteers, Mass., 1st Regiment, Who Was Killed by the Rebels Near Yorktown, April 26, 1862.* Boston: J. M. Hewes, 1862. Private Kingsbury was a bugler for the regiment.

Kinzer, Cal. *The Hardcracker Handbook.* Bixby, OK: Self published, 1996. Compilation of reprinted articles from various reenactment journals for the Western Federal Impression.

Langellier, J. Philip. *Army Blue: The Uniform of Uncle Sam's Regulars, 1848–1873.* Primary sources are combed for an exacting look at uniforms. Not seen.

Lord, Francis. *Civil War Sutlers and their Wares.* New York: Yoseloff, 1969. Accounts of sutlers.

McKee, Paul. "Notes on the Federal Sack Coat." *Military Collector and Historian* 47 (Summer 1995).

Nelson, Dean. "The Union Army Standard Size and Make Shirt." *Military Collector and Historian* 47 (Fall 1995).

Regulations and Notes for the Uniform of the Army of the United States, 1861. Compiled and edited by Jacques Noel Jacobsen, Jr. Union City, TN: Pioneer Press, 1990. Reprint of the 1861 Army Regs on uniforms.

Revised U.S. Army Regulations. Washington, DC: U.S. Government Printing Office, 1863. Reprint. Yuma, AZ: Fort Yuma Press, 1980. Best set of rules for understanding army life. Now hard to find, but still available through interlibrary loan.

Small, Harold A., ed. *The Road to Richmond: The Civil War Memoirs of Major Abner R. Small of the Sixteenth Maine Volunteers: Together with a Diary He Kept while a Prisoner of War.* Berkeley, CA: University of California Press, 1939.

Smith, Robin. *The American Civil War: The Union Army*. London: Brassey's, 1996. The book details army uniforms, as well as militia and American Indian cavalry units.

Stamatelos, James. *Notes on the Uniform and Equipment of the United States Cavalryman, 1861–1865*. The Sutler's Wagon, n.d. Pamphlet on Yankee cavalrymen stuff. Not seen.

Thompson, Jerry D. *Mexican Texans in the Union Army*. El Paso: Texas Western Press, 1986. Account of the Union's 2nd Texas Cavalry of *Tejanos* from the Rio Grande.

Tice, Warren K. *Uniform Buttons of the United States, 1776–1865*. More than 3,500 buttons are illustrated in this in-depth examination of military buttons.

United States War Department. *Revised Regulations of the Army of the United States, 1861. With a Full Index*. Philadelphia: J. G. L. Brown, 1861. Printed by authority of the War Department. Reprint. Harrisburg, PA: National Historical Society. These are the regs in force for the first year of the WBTS. The next item is the revised edition for 1863.

0. *Revised United States Army Regulations: 1861; With an Appendix Containing the Changes and Laws Affecting Army Regulations and Articles of War to June, 1863*. 1863. Reprint. U.S. Government Printing Office, Yuma, AZ: Fort Yuma Press, 1980. 594 pages. The set of rules and regulations governing all aspects of army life, from allotments sent home to courts-martial to dress-uniform requirements. Also useful as a reference for Confederates, who had many of the same regulations.

Weaver, C. P., ed. *Thank God My Regiment is an African One: The Civil War Diary of Col. Nathan W. Daniels*. Baton Rouge, LA: Louisiana State University Press, 1998. Biography of the commander of the 2nd Louisiana Native Guard Volunteers, one of the first black regiments.

Confederate Soldier Life

Battle-fields of the South, from Bull Run to Fredericksburgh, with Sketches of Confederate Commanders, and Gossip of the Camps, by an English Combatant, Lieutenant of Artillery on the Field Staff. 1864. Reprint. Alexandria, VA: Time-Life Books, 1984. ISBN: 0809443929. Interesting account of an Englishman serving in the Confederate army.

Casier, John Overton. *Four Years in the Stonewall Brigade, 4th Edition, Revised and Corrected by and Improved by Jed Hotchkiss, with Notes and Index by James Robertson, Jr.* 1893. Reprint. Dayton: Morningside Press, 1971. An account of a soldier with the 33d Virginia Infantry and the Stonewall Brigade.

Confederate Army Regulations, Richmond, 1861–1864. I haven't seen a copy except on microfilm.

Confederate States of America War Department. *Regulations for the Army of the Confederate States: Corrected and Enlarged with a Revised Index* [the only correct edition]. Richmond: J. W. Randolph, 1863. 420 pages. (Another copy was printed by West and Johnson of Richmond, again in 1863, but with 432 pages. The Randolph edition is considered the more correct and was republished by the National Historical Society, Harrisburg, PA, in 1980.) The how-to book for C.S. Army reenactment.

Czekanski, Tom. *Third Mississippi Infantry Regiment Camp of Instruction.* New Orleans, n.p., 1998. Like *The Hardcracker Handbook,* this is a collection of selected articles from reenactment magazines, but aimed at the Confederate impression.

Dame, William Meade. *From the Rapidan to Richmond and the Spotsylvania Campaign, a Sketch in Personal Narration of the Scenes a Soldier Saw.* Baltimore: Green-Lucas Co., 1920.

Dinkins, James. *1861–1865 by an Old Johnnie: Personal Recollections and Experiences in the Confederate Army.* Cincinnati: Clarke Co., 1897.

Eggleston, George C. *A Rebel's Recollections.* 1887. Reprint. Bloomington, IN: Indiana University Press, 1959.

Field, Ron. *The American Civil War: The Confederate Army.* London: Brassey's, 1996. State-by-state analysis of uniforms.

Fletcher, William Andrew. *Rebel Private, Private Front and Rear.* 1908. Reprint. New York: Dutton Press, 1995. Account of a soldier in the 5th Texas Infantry.

Ford, Athur Peronneau. *Life in the Confederate Army: Being Personal Experiences of a Private Soldier in the Confederate Army.* New York: Neale Publishing Co., 1905.

Hill, Daniel H. *The Confederate Soldier in the Ranks: An Address by Major General D. H. Hill, of North Carolina, before the Virginia Division of the Association of the Army of Northern Virginia, at Richmond, Virginia, on Thursday Evening, October 22, 1885.* Richmond, VA: W. E. Jones, 1885. 28 pages.

Hunton, Eppa. *Autobiography of Eppa Hunton.* Richmond: William Byrd Press, 1933. Biography of an officer, but with good information about army life.

Jensen, Leslie. "A Survey of Confederate Central Government Issue Jackets," Parts 1 and 2. *Military Collector & Historian* 16 (Fall/Winter 1989).

McCarthy, Carlton. *Detailed Minutiae of Soldier Life in the Army of Northern Virginia.* Richmond: C. McCarthy, 1882. (Reprinted several times.) ISBN:0803281978. One of the best resources of the common soldier's life, with good illustrations.

McKim, Randolph Harrison. *A Soldier's Recollection: Leaves from the Diary of a Young Confederate, with an Oration on the Motives and Aims of the South.* 1910. Reprint. Alexandria, VA: Time-Life Books, 1984. ISBN: 080944271X.

Mixson, Frank M. *Reminiscences of a Private.* Columbia, SC: State Co., 1910. Account of a soldier in Company E, 1st Regiment, South Carolina Volunteer Infantry.

Moore, Edward Alexander. *The Story of a Cannoneer Under Stonewall Jackson, in Which is Told the Part taken by the Rockbridge Artillery in the Army of Northern Virginia.* New York: Neale Publishing, 1907. Reprinted by Time-Life Books as *Life in an Artillery Battery from Virginia.*

Stevenson, William G. *Thirteen Months in the Rebel Army.* 1864. Reprint. New York. A. S. Barnes, 1959. Account of a drafted soldier.

Stiles, Robert. *Four Years Under Marse Robert.* 1903. Reprint. Dayton: Morningside Press, 1977. ISBN: 08902904OX.

Toney, Marcus Breckenridge. *The Privations of a Private: The Campaign under Gen. R. E. Lee; the Campaign under Gen. Stonewall Jackson; Bragg's Invasion of Kentucky; the Chickamauga Campaign; the Wilderness Campaign; Prison Life in the North; the Privations of a Citizen; the Ku-Klux Klan; a United Citizenship.* Nashville: M. B. Toney, 1905.

Watkins, Sam R. *Co Aytch, "Maury Grays," First Tennessee Regiment, of a Sideshow of the Big Show.* 1882. Reprint. Jackson, TN: McCowat-Mercer Press, 1952. One of the best-known and more entertaining accounts of Confederate army life.

Watson, William. *Life in the Confederate Army, Being the Observations and Experiences of an Alien in the South During the American Civil War.* New York: Scribner & Walford, 1888. William Watson was from Scotland and served in the Confederate army.

4: CIVILIAN REENACTING

Women in the Civil War

Alcott, Louisa May. *Hospital Sketches.* Reprinted several times. Memoirs of her experiences in Washington hospitals.

Ames, Mary. *From a New England Woman's Diary in Dixie in 1865.* 1906. Reprint. New York: Negro Universities Press, 1963. ISBN: 0837113865.

Andrews, Matthew Page. *The Women of the South in War Times.* Baltimore: Norman, Remington Press, 1920. Personal narrative of women in the Upper South.

Ashkenazi, Elliott, ed. *Civil War Diary of Clara Solomon: Growing Up in New Orleans, 1861–1862.* Baton Rouge, LA: Louisiana State University Press, 1995. Diary narrative of a Jewish teenager in New Orleans.

Baird, Nancy C., ed. *Journals of Amanda Virginia Edmonds, Lass of Mosby's Confederacy, 1859–1867.* Delaplane, VA: N.C. Baird, 1984.

Bernard, Richard M., and Marie A. Vinovskis. "The Female School Teacher in Ante-Bellum Massachusetts." *Journal of Social History* 10 (March 1977): 332–45.

Boykin, Laura N., and Mary W. Stock, eds. *Shinplasters and Homespun: The Diary of Laura Nisbet Boykin.* Rockville, MD: Printex, 1975.

Brock, Sallie A. Putnam. *Richmond During the War: Four Years of Personal Observation.* New York: Carelton Press, 1867. Reprinted by University of Nebraska Press, 1996. Interesting account of the war from the view of a Richmond lady.

Burgess, Lauren Cook. "Typical Soldier May Have Been Red-Blooded American Woman." *Washington Times,* October 5, 1991.

Burgess, Lauren Cook, ed. *An Uncommon Soldier: The Civil War Letters of Sarah Rosetta Wakeman, 153rd Regiment, New York State Volunteers.* New York: Oxford University Press, 1994. Letters home from a woman posing as a man in the Union army.

Chang, Ina. *A Separate Battle: Women and the Civil War.* New York: Lodestar Books, 1991. A good book for young readers on the role of women during the war.

Clark, James Madison. *Luella Blassingame: The Blue and the Gray*. Nashville: McQuiddy Press, 1903.

Culpepper, Marilyn Mayer. *Trials and Triumphs: Women in the American Civil War*. East Lansing: Michigan State University Press, 1991.

Daly, Maria Lydig. *Diary of a Union Lady, 1861–1865*. Edited by Harold E. Hammond. New York: Funk and Wagnalls, 1862. Mrs. Daly was the wife of a New York City judge during the war.

Dannett, Sylvia G. L., ed. *Noble Women of the North*. New York: Thomas Yoseloff, 1959. This is an excellent account taken from diaries and letters of the time.

Davis, Rodney 0. "Private Albert Cashier as Regarded by His/Her Comrades." *Illinois Historical Journal* 82, no. 2 (Summer 1989): 108–12.

Dawson, Sarah Morgan. Her diary has been printed several times under different titles. *Sarah Morgan: The Civil War Diary of a Southern Woman, The Civil War Diary of Sarah Morgan,* or *A Confederate Girl's Diary*. Personal story of a young Louisiana woman, who was only eighteen years old when the war began.

Edmonds, Sarah Emma E. *Nurse and Spy in the Union Army: Comprising the Adventures and Experiences of a Woman in Hospitals, Camps and Battlefields*. Hartford, CT: W. S. Williams & Co., 1865. (Reprinted several times.) Sarah Edmonds, dressed as a man, was a courier on the staff of Gen. Phil Kearney.

Edmondston, Catherine Devereux. *Journal of a Secesh Lady.: The Diary of Catherine Ann Devereux Edmonston, 1860–1866*. Raleigh, NC: Division of Archives and History, 1979. Accounts of a woman running a plantation in Halifax County, North Carolina.

Farnham, Christie Ann. *The Education of the Southern Belle: Education and Socialization in the Antebellum South*. New York: New York University Press, 1994. ISBN: 0814726151.

Faust, Drew Gilpin. *Mothers of Invention: Women of the Slaveholding South in the American Civil War*. Chapel Hill: University of North Carolina Press, 1996. Good overview of Southern women and their problems with their society and the enemy during the war.

Fraser, Walter J., et al., eds. *The Web of Southern Social Relations: Women, Family and Education*. Athens, GA: University of Georgia Press, 1985. ISBN:0820307874.

Hague, Parthenia Antoinette. *A Blockaded Family: Life in Southern Alabama during the Civil War*. 1888. Reprint. Bedford, MA: Applewood Books, 1995. ISBN:1557092478.

Hall, Richard. *Patriots in Disguise: Women Warriors of the Civil War*. New York: Harlowe & Co., 1994. A list of all known women posing as men to join the army.

Hickson, Shirley Ann. "The Development of Higher Education for Women in the Antebellum South." Ph.D. diss., University of South Carolina, 1985. 296 pages.

Jones, Katharine McBeth. *Heroines of Dixie: Confederate Women Tell their Story of the War*. Indianapolis: Bobbs-Merrilll, 1955. Reprinted. Personal accounts of the homefront during the war; many accounts are excerpts from diaries of younger women and teenagers.

————. *Ladies of Richmond, Confederate Capital.* Indianapolis: Bobbs-Merrill, 1962. Personal accounts of Richmond residents during the conflict.

Leisch, Juanita. "Commentary." *Glass House Gazette* 2, no. 1 (January 1987). Produced by the Glass House Gang, 1235 Battery Avenue, Baltimore, MD 21230. Juanita Leisch is one of the nation's experts on civilian clothing during the middle of the nineteenth century.

————. *Costumer's Family Album: 1860–65.* Arlington, VA: Wearlooms, 1983.

————. "Defining Historical Accuracy: Could, Would, Should Test." *Civil War Lady* 1, no. 1 (May-June 1991): 4–7.

————. *Family Album: Ladies' Wear Daily.* Berryville, VA: Wearlooms, 1986.

————. *An Introduction to Civil War Civilians.* Gettysburg, PA: Thomas Publications, 1994. ISBN: 0939631709.

————. *Who Wore What: Women's Wear 1861–1865.* Gettysburg, PA: Thomas Publications, 1995. ISBN: 0939631814. An excellent book on civilian clothing with numerous photographs from the period.

Livermore, Mary Ashton Rice. *My Story of the War: A Woman's Narrative of Four Years Personal Experience As Nurse in the Union Army, and in Relief work At Home, In Hospitals, Camps and at the Front, During the War of the Rebellion.* Reprinted several times. Excellent accounts of the U.S. Sanitary Commission and women's roles during the war. She also wrote *Pen Picture, or, Sketches from Domestic Life.* Chicago: S. C. Griggs Publishing, 1862. An interesting account of domestic life in the North.

Logan, Kate Virginia Cox. *My Confederate Girlhood: The Memoirs of Kate Virginia Cox Logan.* 1932. Reprint. New York: Arno Press, 1980. ISBN: 0405128495. Logan was a resident of central Virginia during the war.

Logan, Mary. *Reminiscences of a Soldier's Life.* Carbondale: Southern Illinois University Press, 1997. From the wife of Union general John A. Logan.

Loughborough, Mary Ann Webster. *My Cave in Vicksburg, with Letters of Trial and Travel.* Spartanburg, SC: Reprint Shop, 1976. ISBN: 0871522179.

Massey, Mary Elizabeth. *Bonnet Brigades: Women in the Civil War.* New York: A. A. Knopf, 1966. Reprinted as *Women in the Civil War.* Good account of women during the Civil War.

Meyer, Eugene L. "The Odyssey of Pvt. Rosetta Wakeman, Union Army: The Soldier Left a Portrait and Her Eyewitness Account." *Smithsonian* 24, no. 10 (January 1994): 96–104.

Middleton, Lee. *Hearts of Fire: Soldier Women of the Civil War, with an Addendum on Female Reenactors.* Franklin, NC: Genealogy Pub. House, 1993. ISBN:1882755006. 254 pages of women combatants.

Mihesuah, Devon A. *Cultivating the Rosebuds: The Education of Women at the Cherokee Female Seminary, 1851–1909.* Urbana, IL: University of Illinois Press, 1993. ISBN: 0252019539.

Moore, Frank. *Women of the War: Their Heroism and Self-Sacrifice.* Hartford, CI: S. S. Scranton, 1866. Early accounts of women who were involved in the war.

Norse, Clifford C. "School Life of Amanda Worthington, Washington County, 1857–1862." *Journal of Mississippi History* 34 (May 1972): 107–16.

Pope, Christie Farnham. "Preparation for Pedestals: North Carolina Antebellum Female Seminaries." Ph.D. diss., University of Chicago, 1977.

Richards, Caroline Cowles. *Village Life in America, 1852–1872, Including the Period of the American Civil War as Told in the Diary of a Schoolgirl.* Williamstown, MA: Corner House, 1972.

Roos, Marita. *An Approach to the Interpretation of Women's History for an Urban Cultural Park in Seneca Falls, New York.* Master's thesis, University of Georgia, 1989. 85 pages.

Thomas, Ella Gertrude Clanton. *The Secret Eye: The Journal of Ella Gertrude Thomas, 1848–1889.* Chapel Hill: University of North Carolina Press, 1990. Social life and customs of women in Georgia.

Thompson, Eleanor Wolf. *Education for Ladies, 1830–1860: Ideas on Education in Magazines for Women.* New York: King's Crown Press, 1947. Also submitted as a Ph.D. thesis to Columbia University.

Vallone, Lynne. *Disciplines of Virtue: Girls' Culture in the Eighteenth and Nineteenth Centuries.* New Haven, CT: Yale University Press, 1995. Vallone contrasts expected behavior of adolescent and preteen boys and girls.

Virginia Historical Society. *Documenting Women's Lives: A User's Guide to Manuscripts at the Virginia Historical Society.* Richmond: The Virginia Historical Society, 1996. Bibliography and instructions on researching women's roles during the Civil War.

Wendel, Vickie. "Washer Woman." *Civil War Times Illustrated* 38, no.4 (August 1999): 31–36. Good information on camp laundresses.

Woolsey, Jane Stuart. *Hospital Day: Reminiscences of a Civil War Nurse.* Reprint of the 1868 edition of her memoir as superintendent of nurses at a Union hospital in Fairfax, Virginia.

The Workwoman's Guide: Containing Instructions to the Inexperienced in Cutting Out and Completing Those Articles of Wearing Apparel, etc., Which Are Usually Made at Home; Also, Explanations of Upholstery, Straw-Platting, Bonnet-Making, Knitting, etc. 1838. Reprint. Guilford, CT: Opus Publications, 1986. ISBN:0940983001. 300 pages with illustrations. The title says it all.

York, Kathleen. *The Victorian Ladies Sketchbook.* 3 vols. Elgin, IL: The House of York, 1980. ISBN: 0939808013.

Children

The American Boy's Book of Sports and Games: A Repository of in-and-out-of-doors Amusements for Boys and Youth, Illustrated with over 600 Engravings. New York: Dick and Fitzgerald, 1864. Tips on games and sports, from arithmetic puzzles to parlor magic tricks. Pretty neat.

Bennett, Daphne. *Queen Victoria's Children.* New York: St. Martin's Press, 1980. Biographies of the childhood of the British queen's children, with interesting accounts of the royal nursery, education, and childcare.

Boggs, Johnny D. "Charge!" *Boys Life* 88, no. 7 (July 1998): 36–39. Boy Scouts at the reenactment of Antietam and how this helps them understand history.

Davis, Sharon, Donk, Karlene M. and Gordon, Lois. "A Feast of Ideas for Thanksgiving." *Schooldays* 18, no. 2 (Nov 1998) 23–25. Reenacting the first Thanksgiving for primary school children.

Early American School Books. Maynard, Mass.: Chandler Press, 1988. Choice pages reprinted from American school books from 1785 to 1880.

Endless Mirth and Amusement: A Capital and Clever Collection of Mirthful Games, Parlour Pastimes, Shadow Plays, Magic, Conjuring, Card Tricks, Chemical Surprises, Fireworks, Forfeits, Etc. Compiled and illustrated by Charles Gilbert, George Cruikshank, et al. London: Dean and Sons, 1867. This teaches children how to have fun and make mischief in historically correct ways.

England, J. Merton, ed. *Buckeye Schoolmaster: A Chronicle of Midwestern Rural Life, 1853-1865*. Bowling Green: Bowling Green State University Popular Press, 1996. Diaries and letters of John M. Roberts, an Ohio schoolteacher in Madison County.

Harten, James Alan. *The Children's Civil War*. Chapel Hill: University of North Carolina Press, 1998. The impact of war on the lives of children.

Marten, James. *Lessons of War: The Civil War in Children's Magazines*. Wilmington, DE/: SR Books, 1999. How the war was portrayed to children through Northern periodicals.

Metzler, Suzanne. *Witness to History: Using Hands-On Activities, A Guidebook for High School History Teachers*. U.S. Dept. of Education, ERIC Report #387416, 1995. Activities for teachers on how to make marbled paper, "Living History Day," quill pens, and other artifacts.

Murphy, Jim. *The Boy's War: Confederate and Union Soldiers Talk about the Civil War*. New York: Clarion Books, 1989. Good photos and pathos of documented accounts of our "seed corn" in the armies.

Nineteenth-Century Clothing and Life

Civilian clothing between 1850 and 1865 is such a large topic that no one book can do it justice. For the reenactor to be knowledgeable about not only the cut and style but also the method of wearing period clothes, a great deal of experimentation and research are necessary. Research into civilian fashion is more arduous than for military uniforms, since less has been written and preserved.

By far the most available source of information about proper clothing is from the women in reenacting. My hat is tipped to them, since I have seen the results of their research far outshine the results of most men, who often look no further than a description of proper uniform cut. Women in their research often investigate children's and men's clothing as well.

The following books are a place to start in your research. Some of these items have been taken from the footnotes and bibliographies of other researchers.

Arnold, Janet. *Patterns of Fashion: Englishwomen's Dresses and Their Construction*. New York: Drama Book Specialists, 1972. 2 vols. ISBN: 0910482500.

Bandel, Eugene. *Frontier Life in the Army, 1854–1861.* The Southwest Historical Series, edited by Ralph P. Bieber, vol. 2. Glendale, CA: Arthur H. Clark Co., 1932. Eugene Bandel was a Prussian immigrant who served in the 6th U.S. Infantry and later worked as a civilian on the military post at Benicia Arsenal, California.

Baumgarten, Linda. "Plains, Plaids and Cotton: Woolens for Slave Clothing." *Ars Textrina* 15 (July 1991): 203–21. Although concerned with an earlier period, this is still a good reference on cloth used for slaves.

"Beadle's Dime Books." This series of books on common topics are being reprinted by different sutlers, such as Bob Sullivan and Virginia Mescher. They include titles such as *Base Ball Player, Dressmaking, Letter Writer, Ball Room Companion,* and several other period titles. There are also large collections of the Beadle Dime books in the New York Public Library and at Harvard University Library. They were very popular during the Civil War period and afterward.

Beaton, Cecil. *Fashion: An Anthology. For the Victoria and Albert Museum.* London: HMSO, 1972.

Beecher, Catherine Ester. *Letters to Persons Who are Engaged in Domestic Service.* New York: Leavitt & Trow, 1842. Advice for domestic servants.

Betts, Vicki. *Clothing Bibliography.* Self-published, 1996. Vicki Betts has put together an excellent bibliography of clothing information from reenactor and other publications.

Bloch, E. Maurice. *The Paintings of George Caleb Bingham.* University of Missouri Press, 1986. Bingham was a mid-nineteenth-century painter of Western scenes, and his antebellum images of civilian clothing styles and how they were worn are fascinating.

Blum, Stella, ed. *Fashions and Costumes from Godey's Lady's Book.* New York: Dover Publications, 1985. ISBN: 0486248410. 91 pages.

———. *Victorian Fashions and Costumes from Harper's Bazaar: 1867 to 1898.* New York: Dover Publications, 1974.

Bradfield, Nancy. *Costume in Detail, Women's Dress, 1730–1930.* London: Harrap Co., 1981. ISBN: 0245536086. 391 pages.

Braun-Ronsdorf, Margarete. *Mirror of Fashion: A History of European Costumes, 1789 to 1929.* New York: McGraw Hill, Co., 1964. Although this is a European fashion study, it does comment on some American fashion.

Breathnach, Sarah Ban. *Mrs. Sharp's Traditions: Nostalgic Suggestions for Recreating the Family Celebrations and Seasonal Pastimes of the Victorian Home.* New York: Simon and Schuster, 1990. ISBN: 067169569X. This is an excellent and highly recommended book on how to capture the spirit of the Victorian age in the twentieth century.

Bronson, L. D. *Early American Specs: An Exciting Collectible.* Glendale, CA: Occidental Pub. Co., 1974. 184 pages. Chaotic history of eyeglasses, with fine illustrations. This book fortunately has an American, rather than European, point of view.

Brooke, Iris. *English Children's Costumes since 1775.* London: A&C Black, Ltd., 1930. 88 pages, color plates. Many urban Americans copied British fashions.

Buck, Anne. *Victorian Costume and Costume Accessories.* 1961. Reprint. Bedford, England: Ruth Bean Co., 1984. ISBN: 0903585170.

Burrows, Adrienne and Ivan Schumaker. *Portraits of the Insane: The Case of Dr. Diamond.* New York: Quartet Books, 1990. Haunting photographic study of insane patients in mid-nineteenth-century England. Excellent but startling resource for examples of working-class clothing and styles.

Button, Jeanne. *A History of Costume in Slides, Notes and Commentaries.* New Haven, CT: Button, 1975.

Calthrop, Dion Clayton. *English Dress from Victoria to George V.* London: Chapman and Hall, Ltd., 1934. 172 pages.

Campbell, Edward D., and Kym S. Rice. *Before Freedom Came: African American Life in the Ante-Bellum South to Accompany an Exhibition Organized by the Museum of the Confederacy with Essays by Drew Gilpin Faust.* Richmond: Museum of the Confederacy, and Charlottesville: University Press of Virginia, 1991. Excellent examination of slave life, clothing, and culture.

Chenoune, Farid. *A History of Men's Fashions.* Paris: Flammarion Press, 1993. Well-photographed look at fashion over time—but only a small section on the 1850s to 1870s.

Chesterfield's Complete Rules of Etiquette and the Usages of Society. New York: Dick & Fitzgerald, 1857. Reprint. Iowa City, IA: Cunningham's Homespun Commissary, 1987. (P.O. Box 789, Iowa City, IA 52240.)

Civil War Ladies: Fashions and Needle Arts of the Early 1860's. ISBN: 0914046098. 348 pages. Primary source material from *Peterson's Magazine,* plus additional hairstyles and hair jewelry.

Clayton, Thomas H. *Close to the Land: The Way We Lived in North Carolina, 1820–1870.* Chapel Hill, NC: University of North Carolina Press, 1983. ISBN:080784103X. An illustrated work on life in the old South.

Compaing, C., and L. Devere. *The Tailor's Guide.* 2d ed. 2 vols. New York: Thomas N. Dale, Co., 1857.

Confederate Receipt Book: A Compilation of Over 100 Receipts, Adapted to the Times. Richmond, 1863. Reprint. Mattituck, NY: Amereon Press, 1983. ISBN:0848800079. This is a good way to find out how people lived during the WBTS. The methods and techniques show how the Southern home front made do with the demands from the army and the coils of the blockade.

Cordy, Ann Elizabeth. "Investigation of Thread Color Change in American Civil War Uniforms." Ph.D. Thesis, University of Maryland, 1983. Sewing stuff and dye colors of the period, and how they change color over time.

The Corset and the Crinoline: A Book of Modes and Costumes from Remote Periods to the Present Time by W.B.L. [William Barry Lord]. London: Ward, Locke and Tyler, 1868. 227 pages.

Corson, Richard. *Fashions in Eyeglasses.* Chester Springs, PA: Dufour Co., 1967. 288 pages.

A Country Kitchen, 1850. Maynard, MA: Chandler Press. 1987. Reprints of kitchen advertisements, recipes, and techniques from 1850.

Crawford, Laurie Casey. "The Analysis of Mid-Nineteenth Century Men's Outer Garments from a Deep Ocean Site." Ph.D. Thesis, Ohio State University, 1994. Accounts of the garments recovered from the 1857 wreck off South Carolina of the *Central America*.

Crinoline und Amazonenhut, oder Anectdoten fuer Freunde und Freinde der Crinoline und des "letzen Versuchs." Nordhausen, 1858.

Cunnington, Cecil Willet. *The Art of English Costume*. London: Collins, 1948. 243 pages.

———. *A Dictionary of English Costume, 900–1900*. Philadelphia: Dufour Editions, 1960. 281 pages.

———. *English Women's Clothing in the Nineteenth Century*. London: Faber and Faber, 1937. Reprint. New York: Dover Press, 1955. 460 pages. This is a treasure that has some good information on hairstyles and fashions for English ladies.

———. *Feminine Attitudes in the Nineteenth Century*. Reprint. 1935. New York: Haskell House, Publishers, 1973. Social customs and attitudes of women in the nineteenth century, with a very English slant that is not necessarily consistent with American attitudes.

———. *Handbook of English Costume in the Nineteenth Century*. Philadelphia: Dufour Editions, 1959. 606 pages. Witty and well-illustrated depiction of English dress. An excellent section on men's clothing.

———. *The Perfect Lady*. London: M. Parrish, 1948. 71 pages.

———. *A Picture History of English Costume*. London: Vista Books, 1960. 160 pages.

———. *Why Women Wear Clothes*. London: Faber and Faber, 1941. 261 pages.

———. *Women*. London: Burke Publishers, 1950.

Cunnington, Cecil Willet, and Phyllis Cunnington. *The History of Underclothes*. London: M. Joseph Co., 1951. 266 pages.

Dallas, George. "New York 1865." *History Today* 37 (December 1987): 17–22. Excellent account of the health and politics of America's largest city in 1865. Good background information for New York reenactors, both military and civilian.

Dangers of Crinoline, Steel Hoops, Etc. London: Vickers Publishers, 1858. 16 pages. Polemic against crinolines.

Davenport, F. Garvin. *Cultural Life in Nashville on the Eve of the Civil War*. Chapel Hill, NC: University of North Carolina Press, 1941. Interesting discussion on antebellum society on the western side of the Appalachians.

Davidson, Derek C. *Spectacles, Lorgnettes and Monocles*. Privately printed. 32 pages. Good pamphlet about the history of glasses.

Davis, R. I. *Men's Garments, 1830–1900: A Guide to Pattern Cutting and Tailoring*. Studio City, CA: Players' Press, 1994. Diagrams and other illustrations show how to cut and sew men's fashions.

de Marly, Diana. *Fashion for Men: An Illustrated History.* London: B. T. Batsford, 1989. History of men's clothing.

Deetz, James. *In Small Things Forgotten: Archaeology of Early American Life.* New York: Anchor Books/Doubleday, 1996. Excellent examples of how small, often-overlooked artifacts add new interpretations to American life in New England and Virginia.

DeLeon, Thomas Cooper. *Four Years in Rebel Capitals: An Inside View of Life in the Southern Confederacy, from Birth to Death, From Original Notes, Collated in the Years 1861 to 1865.* Mobile, AL: Gossip Printing, 1890. Reprinted 1968. Personal narrative of life and travels in the South.

Delo, David M. *Peddlers and Post Traders: The Army Sutler on the Frontier.* Salt Lake City: University of Utah Press, 1992. Reprinted by Kingfisher Books, 1998. Good account of sutlers and other army civilians during the war.

Durand, Sally Graham. "The Dress of the Ante-Bellum Field Slave in Louisiana and Mississippi from 1830 to 1860." Master's thesis, Louisiana State University, 1977.

Eales, Anne Bruner. *Army Wives on the American Frontier: Living by the Bugles.* Boulder, CO: Johnson Books, 1996. A rare glimpse into the lives of women living out West in the second half of the nineteenth century.

Ewing, Elizabeth. *Dress and Undress: A History of Women's Underwear.* London: Batsford Press, 1989. History of lingerie.

Fennelly, Catherine. *The Garb of Country New Englanders, 1790 to 1840.* Sturbridge, MA: Old Sturbridge Village, 1966. Although this stops before the WBTS period, it is a good discussion of early-nineteenth-century clothing worn by average Americans.

Forty, George and Anne Forty. *They Also Served: A Pictorial Anthology of Camp Followers through the Ages.* Speldhurst, England: Midas Books, 1979. History of wives, servants, sutlers, tradesmen, entertainers, and canteen staff, who followed the troops.

Foster, Vanda. *A Visual History of Costume: The Nineteenth Century.* New York: Drama Book Publishers, 1984. ISBN: 0713440953.

Frank Leslie's New Family Magazine. New York: Frank Leslie, 1857–60. Fascinating to flip through, page by page.

Fry, Gladys-Marie. *Stitched from the Soul: Slave quilts from the Ante-Bellum South.* New York: Dutton Studio Books in Association with the Museum of American Folk Art, 1990. Although this work is on quilts, it has several good photographs of slave laborers and clothing.

Fun and Games of Long Ago. Maynard, MA: Chandler Press, 1988. ISBN:0944593100. Reprinted selections from an 1864 book on games for boys and girls.

Gardner, James B., and Adam George Rollis, eds. *Ordinary People and Everyday Life: Perspectives on the New Social History.* Nashville: American Association for State and Local History Press, 1983. ISBN: 091005066X. Discusses the need to interpret the lives of the average class member, rather than the uncommonly rich or talented people of history.

Gernsheim, Alison. *Victorian and Edwardian Fashion: A Photographic Survey.* New York: Dover Publications, 1981. ISBN: 0486242056. 104 pages. Originally published as *Fashion and Reality, 1840–1914,* by Faber and Faber of London, 1963. Gernsheim does an excellent job of describing the fashions of the period, as well as the social milieu that led to the development of those fashions. Good background material for living history and period clothing.

Gibbs-Smith, Charles H. *The Fashionable Lady in the Nineteenth Century. For the Victoria and Albert Museum.* London: HMSO, 1960. 184 pages.

Gladstone, William, A. *Men of Color.* Gettysburg: Thomas, 1993. Examines the role of black men during the Civil War.

Godey's Magazine. Edited by L. A. Godey and Sarah J. Hale. Vols. 1–137. New York: The Godey Company, 1830–98. This magazine caught the spirit of the age. Of all the works, this is the most interesting to thumb through and peruse. The advice is sometimes wise, sometimes silly, but always insightful into the mores and manners of the Victorians.

Goodman, Deborah Lerme. "Paisley Shawls: A Democratic Fashion" *Fiberarts* 12 (May 1985): 52–53.

Graham's Illustrated Magazine. Edited by George R. Graham and Edgar Allan Poe. Philadelphia, 1844–58. 32 volumes, title varies.

Harper's Bazaar. Philadelphia, 1867–1901. Although after the Civil War period, this weekly fashion magazine is a good source for information on the society of the general period.

Harris, Joseph E. *Afro-American History Interpretation at Selected National Parks.* Washington, DC: Howard University, 1978. Prepared by the History Department Research Team, Howard University, September 1978. 238 pages.

Hartley, Florence. *The Ladies' Handbook of Fancy and Ornamental Work: Civil War Era.* Reprinted 1991 from the 1859 edition by R. L. Shep.

Hawks, Alta Marcellus. "Food, Clothing and Shelter of the American Slave." Ph.D. thesis, Southern Methodist University, 1936.

Holden, Angus. *Elegant Modes in the Nineteenth Century.* London: G. Allen and Unwin, Ltd., 1935. 123 pages.

How to Dance Through Time: The Romance of the Mid-19th Century Couple Dances Including the Waltz, Gallop, Polka, Schottische and Polka Mazurka. Privately printed. One-hour video, Dance Time Publications. Not seen.

Hoy, Suellen M. *Chasing Dirt: The American Pursuit of Cleanliness.* New York: Oxford University Press, 1995. Documents the changes in American habits of hygiene and cleanliness from the "malodorous" 1850s to the squeaky clean 1950s.

Hundley, Daniel Robinson. *Social Relations in Our Southern States.* 1860. Reprint. New York: Arno Press, 1973. Contemporary study of Southern social classes, life, and customs in the period just before the war.

Hunt, Patricia K. "Fabric Production in the 19th Century African American Slave Community." *Ars Textrina* 15 (July 1991): 83–92. The weaving, manufacture, and dyeing of slave clothing.

———. "Textile Fragments Recovered from a Slave Cemetery in South Carolina." *Ars Textrina* 22 (December 1994): 87–105. Account of rings, buttons, and cloth fragments from slaves buried in 1863 in South Carolina.

Iobst, Richard. *Civil War Macon*. Account of Macon, Georgia, on the eve of the Civil War.

Kohler, Carl. *History of Costume*. London: Harrap, 1928. 463 pages, 600 illustrations.

Korn, Bertram Wallace. *American Jewry and the Civil War*. Philadelphia: Jewish Publication Society of America, 1951. Description of the Jewish community and its reaction to the crisis.

Kramrisch, Bernard. "Color in Clothing—Past and Present." *American Dyestuff Reporter* 74 (March 1974): 15.

Krockover, Gerald H., and Jeanette Hauck. *Training for Docents: How to Talk to Visitors*. Technical Leaflet #125. Nashville: American Association for State and Local History, 1980.

Kunciov, Robert. *Mr. Godey's Ladies' Book*. Princeton, NJ: Pyne Press, 1971. ISBN:087861009X. 183 pages.

Laver, James. *Children's Fashions in the Nineteenth Century*. London: B. T. Batsford, Ltd., 1951. Color drawings of children's clothing taken from European magazines.

———. *Costume Illustration. The Nineteenth Century*. London: H.M. Stationery Office, 1947. Produced by the Victoria and Albert Museum. 68 pages.

———. *English Costume of the Nineteenth Century*. 1929. Reprint. London: A. and C. Black, 1947. 88 pages.

———. *Fashions and Fashion Plates 1800–1900*. London: Penguin Books, 1943. 30 pages.

———. *Taste and Fashion from the French Revolution to the Present Day*. London: G. G. Harrap Co., 1945. 232 pages.

Leisch, Juanita. *Everyday Clothing of Rural Women*. and *Family Album: Children's Wear Daily*. Gettysburg: Thomas Publications, 1994. Berryville, Va.: Wearlooms, 1993. History and description of children's clothing.

———. *Ladies Wear Daily: 50 Original, American, Civil War Period Photographs of Civilians*. Berryville, VA: Wearlooms, 1986. (Route 3, Box 6025, Berryville, VA 22611.)

Lewenhaupt, Tony. *Crosscurrents: Art, Fashion, Design, 1890 to 1989*. New York: Rizzoli, 1989. ISBN: 0847811379.

Lowry, Thomas P. *Civil War Bawdy Houses of Washington, DC*. Fredericksburg, VA: Sergeant Kirkland's, 1997. Locations and histories of more than 60 bawdy houses of the capital during the war.

———. *The Story the Soldiers Wouldn't Tell: Sex in the Civil War*. Mechanicsburg, PA: Stackpole Books, 1994. Sex, North and South.

Lum, Ruthann. "Chinese in the Civil War: Ten Who Served." *Chinese America: History and Perspectives*. (1996): 149–181. For people curious about participation in the Civil War by real "Down Easterners."

MacDonald, Anne L. *No Idle Hands: The Social History of American Knitting*. New York: Ballantine Books, 1988.

Malcolm-Davies, Jane. "Keeping it Alive: The Use of Live Interpreters in Historical Museums; A Conference Sponsored by Cadbury's, Birmingham, England." *Museums Journal* 90 (1990): 25–29.

Marsh, Heidi. *Hair, Hat, Hood and Bonnet, Too: Of The Era of the Hoop; Knit, Net, Crochet and More of the Era of the Hoop; Ladies' Sports of the Era of the Hoop; Riding Habits of the Era of the Hoop; Sew and So Forth of the Era of the Hoop; Styles for Mourning of the Era of the Hoop; Styles and So Forth of the Era of the Hoop; Wedding Suggestions of the Era of the Hoop;* and *What Children Wore (Or Wished They Could) of the Era of the Hoop.* Greenville, CA: Self-published, 1993. These books are reproductions from fashion magazines and other sources of the period, with excellent descriptions of clothing and styles.

Martin, Linda, comp. *The Way We Wore: Fashion Illustrations of Children's Wear 1870 to 1970.* New York: Scribner Co., 1978. ISBN: 0684156555.

Massey, Mary Elizabeth. *Erzatz in the Confederacy: Shortages and Substitutes on the Southern Homefront.* Columbia: University of South Carolina Press, 1993. Economics and substitute life in the South. Good background for civilian impressions.

———. *Refugee Life in the Confederacy.* Baton Rouge: Louisiana State University Press, 1964. Descriptions of refugee life and social conditions of civilians during the war using period accounts. A surprising section on social activities and even weddings for refugees.

McClellan, Elizabeth. *Historic Dress in America, 1800–1870.* New York: George Jacobs, 1910. Excellent illustrations and accounts of dress, especially on children's clothes.

McMillan, Sally Gregory. *Motherhood in the Old South: Pregnancy, Childbirth and Infant Rearing.* Baton Rouge, LA: Louisiana State University Press, 1990. Accounts of obstetrics, pregnancy, childbirth, breastfeeding, and childcare in the South, with some chilling statistics.

McPherson, James. *Marching Toward Freedom: Blacks in the Civil War., 1861–1865.* Gripping tales of the black man's fight for freedom.

Merrifield, Mary Philadelphia. *Dress as a Fine Art, with Suggestions on Children's Dress.* Boston: J. P. Jewett & Co., 1854. Reprinted from articles in the *Art Journal* and *Sharpe's London Magazine.*

Mery, Joseph. *Les Parures; fantaisie par Gavarni.* Paris: G. de Gonet, 1850.

Mescher, Virginia. *Dates of Selected Inventions and Occurrences During the Later Part of the 18th Century and During the 19th Century.* Self-published.

———. Several books and pamphlets are available from the Ragged Soldier Sutlery: *Children's Games of the Mid-Nineteenth Century* (1997); *Mid-Nineteenth Century Parlour Games* (1998); *Did They Eat That? Brand Name Foods Through Four Centuries* (1999); *Foods in the South During the Mid-Nineteenth Century* (1993); *Historic Uses of Herbs in the Mid-Nineteenth Century and Home Remedies, Including Medicinal, Beauty, and Household Usage of Herbs* (1993); *Laundry Handbook: A Manual for Creating a Civilian or Military Laundress Impression or Laundry Exhibit* (1999); *Laundry Methods and Equipment Used in the Nineteenth Century* (1994); *Making Do or Substitutions of Scarce Items During the Civil War* (1993); *Price Comparisons, Price Increases and Salaries of Jobs in the South During the Civil War* (1993). Privately printed.

Mitchell, Patricia B. *Civil War Celebrations.* Privately printed. Interesting little pamphlet on holiday celebrations, recipes, and other miscellaneous facts. Includes a curious account of Union soldiers firing Rebel fuses from their muskets to imitate Roman Candle fireworks.

Mohr, James., ed. *The Cormany Diaries: A Northern Family In the Civil War.* Pittsburgh: University of Pittsburgh Press, 1982. Social life and customs of a Northern family.

Montgomery, Florence M. *Textiles in America 1650–1870: A Dictionary Based on Original Documents.* New York: Norton, 1984. ISBN: 0393017036.

Music and the Art of Dress. London: Murray, 1852. Two essays reprinted from the "Quarterly Review " by Lady Elizabeth R. Eastlake (March 1847).

Neville, Ralph Henry. *Fancies: Fashions and Fads.* London: Metheun & Co., 1913.

———. *The World of Fashion, 1837 to 1922.* London: Metheun & Co., 1923.

Newton, Stella Mary. *Health, Art and Reason: Dress Reformers of the Nineteenth Century.* London: J. Murray Co., 1974. ISBN: 0719524245.

Olian, JoAnne. *80 Godey's Full Color Fashion Plates, 1838–1880.* Evolution of American clothing styles.

Orr, Hugh. *Illustrated History of Early Antique Spectacles.* Beckenham, Kent, England: H. Orr, 1985. 172 pages. Fantastic photographic history of specs. Unfortunately, no bibliography, and mostly European and English styles.

Paquin, Worth. *Fashion Drawings 1865 to 1956.* Microfilm. Hastemere, Surrey, England: Emmett Microform Company, 1982. ISBN: 0907696058.

Perrot, Philippe. *Les dessus et les dessous de la bourgeoisie: une historie du vetement au 19e siecle.* Paris: Fayard, 1981. ISBN: 2213009589.

Peterson's Monthly Magazine. Philadelphia, 1847–1892. A fashion magazine from the land of the bluestockings.

Petroski, Henry. *The Evolution of Useful Things: How Everyday Artifacts—from Forks and Pins and Paper Clips and Zippers—Came to be as They Are.* New York: Vintage Press, 1994. Excellent essay on the evolution of forks, tin cans, and other daily-used items.

Philpot, Edward. *Crinoline from 1730 to 1864: Crinoline in Our Parks and Promenades from 1710 to 1864.* London: E. Philpot, 1864. 23 pages.

Piton, Camille. *Le Costume civil en France du XVIIIe au XIXe siecle.* Paris: E. Flammarion, 1926. 380 pages.

Preyer, Norris W. "The Historian, the Slave and the Ante-Bellum Textile Industry." *Journal of Negro History* 44, no. 2 (April 1961): 68–82. Accounts of the use of slave labor in textile mills throughout the South.

Price, Julius Mendes. *Dame Fashion: Paris-London (1786–1912).* New York: Scribner, 1913. 180 pages.

Randolph, Mary. *The Virginia House-Wife.* Reprinted from the 1824 edition by the University of South Carolina Press, 1984. Although this book predates the Civil War, it does give an excellent account of domestic life of the period.

Rawlings, Kevin. *We were marching on Christmas Day: A History and Chronicle of Christmas during the Civil War.* Baltimore, MD: Toomey Press, 1995. ISBN:0961267046. Life in the army and back home during the holidays. A good read.

Reed, John Shelton. *Southern Folk, Plain and Fancy: Native White Social Types.* Atlanta: University of Georgia Press, 1986. A modern look at Southerners.

Reibel, Daniel B., and Patricia B. Reibel. *A Manual for Guides, Docents, Hostesses, and Volunteers of Old Economy.* Ambridge, PA: Harmonie Associates, Inc., 1974.

Rice, Judith Cambell. "Pattern Drafts of Men's Costume in America, 1850 to 1900." Master's thesis, Southern Illinois University, 1979. Examination of tailoring and sewing styles in men's clothing.

Rickman, David A. *Costume Manual: A Guide to the Clothing Worn in California and the Far West, Circa 1845.* Sacramento, CA: Sutter's Fort State Historic Park, n.d. Good information for civilians for the time shortly before the Civil War.

Saum, Lewis O. *The Popular Mood of Pre-Civil War America.* Westport, CT: Greenwood Press, 1980. Good account of civilian opinions (spiritual and temporal) involving life before the war.

Schenkman, David. "Civil War Sutler Tokens and Cardboard Script." Turtle Hill Book Co., 1983.

Severa, Joan. *Authentic Costuming for Historic Site Guides.* American Association of State and Local History Leaflet #113. Nashville: Association of State and Local History, 1979.

Shackel, Paul A. *Culture Change and the New Technology: An Archaeology of the Early American Industrial Era.* New York: Plenum Publishing, 1996. Interesting account about how changes in technology influenced changes in society and living in Harpers Ferry, West Virginia.

Shep, R. L. *Civil War Gentlemen: 1860's Apparel Arts and Uniforms.* Self-published, 1994. Cutting patterns and examples for tailors of period uniforms and civilian clothing for men.

———. *Civil War Ladies: Fashions and Needle Arts of the Early 1860's.* Reprinted from *Peterson's Magazine,* with guidance on sewing, embroidery, crochet, and other needlecrafts.

Skinner, A. *The Death of a Confederate: Selections from the Letters of the Archibald Smith Family of Roswell, Georgia.* Athens: University of Georgia Press, 1996. Insights into the life of a southern agricultural family.

Sloat, Caroline, ed. *Old Sturbridge Village Cookbook: Authentic Early American Recipes.* Chester, CT: Globe Pequot Press, 1984. Good recipe book for "open hearth" or firepit cooking, based on earlier accounts.

Smithsonian Institution. *Basic Principles for the Care and Handling of Period Costumes.* Museum of History and Technology, Division of Costume, Washington, DC: Smithsonian Institution, n.d.

Snyder-Haug, Diane. *Antique and Vintage Clothing: A Guide to Dating and Valuation of Women's Clothing, 1850–1940.*

Spaulding, Lily May and John Spaulding, eds. *Civil War Recipes: Receipts from the pages of Godey's Lady's Book.* Lexington: University of Kentucky Press, 1999. Includes modern equivalents of Civil War cooking measures.

Stachiw, Myron O. *Negro Cloth: Northern Industry and Southern Slavery.* Boston: Boston National Historical Park, and North Andover, Mass.: Merrimack Valley Textile Museum, 1981. Accounts of clothing for slaves, and how the cloth for slave's clothing was manufactured in Northern textile mills.

Stansell, Christine. *City of Women: Sex and Class in New York, 1789–1860.* New York: Knopf, 1986. Study on the lives, employment, and economics of working-class women in New York City.

Steamburg, Ary van. *Everyday Clothing of Rural Women at the Time of the Civil War.* Available from Fall Creek Sutlery.

Stewart, Doug. "The Old Ball Game." *Smithsonian* 29, no. 7 (Oct. 1998): 99–106. Living history of nineteenth-century baseball at the Old Bethpage Restoration Village in New York.

Stolz, Craig. "Lawyers on Stage: Re-enactment of Famous Trials at the Smithsonian Institution's Folklife Festival." *Association Management* 38 (November 1986): 34–36.

Stover, Kate F. "Is it Real History Yet? An Update on Living History Museums." *Journal of American Culture* 12 (Summer 1989): 13–17.

Sykas, Philip. "Caring or Wearing: Wearing Costume in Museum Collections." *Museums Journal* 87 (December 1987): 155–57.

Tandberg, Gerilyn G. "Dress-up Clothes for Field Slaves of Ante-Bellum Louisiana and Mississippi." *Costume* 15 (1981): 40–48.

———. "Field Hand Clothing in Louisiana and Mississippi During the Ante-Bellum Period." *Dress* 5 (1980): 89–104.

Tarrant, Naomi. *The Development of Costume: Costumes on Display.* New York: Routledge, 1998. Guide to the history, use, and preservation of historical apparel.

Tennent, William Lawrence. *The John Jarvie Ranch: A Case Study in Historic Site Development and Interpretation.* Master's thesis, Utah State University, 1980. 180 pages.

Thieme, Otto C. "On Collecting Costumes." *The Cincinnati Art Museum Bulletin* 13 (December 1986): 20–24.

Urbanski, Mary Ellen. "A Study of Civil War Era Women: A Fashion Overview." *Camp Chase Gazette* (n.d.): 32–33. Urbanski has written several articles on Victorian dress, which appear in a number of publications.

Varhola, Michael J. *Everyday Life During the Civil War.* Cicinnati: Writer's Digest Books, 1999. Excellent portrayal of everday life for civilians and soldiers.

Victoria & Albert Museum, Department of Textiles and Dress. *Four Hundred Years of Fashion.* London: Victoria and Albert Museum, 1984. Good examples and photos of English women's dresses and men's clothing from the period.

von Boehn, Max. *Modes and Manners.* 2 vols. Translated by John Joshua. New York: B. Blom, 1971. Manners and customs of clothing through history. Very thorough.

Walkley, Christina, and Vanda Foster. *Crinolines and Crimping Irons: Victorian Clothes—How They Were Cleaned and Cared For.* London: Owen Press, 1978. ISBN: 0720605008. An excellent account of nineteenth-century civilian fashions and cleaning clothes authentically, as well as an interesting history of laundry.

Warner, Deborah Jean. "Optics in Philadelphia during the Nineteenth Century." *Proceedings of the American Philosophical Society* 129, no. 3 (1985): 291–99. Nice overview of the history of glasses, but little emphasis on the Civil War period.

Waugh, Norah. *Corsets and Crinolines.* New York: Theater Arts Books, 1954. Examination of corsets and crinoline dresses from a costumer's perspective.

———. *The Cut of Men's Clothes, 1600 to 1900.* New York: Theater Arts Books, 1964.

———. *The Cut of Women's Clothes, 1600 to 1900.* New York: Theater Arts Books, 1968.

Wehinger, Brunhilde. *Paris-crinoline: zur Faszination des Boulevardtheatres und der Mode in Kontext Urbanitat und der Modernitat des Jahres 1857.* Munchen: Wilhelm Fink Verlag, 1988.

Williams, William G. *Days of Darkness: The Gettysburg Civilians*. New York: Berkely Books, 1990. ISBN: 0425123537. Accounts of Gettysburg from the viewpoints of civilians.

Winter, Janet, and Carolyn Schultz. *Victorian Costuming 1840–1865*. Oakland, CA: Other Times Productions, 1980.

York, Kathleen. *The Civil War Ladies' Sketchbook*. 3 vols. Elgin, IL: The House of York, 1980. (32 North Union Street, Elgin, IL 60123.)

5: REENACTING ETIQUETTE

Many books on Civil War etiquette are available. Nevertheless, it is enormously difficult to get into the "mindset" of another period.

At a recent event, a new recruit who arrived after dark went to sleep in a camp filled with hard-core authentics. When they awoke and found him sleeping in their camp with nonperiod blankets, they swore at him and told him to remove himself and his "farb" blankets from their presence or they would throw his blankets in the fire. No matter how authentic their attire and supplies, reenactors who are this rude and uncivil are totally incompatible with the nineteenth-century attitudes of both military and civilian courtesy to strangers.

"Farb" attitudes and language are even worse than "farb" clothing. Discourtesy is bad enough when directed against other reenactors; it is inexcusable when directed against the public, and reprehensible when directed against children.

Adburgham, Alison. *A Punch History of Manners and Modes: 1841–1940*. London: Hutchinson Co., 1961. Social life and customs in Great Britain from the magazine *Punch*. Some good cartoons.

Aldrich, Elizabeth. *From the Ballroom to Hell: Grace and Folly in Nineteenth Century Dance*. Evanston, IL: Northwestern University Press, 1991. Dancing, etiquette, and social mores from period accounts. Good annotated bibliography.

Beadle Dime Book of Practical Etiquette for Ladies and Gentlemen. New York: Beadle, 1850. Seventy some pages of "practical" advice.

Beecher, Catharine Ester. *A Treatise on Domestic Economy, for the Use of Young Ladies at Home, and at School*. New York: Marsh, Capen and Lyon, 1841. Reprinted 1970, 1977. Taking care of family and home, with several chapters on etiquette and manners.

Bowie, Catherine A. *Manners and Society in the Victorian Era*. Amherst, MA: n.p. Typescript. A Division III examination in the School of Social Science, Hampshire College, May 1995. British social life and customs in the nineteenth century.

Campbell, Erin E. *Writing Against Tradition, Gentility, Manners, and the Awakening*. Master's thesis, University of North Carolina at Greensboro, 1993. Women in literature in the Southern states and etiquette for women.

Chesterfield's Complete Rules of Etiquette and the Usages of Society. New York: Dick & Fitzgerald, 1857. Republished in 1987 by Cunningham's Homespun Commissary, P.O. Box 789, Iowa City, IA 52240.

Civil War Era Etiquette. Martine's Handbook of Etiquette Combined with a Dictionary of Vulgarisms, with Added Illustrations from Godey's Lady's Book and Other Civil War Sources. Mendocino, CA: R. L. Ship Co., 1982. 0914046071. This is a nice reprint of one of the first "manners" books in America. Such a book was needed as more people left the farms and moved to the larger cities and social classes became more fluid.

Conkling, Margaret Cockburn. *The American Gentleman's Guide to Politeness and Fashion by Henry Lunette* (pseudonym). Philadelphia: Claxton, Remsen & Hafflefinger, 1868.

Cunnington, Cecil Willett. *Feminine Attitudes in the Nineteenth Century.* New York: Haskell House, Publishers, 1973. First published August 1935. Social customs and attitudes of women in the nineteenth century, with a very English slant that is not necessarily consistent with American attitudes.

Curtin, Michael James. *Etiquette and Society in Victorian England.* Doctoral thesis, University of California, Berkeley, 1981.

———. *Propriety and Position: A Study of Victorian Manners.* New York: Garland Publishers, 1987. Etiquette in Great Britain.

Davenport, F. Garvin. *Cultural Life in Nashville on the Eve of the Civil War.* Chapel Hill, NC: University of North Carolina Press, 1941. Interesting discussion on antebellum society on the western side of the Appalachian mountains.

Fisher, Mary Rosalie. *Models for Manners: Etiquette Books and Etiquette in Nineteenth Century France.* Doctoral thesis, New York University, 1992.

Good Behavior for Young Gentlemen: Founded on Principles of Common Sense, and the Usage of Good American Society: Containing Also Instructions on Letter Writing By an American Gentleman. Rochester, NY: D. M. Dewey, 1850.

Habits of Good Society: A Handbook for Ladies and Gentlemen. New York: Carleton, 1841, 1865. Reprinted 1970 by Source Book Press.

Hartley, Florence. *The Ladies' Book of Etiquette and Manual of Politeness.* Boston: J. S. Locke, 1860. Reprinted 1993.

Henry, Ann. *Pre-Post: Etiquette Books in America, 1830–1860.* Thesis, Harvard University, 1986. Etiquette in the United States.

Hilgrow, Thomas. *Hilgrow's Call Book and Dancing Master.* New York: DaCapo Press, 1864. Reprinted.

Hill, Thomas Edie. *The Essential Handbook of Victorian Etiquette.* San Francisco, CA: Bluewood Books, 1994. Etiquette, adapted directly from material written and published by Professor Thomas E. Hill between 1873 and 1890.

Kasson, John F. *Rudeness and Civility: Manners in 19th Century Urban America.* New York: Hill and Wang, 1990. Also translated into the French as *Savoir-faire et Societé aux États-Unis* in 1993.

Mike Mescher *Parlour Games.* Burke, VA: Ragged Soldier Sutlery.

Morgan, Marjorie. *Manners, Morals, and Class in England, 1774–1858.* New York: Macmillan Press; St. Martin's Press, 1994. English social life and customs of the nineteenth century.

Mulvey, Christopher. *Transatlantic Manners: Social Patterns in Nineteenth-Century Anglo-American Travel Literature.* New York: Cambridge University Press, 1990.

Pine, Richard. *The Dandy and the Herald: Manners, Mind and Morals from Brummell to Durrell.* New York: Macmillan, 1988. Dandies in literature.

The Rambler in Georgia: Desultory Observations on the Situation, Extent, Climate, Population, Manners, Customs, Commerce, Constitution, Government, etc., of the State from the Revolution to the Civil War Recorded by Thirteen Travellers. Edited by Mills Lane. Savannah, GA: The Library of Georgia, 1973. Georgia description and travel from 1775 to 1950.

St. George, Andrew. *The Descent of Manners: Etiquette, Rules & the Victorians.* London: Chatto & Windus, 1993. Etiquette in Great Britain.

Sessions, Sarah J. *What Was What and Who Was Who: An Analysis of Nineteenth Century Etiquette Books.* Honors paper, Lawrence University, 1988.

Stowe, Catharine Beecher, and Harriet Beecher Stowe. *The American Woman's Home, or, Principles of Domestic Science, Being a Guide to the Formation and Maintenance of Economical, Healthful, Beautiful, and Christian Homes.* Boston: Brown & Co., 1869. Reprinted 1996 by the Stowe-Day Foundation, Hartford, Connecticut.

Stowe, Catharine Beecher. *A Treatise on Domestic Economy, American Family Home.* Boston: Marsh, Capen Lyon & Webb, 1841. Reprinted 1977 by Schocken Books, New York.

Trollope, Frances. *Domestic Manners of the Americans.* New York: Vintage Books, 1949. Although she traveled in the United States during the 1820s, and is thus a bit dated for the 1860s, her account of American life is one of the more readable.

6: HEALTH AND COMFORT

The best book to look at for advice on how to camp is an older copy of the *Boy Scout Handbook*. If you can't locate one, look at books on camping while mountain climbing, in the Arctic, or in the jungle. U.S. Army military training manuals can be very informative.

Nevertheless, the best teacher is experience. How to keep the rain out of your tent can be described any number of times in books, yet nothing but experience will teach you what is best for your situation. The learning of these lessons is part of reenacting. You will always learn most from your pards, then from your own experience, then from books.

For general outdoor information, try the following books.

Boga, Steven. *Camping and Backpacking with Children.* Mechanicsburg, PA: Stackpole Books, 1993.

Darman, Peter. *The Survival Handbook.* London: Greenhill Books, 1996.

Geary, Don. *Using a Map and Compass*. Mechanicsburg, PA: Stackpole Books, 1995.

Hampton, Bruce, and David Cole. *NOLS Soft Paths: Revised and Updated*. Mechanicsburg, PA: Stackpole Books, 1995.

Hodgson, Michael. *Wilderness with Children: A Parent's Guide to Fun Family Outings*. Mechanicsburg, PA: Stackpole Books, 1992.

Meyer, Kathleen. *How to Shit in the Woods: An Environmentally Sound Approach to a Lost Art*. Berkeley, CA: Ten Speed Press, 1994. The title says it all—great for people who are unfamiliar with woodsmanship and the "unspoken arts."

Powers, Phil. *NOLS Wilderness Mountaineering*. Mechanicsburg, PA: Stackpole Books, 1993.

Schimelpfenig, Tod, and Linda Lindsey. *NOLS Wilderness First Aid*. Mechanicsburg, PA: Stackpole Books, 1991.

7: HOSTING A CIVIL WAR REENACTMENT

American Civil War Commemorative Committee, Inc. *Commemorative Program: The Battle of First Manassas*. Alexandria, VA: ACWCC, 1986.

———. *125th Anniversary Commemorative Program: The Battle of Antietam*. Alexandria, VA: ACWCC, 1987.

———. *125th Anniversary Commemorative Program: The Battle of Gettysburg*. Alexandria, VA: ACWCC, 1988.

———. *125th Anniversary Commemorative Program: 125th Anniversary Re-enactment Battle of Chickamauga*. Richmond, VA: ACWCC, 1988.

———. *Commemorative Program: The Spring Campaign of 1864*. Richmond, VA: ACWCC, 1989.

Battle of Cedar Creek. Hagerstown, MD: Video Vision Co., 1991. 45-minute video of the battle reenactment.

Battle of Franklin: 125th Anniversary Re-enactment, December 1–3, 1989. Nashville: Tom Jackson and Assoc., 1989. Official program of one of the coldest events I've ever been to.

Battle of Lexington, MO. Lexington, MO: Oran Green Productions, 1991. Video of the September 1991 reenactment of Lexington.

Battle of Selma Re-enactment. Selma, AL: Kiwanis Club, 1994. Sponsored by the Kiwanis Club and the 33d Alabama Infantry Regiment.

Battle of Wilson's Creek Reenactment, August 1991. Videotape of the August 10, 1991, reenactment near Springfield, Missouri.

Belmont: 132nd Anniversary Re-enactment. Belmont, MO: 1993. Hour-long videotape of the reenactment.

Burning of the Arsenal at Harpers Ferry: April 18, 1861: A Souvenir Booklet of the Re-enactments of the Burning of the Arsenal, April 22, 1961. Sponsored by the Jefferson County, West Virginia, Chamber of Commerce, 1961. 12 pages.

Carpenter, Keith. *The Battle of Shiloh: 125th Anniversary Reenactment Official Souvenir Program, a Living History Event*. Sponsored by the Shiloh Reenactment Association, 1987.

"Charging into Civil War History." *The Retired Officer* (August 1995): 38–43. ISSN:1061–3102 or 0737–724X.

Civil War Battle of Lexington, Missouri's Civil War Centennial Feature. Re-enacted by the Cadet Battle Group of Wentworth Military Academy, Assisted by Regular Army, National Guard and ROTC Units. Lexington, MO: Battle Re-enactment Committee, 1961.

Classic Images Productions, Inc. Classic Images (P.O. Box 2399, Columbia, MD 21045) has videotaped a number of Civil War reenactments and 125th Anniversary events. These videotapes are sometimes disappointing but they always have good photography and action scenes. Reenactors often get a special edition that has some living-history cuts and action outtakes added to the general videotape.

Cullen, Jim. *The Civil War in Popular Culture: A Reusable Past.* Washington, DC: Smithsonian Institution Press, 1995. ISBN: 1560984597. The last chapter is on reenactments.

Daily, Brian. *The Basics: How to Get Started in Civil War Reenacting.* Illustrated by Ward Williams. Austin, IN: Privately printed by the author, 1984. This is an excellent little pamphlet and is an outstanding example of a recruiting tool for reenactment regiments. It not only explains the hobby somewhat, but also tells the reader who to call to join a unit (the 49th Indiana).

Dennison, Will. *Springing to the Call! How to Get Started in Civil War Reenacting.* Marietta, OH: Camp Chase Publishing Company, 1990. 36 pages. An excellent book, with much needed information and advice on how to get started. Recommended as a first purchase.

Helwig, Richard M. *Soldiers in Blue from the Maumee Valley: Student Study Guide for "A River of History—The Maumee": Unit 11.* Archbold, OH: Northwest Technical College, 1976.

Horwitz, Tony. "For Hard-Core Few, Replaying Civil War Ain't Whistling Dixie: They Don Period's Clothes, Eat Era's Grub and Sneer at Less-Exacting Brethren." *Wall Street Journal,* June 2, 1994.

Johnson, Neil. *The Battle of Gettysburg.* New York: Four Winds Press, 1989. ISBN:0027478319. 56 pages. A book for younger buffs and reenactors, with excellent photographs taken of the 1988 reenactment of the 125th Anniversary of the battle.

Kietz, Bill. *Bi-Annual Reenactor's Directory.* Lancaster, OH: Privately printed, 1989. An incomplete listing of reenactors, mostly concentrated in the Midwest.

———. "The Reenactor's Art." *Civil War Times, Illustrated* (March 1987): 22–36. ISSN: 0009–8094. A good, brief article on how to get started.

The Last Gettysburg Reunion, June 30, 1938. Civil War Veterans Speak. Green Valley, AZ: Radio Gem, 1987. Audiotape of the "real" reenactors—the veterans themselves.

Loomis, David. *The Hobby: An Illustrated Guide to Having a "Civil" Reenactment.* Vol. I. Garrettsville, OH: Battlefield Promotions, 1992. Humorous introduction to the hobby by a "high private" of the 66th Ohio Volunteer Infantry.

Louisiana Civil War Centennial Commission. *The Reenactment of Louisiana's Secession from the Union*. Baton Rouge, LA: Louisiana Civil War Centennial Commission, 1960. A 16mm black-and-white film, one reel. Good introduction to the period, with emphasis on politics.

Napoleonic Tactics, Inc. *125th Anniversary Reenactment of the Battle of Monocacy: The Battle That Saved Washington*. Newark, NJ: Video Vision, 1990. There were more than two thousand participants in this reenactment held near the original battlefield and current shopping mall.

———. *125th Anniversary Re-enactment of the Battle of New Market [VA]: Field of Honor*. Hagerstown, MD: Video Vision, 1989. Hour-long videotape of the reenactment.

O'Sullivan, Richard. "Red Badge Revivalists." *History Today* 37 (December 1987): 6–8. Author looks at reasons for reenacting but does not believe it has much use to historians.

Philips, Herb. "Here and There: Playing Soldier: History Hobbyists Relive the Battle of the Blue and the Gray." *Travel-Holiday* 172, no. 2 (August 1989): 106. Discusses "magic moments" at reenactments and how emotions combine with action to make memorable experiences.

Pressly, Thomas. *Americans Interpret Their Civil War*. New York: Collier Books, 1962.

Price, Lawrence G. *Yankee Reflections; Civil War Reenactments, Rockville, Burlington, Owensboro, Fort Wayne (1978–1980)*. Greencastle, IN: Privately published.

Re-enactment of the Battle of Bee Creek, Platte County, Missouri, June 11th and 12th, 1994. Shawnee, KS: Video Lab. Hour-long videocassette souvenir of the reenactment.

Reenactment of Louisiana's Secession from the Union. Baton Rouge, LA: Louisiana Civil War Centennial Commission, 1961. 30-minute 16mm film.

Sayler's Creek Reenactment and Preservation Committee. *The Final Chapter: The 125th Anniversary of the Battle of Sayler's Creek and the Stacking of Arms at Appomattox Court House*. Farmville, VA: Jesse Frank Jackson, 1990. Commemorative program.

Seley, Shane. *Gettysburg*. Civil War Series, vol. 2. Springfield, MO: Video Post, 1993. Videocassette of the 1993 reenactment at Gettysburg.

Severa, Joan. *Authentic Costuming for Historic Site Guides*. Nashville: American Association of State and Local History, 1979. Leaflet #113. Excellent pamphlet on costuming for museums.

Skow, John, Beth Austin, and Joseph L. Kane. "Bang, Bang! You're History, Buddy." *Time* 128, no. 6 (August 11, 1986): 58. Account of the 125th commemorative reenactment at Manassas.

Souvenir Program: Reenactment, Abbeville (South Carolina) District Meeting, November 22, 1860–November 27, 1960. Magazine Hill, South Carolina. Abbeville, SC: Privately printed, 1960.

Sylvia, Stephen W. *North-South Trader's Association Manassas Reenactment Commemorative: 125th Civil War Anniversary*. Fredericksburg, VA: North-South Press, 1986.

Sylvia, Stephen W., and Mike O'Donnell. *Civil War Reenactments*. Orange, VA: Moss Press, 1985. Nice photo album of more than twenty years of Civil War reenacting, including scenes from the 1961 reenactment at Manassas.

Thomas, Michael R. *A Confederate Sketchbook*. Privately printed, 1980.

Turner, Rory Peter Benedict. "Sociability, Metaphor, and Time Warps in the Experience of Civil War Reenactments." Master's thesis, Indiana University, 1990. Unfortunately, this copy has disappeared from the Indiana University Library and is no longer available for interlibrary loan. This is a shame, since many people want to read it. So if you've got it, give it back!

Video Vision Presents the 125th Anniversary Reenactment of the Battle of New Market, Field of Honor Sponsored by the New Market Battlefield Park, Virginia Military Institute; Managed by Napoleonic Tactics, Inc. Hagerstown, MD: Video Vision, 1989. The New Market reenactment suffered from a bad reputation because of unauthentic regiments. This has greatly improved in recent years, as seen in this work.

Wexler, Henrietta. "The Way Things Really Were: Living History Museum Researchers Delve Deeper." *Museum News* 66 (January-February 1988): 62–63. Interesting article on how things were as opposed to modern thinking.

Wright, Willie Ann. *Civil War Redux Pinhole Photographs of Civil War Reenactments*. Norfolk, VA: Willoughby Productions, 1990. 7-minute videocasette. Virginia artist Willie Ann Wright discusses her art of pinhole photography of Civil War reenactments.

Index

A-frame tents, 88
ad-libbing, 18
Alderson, William T., 24
American Civil War Commemorative Committee, 169–175
ammunition, live, 114
Antietam, battle of, 9–10
Antietam, reenacting at, 159–168
antiques, use of, 58–59, 115, 131–132, 155–156
apples, authentic varieties, 122
aprons, 104, 107
arms. *See* weapons
armscyes, 174
Army of Northern Virginia (ANV), 137
Army of the Pacific, 137
army regulations, books about, 240–244
artillery, 49, 114, 170
auctions, 43

authenticity,
accuracy in interpretive talk, 29
at Antietam reenactment, 160–161
for civilians, 173–175
documenting, 10, 152
in early reenactments, 4
for gear and clothing, 36–37, 100
generic regiments, 139–140
at Gettysburg reenactment, 173–175
hardcore movement, 138–140
in portraying common soldier, 35–37
rules regarding, 109–110

Band-Aids, use of, 55
bandanas, 107, 164
barbers, 71
bare feet, 57

Barlow knives, 69
Battle Cry of Freedom, 30
Battle of Gettysburg, The, 30
battle reenactments, standards for, 143–158
bayonets, 54, 63–64, 115, 171, 185
belt buckles, 54, 165
belts, 53–54, 165
Berdan's sharpshooters, 46, 58
beverages, 35
Bible, 70
Bicentennial, impact of, 5
Bingham, George Caleb, 136–137
black powder, 60–61, 147–148, 153–154, 171. *See also* cartridges
black powder shooting, 5
blanket roll, 43, 68
blisters, 55, 123
bonnets, 104, 117